PENGUIN CLASSICS

THOUGHTS AND SENTIMENTS ON
THE EVIL OF SLAVERY

Quobna Ottobah Cugoano, the most radical African opponent of slavery in the eighteenth century, was born about 1757 on the coast of what is present-day Ghana, in the Fante village of Agimaque or Ajumako. In 1770 he was kidnapped by fellow Africans, sold into slavery to Europeans, and transported to the West Indies. At the end of 1772 he was taken to England, where he was baptized as "John Stuart" in 1773. By 1784, he was employed as a servant by the fashionable painters Richard and Maria Cosway, through whom he came to the notice of prominent politicians, artists, and writers, including William Blake.

Cugoano soon became one of the first Afro-Britons who fought against slavery. In 1786 he helped to save Harry Demane from being forced into West Indian slavery. With Olaudah Equiano and other "Sons of Africa," Cugoano continued the struggle against slavery with published letters to newspapers. In 1787, Cugoano published *Thoughts and Sentiments on the Evil and Wicked Traffic of the Slavery and Commerce of the Human Species*, perhaps written with help from Equiano.

In this jeremiad, Cugoano raises the most overt and extended challenge to slavery ever made by an English-speaking person of African descent. He is also the first Anglophone-African historian of slavery and the slave trade, and the first African to criticize European imperialism in the Americas. His recognition of John Marrant and James Albert Ukawsaw Gronniosaw as his predecessors helped establish a tradition of Afro-British writings by converts to Christianity. In *Thoughts and Sentiments* Cugoano powerfully refutes the religious and secular arguments made by proponents of slavery; he believes that slaves have not only the right but the obligation to rebel against their owners, "the servants of the devil." Every Briton, he says, shares the blame for the evil of slavery, which threatens Great Britain with divine retribution. He also calls for the conversion of non-Christians and the substitution of trade *with* Africans for the trade *in* Africans.

In 1791, in a shorter version of his 1787 book, "Addressed to the Sons of Africa, by a Native," Cugoano announced his intention to open a school for Afro-Britons. About 1791, he also asked the abolitionist Granville Sharp to send him to Nova Scotia to recruit settlers for a second attempt to settle free Afro-Britons in Sierra Leone. No record has been found of either Cugoano's proposed school or participation in settling Sierra Leone. After 1791, Cugoano seems to have dropped out of history, leaving no record.

Vincent Carretta is a professor of English at the University of Maryland, College Park. His publications include *"The Snarling Muse": Verbal and Vi-*

sual Satire from Pope to Churchill (1983); *George III and the Satirists from Hogarth to Byron* (1990); and *Unchained Voices: An Anthology of Black Authors in the English-Speaking World of the Eighteenth Century* (1996). Professor Carretta edited the Penguin Classics editions of *The Interesting Narrative and Other Writings* by Olaudah Equiano and *Letters of the Late Ignatius Sancho, An African.*

THOUGHTS AND SENTIMENTS ON THE EVIL OF SLAVERY

AND OTHER WRITINGS

QUOBNA OTTOBAH CUGOANO

EDITED WITH AN INTRODUCTION AND NOTES
BY VINCENT CARRETTA

PENGUIN BOOKS

PENGUIN BOOKS

Published by the Penguin Group

Penguin Group (USA) Inc., 375 Hudson Street, New York, New York 10014, U.S.A.
Penguin Group (Canada), 90 Eglinton Avenue East, Suite 700, Toronto,
Ontario, Canada M4P 2Y3 (a division of Pearson Penguin Canada Inc.)
Penguin Books Ltd, 80 Strand, London WC2R 0RL, England
Penguin Ireland, 25 St Stephen's Green, Dublin 2, Ireland (a division of Penguin Books Ltd)
Penguin Group (Australia), 250 Camberwell Road, Camberwell,
Victoria 3124, Australia (a division of Pearson Australia Group Pty Ltd)
Penguin Books India Pvt Ltd, 11 Community Centre, Panchsheel Park,
New Delhi – 110 017, India
Penguin Group (NZ), 67 Apollo Drive, Rosedale, North Shore 0632, New Zealand
(a division of Pearson New Zealand Ltd)
Penguin Books (South Africa) (Pty) Ltd, 24 Sturdee Avenue, Rosebank,
Johannesburg 2196, South Africa

Penguin Books Ltd, Registered Offices: 80 Strand, London WC2R 0RL, England

*Thoughts and Sentiments on the Evil and Wicked Traffic of the Slavery and
Commerce of the Human Species* first published in Great Britain 1787
This edition with an introduction and notes by Vincent Carretta published
in Penguin Books 1999

7 9 10 8 6

Introduction and notes copyright © Vincent Carretta, 1999
All rights reserved

LIBRARY OF CONGRESS CATALOGING-IN-PUBLICATION DATA
Cugoano, Ottobah.
[Thoughts and sentiments on the evil and wicked traffic of the slavery and commerce of
the human species . . .]
Thoughts and sentiments on the evil of slavery and other writings / Quobna Ottobah
Cugoano ; edited with an introduction and notes by Vincent Carretta.
   p. cm. — (Penguin classics)
Originally published : Thoughts and sentiments on the evil and wicked traffic of the
slavery and commerce of the human species . . . London, 1787.
ISBN 978-0-14-044750-7 (pbk.)
1. Slavery. I. Carretta, Vincent. II. Title. III. Series.
HT871.C8 1999
306.3'62—dc21   98-41172

Printed in the United States of America
Set in Stemple Garamond
Designed by Sabrina Bowers

For Krista, Michael, Marc, and Owen

CONTENTS

INTRODUCTION

Of the four major writers of African descent—Ignatius Sancho, John Marrant, Quobna Ottobah Cugoano (John Stuart), and Olaudah Equiano (Gustavus Vassa)—whose works were first published in London during the 1780s, Cugoano remains the most radical and the least familiar. His known writings consist of several co-signed letters printed in London newspapers between 1787 and 1789, a few manuscript letters, and two published books. His *Thoughts and Sentiments on the Evil and Wicked Traffic of the Slavery and Commerce of the Human Species, Humbly Submitted to the Inhabitants of Great-Britain, by Ottobah Cugoano, a Native of Africa* appeared in 1787, and in 1791 an abridged version of it, including some new material, was published as *Thoughts and Sentiments on the Evil of Slavery; or, the Nature of Servitude as Admitted by the Law of God, Compared to the Modern Slavery of the Africans in the West-Indies; In an Answer to the Advocates for Slavery and Oppression. Addressed to the Sons of Africa, by a Native.*

Cugoano remains the least studied of the four writers, in part because the least is known about his life. All we know with certainty about him occurred between 1787 and 1791. Cugoano is representative of the difficulty a biographer frequently faces in trying to reconstruct the life of a specific, relatively obscure person of African descent (or of any specific poor person) who lived in eighteenth-century Britain. Unless the person had an unusual name given at baptism or later—Ignatius Sancho or Gustavus Vassa, for examples—his or her slave or Christian name can make the subject impossible to trace. Unfortunately for researchers, public records, except for baptisms of non-infants, rarely identify subjects by ethnicity, or what we call race. For example, if one did not already know that Ignatius and Anne Sancho and their children were Black, that fact could not be gleaned from the parish records of their marriage, births, or burials. Similarly, Equiano's naval records identify him only as Gustavus Vassa (with various spellings). Cugoano's Christian name alone—John Stuart (variously spelled)—is too common to be of much help to the biographical researcher.

Almost all the biographical data we have for Cugoano are found in his *Thoughts and Sentiments* (1787). He was born on the coast of present-day Ghana about 1757, in the Fante village of Agimaque or Ajumako. In 1770, when about thirteen, he was kidnapped by fellow Africans, sold into slavery to Europeans, and transported to Grenada. In a paragraph added to some issues of his *Thoughts and Sentiments* in 1787, Cugoano informs us that after having been "about nine or ten months in the slave-gang at Grenada, and about one year at different places in the West-Indies, with Alexander Campbell, Esq.," Campbell took him to England at the end of 1772. This Campbell was probably the same Alexander Campbell, Esquire, who testified in favor of the slave trade before a committee of the House of Commons on 13–18 February 1790. He said that he owned many slaves in the West Indies on plantations on several islands, with his largest holdings on Grenada, and that he had divided his time before his retirement to England in 1788 between the Caribbean and England. Campbell also mentioned that from 1753 to 1759 he lived mostly in North America, and he indicated that part of that time he lived in Virginia, where Equiano had been bought during that period by a Mr. Campbell, who soon sold him to Michael Henry Pascal, an officer in the British Royal Navy. Consequently, Equiano and Cugoano may have shared the same slave owner in the British colonies, though at different times and in different places.

Cugoano arrived in England only months after the Mansfield decision in the *Somerset* case on 22 June 1772, which was greeted by euphoria in London's Afro-British community. The Mansfield decision was popularly received as a virtual emancipation proclamation for the approximately fourteen to twenty thousand Blacks living in Britain, about 0.2 percent of the national population, but perhaps as much as 2 percent of London's population. By comparison, the *Declaration of Independence*, signed four years later in

Philadelphia, offered nothing to the nearly five hundred thousand
Blacks in North America, or 20 percent of the total population.
(The five hundred thousand Blacks in the British West Indies,
more than 90 percent of the population, were unaffected by either
the Mansfield ruling or the *Declaration of Independence*.) Lord
Mansfield, Lord Chief Justice of the King's Bench, the highest
common-law court in England, declared that James Somerset, a
slave brought to England in 1769 from Massachusetts by his master, Charles Stewart, a customs official, could not legally be forced
by his master back to the colonies. Somerset had run away from
Stewart in 1771 but was recaptured on 26 November 1771 by his
master, who tried to send him out of the country on a ship bound
for Jamaica under the command of Captain John Knowles. When
the abolitionist Granville Sharp and others learned of Somerset's
predicament, they quickly convinced Mansfield to issue a writ of
habeas corpus ordering the captain to bring him before the court.
Sharp also convinced several lawyers to argue Somerset's case free
of charge. The inexperienced Francis Hargrave, who wrote an in-
fluential account of his defense and who went on to establish a
distinguished legal career, volunteered his legal services on behalf
of Somerset. Although technically Mansfield's ruling established
only that a slave could not be seized by his master and forced
against his will to leave England and that a slave could get a writ of
habeas corpus to prevent his master's action, Mansfield's judgment
was widely considered, then and since, as the moment slavery was
abolished in England.

The Mansfield ruling may have been one of the reasons Sancho
thought his friend Julius Soubise, who like Sancho was an Afro-
British domestic servant in an aristocratic house, should be grateful that he had not shared the fate of many Africans: "Happy,
happy lad! what a fortune is thine!—Look round upon the miserable fate of almost all of our unfortunate colour—superadded to
ignorance,—see slavery, and the contempt of those very wretches
who roll in affluence from our labours superadded to this woeful
catalogue" (11 October 1772).

In 1777, Edmund Burke saw the judgment as meaning that
"every man putting his foot on English ground, every stranger
owing only a local and temporary allegiance, even a negro slave,

who had been sold in the colonies and under an act of parliament, became as free as every other man who breathed the same air with him" (*Letter to the Sheriffs of Bristol*). Following Mansfield's precedent, the Scottish court declared slavery illegal in 1778. Disputed since the *Cartwright* case of 1569, which concerned the status of a Russian slave, and long ignored de facto (in practice), the legality of slavery in England was now apparently definitively rejected de jure (by law) as well. Advertisements for sales of slaves, notices of runaway slaves, and attempts to enforce colonial slave laws in Britain—all already rare in England—disappeared after the Mansfield ruling. During dinner at the home of the Lord Chief Justice on 29 August 1779, Thomas Hutchinson, who had been governor of Massachusetts at the time of the ruling but was now an exiled Loyalist, told Mansfield that "all Americans who had brought Blacks [to England after *Somerset*] had, as far as I knew, relinquished their property in them, and rather agreed to give them wages, or suffered [allowed] them to go free."

Cugoano celebrates the perceived significance of the Mansfield judgment to Afro-Britons in his 1791 *Thoughts and Sentiments on the Evil of Slavery*:

> For so it was considered as criminal, by the laws of Englishmen, when the tyrannical paw and the monster of slavery took the man [Somerset] by the neck, in the centre of the British freedom, and thought henceforth to compel him to his involuntary subjection of slavery and oppression; it was wisely determined by some of the most eminent and learned counsellors in the land. The whole of that affair rested solely upon that humane and indefatigable friend of mankind, GRENVILLE [*sic*] SHARP esq. whose name we should always mention with the greatest reverence and honor. The noble decision, thereby, before the Right Hon. Lord Chief Justice MANSFIELD, and the parts taken by the learned Counsellor HARGRAVE, are the surest proofs of the most amiable disposition of the laws of Englishmen [5].

If the Mansfield ruling did not abolish slavery de jure it certainly undermined it de facto by indisputably denying slave masters the coercive power of removal to the colonies. Even if the ruling did not render slavery illegal, lacking that power, slave owners could no longer enforce their claims of possession, because slaves on English soil could legally emancipate themselves by flight. To many people, prior to Mansfield's decision the legal status of slavery in England had been established in 1729, when Attorney General Sir Philip Yorke and Solicitor General Charles Talbot unofficially offered their opinion that slavery was legal in England, that a slave's status was not affected by baptism, and that "the master may legally compel him to return again to the plantations." But the authority of the Yorke-Talbot opinion as legal precedent was disputed and challenged by other rulings prior to 1772. And the de facto status of slavery was also unclear before 1772, as a comment by Sir John Fielding in his *Extracts from Such of the Laws, as Particularly Relate to the Peace and Good Order of this Metropolis. . . . A New Edition. . . .* (London, 1768) indicates:

The immense Confusion that has arose in the Families of Merchants and other Gentlemen who have Estates in the *West-Indies*, from the great Number of Negro Slaves they have brought into this Kingdom, also deserves the most serious Attention; many of these Gentlemen have either at a vast Expence caused some of these Blacks to be instructed in the necessary Qualifications of a domestic Servant, or else have purchased them after they have been instructed; they then bring them to *England* as cheap Servants, having no Right to Wages; they no sooner arrive here, than they put themselves on a Footing with other Servants, become intoxicated with Liberty, grow refractory, and either by Persuasion of others, or from their own Inclinations, begin to expect Wages according to their own Opinion of their Merits; and as there are already a great Number of black Men and Women who have made themselves so troublesome and dangerous to the Families who brought them over as to get themselves discharged; they enter into Societies, and make it their Business to corrupt and dissatisfy the Mind of every fresh black Servant that comes to *England*; first, by getting them christened or married, which they inform them makes them free (tho' it has been adjudged by our most able Lawyers, that neither of these Circumstances alter the Master's Property in a Slave). However it so far answers their Purpose, that it gets the Mob on their Side, and makes it not only difficult but dangerous to the Proprietor of these Slaves to recover the Possession of them, when once they are spirited away [143–45].

Thus, even before *Somerset*, colonial slaves considered England a sanctuary. But not surprisingly, after the Mansfield ruling, some slaves brought from the colonies to England still tried to reinforce their claims to freedom by baptism or marriage, seeking to take out extra insurance, as it were. Having arrived in England in the wake of the Mansfield decision and perhaps having emancipated himself by leaving Campbell because of it, Cugoano was nevertheless "[a]dvised by some good people to get myself baptized, that I might not be carried away and sold again." Consequently, he was baptized "John Stuart—a Black, aged 16 Years" at St. James's Church, Piccadilly, on 20 August 1773. The assumption that conversion would, or at least should, guarantee freedom is understandable because traditionally societies that practiced slavery enslaved outsiders, and one of the most common indicators of an outsider was religious difference. For example, ancient Hebrews, and Muslims in Cugoano's own day, reserved the condition of chattel slavery for unbelievers. As the rate of slave conversions grew, apologists were under increasing pressure to find another measure of difference. Ethnicity, color, and law became the principal means to alienate those who had become religiously assimilated and thus likely to claim to have become social insiders.

The Mansfield judgment brought to public attention the legal status of people like Equiano, Cugoano, Marrant, and Sancho, who were residents of Britain yet not ethnically English. Their political status became a subject for public argument in light of the ideological conflict during the American Revolution, and their status as human beings was disputed during the late-eighteenth-century crusade to end British involvement in the slave trade with Africa. In *Thoughts and Sentiments*, Cugoano notes several recent developments suggesting to him that progress was being made toward the eradication of involuntary servitude in America and Europe: in the northern states of the post-Revolutionary United States, the immediate prohibition of slavery as well as the legal provision for gradual emancipation seemed to realize the egalitarian promise found in the *Declaration of Independence*, albeit slowly and often only partially; the outlawing of serfdom in Prussia by Frederick the Great in 1773 and in Austrian Poland by Emperor Joseph II in 1782 demonstrated to Cugoano that enlightened rulers desired free subjects. Destruction of the system of chattel slavery found in the Americas appeared to be within reach.

Although we do not know how Cugoano gained his own free-dom, by the mid-1780s he was employed as a servant by the fash-ionable painters Richard and Maria Cosway in Schomberg House, which still stands on the south side of Pall Mall, where they had taken up residence in 1784. During the eighteenth century, Blacks were often desired as servants in wealthy or status-conscious households because they were associated with the exotic riches of the empire and thus acted as one of the most obvious indicators of their employer's social standing. Visual and verbal representations of Cugoano can be identified in several portrayals of Cosway and his wife. As early as 1784, the probable date of the artist and poet William Blake's unpublished satire "An Island in the Moon," Cu-goano is almost certainly one of the "black servants" referred to in Blake's mockery of the social pretensions of Richard Cosway ("Mr. Jacko"):

> And I hardly know what a coach is, except when I go to Mr. Jacko's. he knows what riding is & *he will ride* & his wife is the most agreeable woman you hardly know she has a tongue in her head, and he is the funniest fellow. & I do believe he'll go into part-nership with his master [the Prince of Wales]. & they have black servants lodge at their house . . . .

And Cugoano appears in Richard Cosway's 1784 etching *Mr. and Mrs. Cosway*. Cugoano was also the model for "Pompey" (a stereotypical name for a Black servant) in another satirical repre-sentation of Cosway, *The Royal Academicians—a Farce* (1786), by "Anthony Pasquin" (John Williams). Through Richard Cosway, who was appointed *Primarius Pictor* (Principal Painter) to the Prince of Wales in 1785, Cugoano probably met the artists who subscribed to his 1791 book—Sir Joshua Reynolds and Joseph Nollekens—as well as the public figures to whom he wrote let-ters—King George III, the Prince of Wales (later King George IV), Edmund Burke, Sir William Dolben, and Granville Sharp.

Cugoano worked for the Cosways at a time of rising concern about the number and condition of Blacks living in Britain. The

Americans' victory in the civil war that we now call the American Revolution led to a great and very visible increase after 1783 in the numbers of free Blacks accompanying their Loyalist former masters as they left the former thirteen colonies for Canada and London, along with the many slaves who had emancipated themselves by joining the British forces in the war. The sight of unemployed and impoverished Blacks in London prompted the formation in 1786 of the Committee for the Relief of the Black Poor, which promoted the project for resettlement in Sierra Leone in whose initial stages Equiano briefly played a major role. According to a report in the newspaper *The Public Advertiser* (6 January 1787), sympathy for the Black poor was so widespread that White beggars disguised themselves as Blacks to increase their incomes. Unfortunately, as Cugoano feared, the first attempt at African resettlement soon ended in disaster when a local African chieftain, King Jimmy, destroyed the settlement of Granville Town in December 1789 in misdirected retaliation for the abduction of some of his people by a United States slave trader.

The aftermath of the defeat by the colonists was a time for national reassessment in Britain, a time well suited for the potentially spiritually regenerating moral crusade initiated by the publication in 1784 of the Reverend James Ramsay's *An Essay on the Treatment and Conversion of African Slaves in the Sugar Colonies* (London, 1784), the first attack on slavery by a former West Indian slave owner. Ramsay's work was quickly followed by Thomas Clarkson's *An Essay on the Slavery and Commerce of the Human Species, Particularly the African* (London, 1786), a translation of Clarkson's prizewinning Latin essay on the question "Is It Right to Make Others Slaves against Their Wills?," written at Cambridge in 1785. The loss of the thirteen colonies both weakened the political base of slavery in Parliament and concentrated attention on the slave trade, without which West Indian slavery apparently could not survive. The Committee for Effecting the Abolition of the Slave Trade, most of whose members were Quakers, was created in London in 1787 and began distributing anti-slave-trade pamphlets throughout the country at the peak of the African trade, when approximately eighty thousand Africans, more than half of them in British ships, were being brought annu-

ally to the Americas in the late 1780s. The committee, allied with
other dissenting sects as well as with the evangelical Methodists of
the Anglican Church, formed the base for the wider movement
that exploited the extraparliamentary methods of political pressure and petitioning that had been developed by supporters of
John Wilkes during the 1760s. Between 1788 and 1792, hundreds
of petitions from around the country were presented to Parliament in support of the movement to abolish the African slave
trade.

Emancipationists like Cugoano, who wanted to outlaw slavery
and free all slaves immediately, were relatively rare during the period. In the eighteenth-century British context, *abolition* almost
always referred to abolition of the trade in slaves from Africa to
the remaining British colonies in the West Indies, not to the abolition of the institution of slavery itself, though many of the slave-
trade abolitionists no doubt saw slavery as the ultimate target. In
response to the growing public interest in the controversy over
the African slave trade, in February 1788 George III ordered the
Privy Council Committee for Trade and Plantations to begin in-
vestigating the nature of the slave trade and British commercial relations with Africa. The committee, as well as the House of
Commons from 1789 to 1792, heard evidence for and against the
trade. From 1789 on, William Wilberforce led attempts in the
House of Commons to pass an abolition bill, only to see it either
fail by narrow margins or be blocked in the House of Lords in
1792, after the Commons had voted in that year to end the trade in
1796. The outbreak of the French Revolution and the subsequent
Terror during the period from 1789 to 1794 made Britons reluc-
tant to pursue any major social reforms lest they lead to revolu-
tionary results, and the slave revolts in the West Indies during the
1790s seemed to justify conservative fears. The threat posed by
Napoleonic France to national survival then eclipsed all other issues until 1804, when the agitation for abolition, relatively quies-
cent since 1796, revived with the renewal of war with Napoleon,
who in 1802 had reintroduced slavery in the French Caribbean
colonies. In 1807 the British slave trade was legally abolished, and
the British navy actively tried to stop the transatlantic slave trade
of other nations; in 1838 nonindigenous slavery itself was abol-

ished by law, and colonial slaves in the British Empire were emancipated.

Although the sustained political struggle to end the slave trade
(and later slavery itself) in the British Empire did not begin until
1787, slavery was a topic of public discussion throughout the century. Many of these discussions did not directly treat the subject
of abolishing the trade in slaves, let alone the abolition of the institution of slavery itself. Typical of the abolitionist's public position
was that expressed by Ramsay, writing in 1786 of his earlier *Essay
on the Treatment and Conversion of African Slaves*: "Though I
sincerely hope, that *some* plan will be devised for the future gradual abolition of slavery; and though I am convinced that this may,
without any prejudice to the planter, or injury to commerce, be
brought about by some such progressive method as is pointed out
in the Essay; yet this was not the first, or immediate object of that
book." Such circumspection reappears in Equiano's *Narrative*,
where he concentrates on the evils of the slave trade, though in
some of his letters to the newspapers his opinion of slavery is
more directly and forcefully stated. Even by the end of the century, the British abolitionist movement was almost always directed to abolishing the trade, not the institution. Some advocates
of the abolition of the trade no doubt saw that as the first step toward total emancipation of the slaves in the British Empire, but
they were usually careful not to diminish the size of their potential
audience by appearing too radical, Cugoano being the most no-
table exception.

Cugoano was one of the first identifiable Afro-Britons actively
engaged in the fight against slavery. On 28 July 1786 he joined
William Green, another Afro-Briton, in appealing to Granville
Sharp to save another Black, Harry Demane, who had been forced
by his employer, a Mr. Jeffries, aboard a ship bound for the West
Indies. On the twenty-ninth, Sharp sent Joseph Irwin and Patrick
Fraser to Jeffries, whom they frightened into telling them the
names of the ship and its master. Sharp obtained a writ of habeas
corpus and rescued Demane while the ship was under sail. In 1787
Demane became one of the Sierra Leone settlers, but, to Sharp's
dismay, by 1789 Demane was himself engaged in the slave trade.
With Equiano and other "Sons of Africa," Cugoano continued the

struggle against slavery with published letters to newspapers. (Cugoano and Equiano, another domestic servant, may have encountered each other before their collaborations during the 1780s: Equiano tells us that one of the churches at which he worshipped between September 1773 and September 1774 was Saint James's, Piccadilly, the church in which Cugoano was baptized. Sancho and Cugoano may have met through mutual friends, such as the sculptor Joseph Nollekens.)

While living with the Cosways in Schomberg House in 1787, Cugoano published *Thoughts and Sentiments on the Evil and Wicked Traffic*, perhaps written with help from Equiano. The book appeared in at least three issues during 1787 and was sold through several booksellers, including James Phillips, the Quakers' principal printer and bookseller in London. It was also sold by "the AUTHOR" and available "at Mr. *COSWAY*'s, No. 88, *Pall-Mall*." A French translation was published in Paris in 1788. But Cugoano's book apparently went unreviewed in Britain.

In 1791 Cugoano published a shorter version of his 1787 book entitled *Thoughts and Sentiments on the Evil of Slavery*, in which he thanks Sharp and Wilberforce for their efforts against slavery. In a postscript, he announces his intention to open a school for Afro-Britons. The book's imprint says that it was "Printed for, and sold by, the AUTHOR," which means that Cugoano bore the costs of its publication and accounts for why he sold it by subscription, receiving money in advance to support his expenses from the subscribers listed at the back of the work. *Letters of the Late Ignatius Sancho, An African* (London, 1782) and Equiano's *The Interesting Narrative of the Life of Olaudah Equiano, or Gustavus Vassa, the African* (London, 1789) had also been sold by subscription. (Cugoano and Richard Cosway subscribed to Equiano's work.) Cugoano again distributed his 1791 book through several booksellers as well as selling it himself from "No. 12, *Queen-Street, Grosvenor-Square*" [present-day Lumley Street], just a couple of blocks west and on the other side of Oxford Street from Stratford Place, where Richard Cosway had moved in 1791. Maria Cosway had moved to Europe in 1790, a few weeks after the birth of their daughter, Louisa Paolina Angelica, leaving Louisa with her husband. Cugoano's proximity to

Cosway and Cosway's name on the subscription list suggests that
Cugoano remained in his employ though no longer in his house,
perhaps having moved out because he had married or because
Cosway was trying to reduce his living expenses. Before moving
to Stratford Place, Cosway had sold much of his art collection.
Cugoano's second book, like his first, appears to have gone unreviewed. Increased financial need probably prompted both Cugoano's desire to open a school and the request he made to
Sharp, probably in 1791, asking to be sent to Nova Scotia to recruit settlers for a second attempt to settle free Afro-Britons
in Sierra Leone. No record has been found of Cugoano's either
having opened a school or having participated in settling Sierra
Leone. After 1791, Cugoano seems to have dropped out of
history, leaving no record. The absence of Cugoano's name on
the subscription list to Equiano's *Interesting Narrative* after its
fourth edition (Dublin, 1791) may indicate that he died in 1791 or
1792.

Additional and sometimes contradictory biographical information on Cugoano is found in Henri Grégoire's *An Enquiry Concerning the Intellectual and Moral Faculties and Literature of
Negroes: Followed with an Account of the Life and Works of Fifteen Negroes and Mulattoes Distinguished in Science, Literature
and the Arts*, translated by David Bailie Warden (Brooklyn, New
York, 1810). Citing as his source Scipione Piàttoli, an Italian abbot
who may have lived in England between 1800 and 1803, Grégoire
says that Cugoano was brought to England by a Lord Hoth and
that he married an Englishwoman. The account by the often unreliable Grégoire, however, remains uncorroborated.

In his *Thoughts and Sentiments* (1787), Cugoano raised the most
overt and extended challenge to slavery ever made by a person of
African descent. He was also the first English-speaking African
historian of slavery and the slave trade and the first to criticize European imperialism in the Americas. The title of his book clearly
alludes to Clarkson's *An Essay on the Slavery and Commerce of
the Human Species, Particularly the African*, and the work itself,
full of acknowledged and unacknowledged debts to the writings
of others, demonstrates that he saw the struggle against the trade

as a kind of group project. His recognition of Marrant and James Albert Ukawsaw Gronniosaw as his predecessors also places his work within an established tradition of Afro-British writings by converts to Christianity. In *Thoughts and Sentiments*, Cugoano refutes the pro-slavery arguments that slavery was divinely sanctioned, that Africans gladly sold their own families into slavery (though he acknowledges African complicity in the transatlantic trade), that Africans were especially well suited for slavery, and that West Indian slaves led better lives than the European poor. Cugoano believes that slaves have not only the right but the obligation to rebel: "It is the duty of every man to deliver himself from rogues and villains if he can." The "enslavers of men are the servants of the devil" and the breakers of God's law, and thus "the only men that others have any right to enslave." Every Briton shares the blame for the evil of slavery, which threatens Great Britain with divine retribution. He also condemns European imperialism throughout the world and especially in the Americas, and calls for the conversion of non-Christians. Defending his friend Equiano, Cugoano criticizes the implementation of the settlement at Sierra Leone in the midst of a slave-trading area, but he supports the principle behind it, believing that trade *with* Africans should replace trade *in* Africans.

By far the most radical assault on slavery as well as the slave trade by a writer of African descent, at a time when attacks on slavery as an institution were very rare, Cugoano's work apparently went unadvertised. For example, James Phillips's advertisements in other anti-slave-trade books he distributed make no reference to Cugoano's *Thoughts and Sentiments*. Perhaps Cugoano's work was not reviewed, as were the works of Sancho and Equiano, because it was not considered to fall within any of the recognized genres normally covered by the contemporaneous literary reviews. Or its message may simply have been too radical for the reviewers to want to circulate, though this explanation seems less likely.

Lacking much documentary biographical evidence and having only a few representations by others of Cugoano's life, we are largely limited in what we can say about him to the ways he represents himself in *Thoughts and Sentiments* and elsewhere. His work has received very little critical treatment, and that often dismissive. His first known critic, Grégoire, says,

> His work is not very methodical. There are repetitions, because grief is verbose. An individual deeply affected, is always afraid of not having said enough—of not being sufficiently understood. We see talents without cultivation, and to which a good education would have given great progress.

Grégoire's emphasis on Cugoano's use of rhetorical pathos—the appeal to his readers' feelings and emotional response—underestimates his reliance on logic and his use of authority in the work. And Grégoire's stress on Cugoano's probable lack of formal education ignores the role secondary sources play in supporting his argument, demonstrating a knowledge of relevant history and theological commentary. Even his modern editor, Paul Edwards, thought that Cugoano's published writing must have been edited and improved by Equiano. Edwards felt that Cugoano's holograph private letters, all then-known copies of which Edwards transcribed and published, reveal his inadequacies as a writer. But to be fair to Cugoano, one should point out that his surviving holograph letters are not significantly less polished than those by Equiano, transcribed in the Penguin edition of *The Interesting Narrative*.

And one should also point out that many of the formal qualities of Cugoano's *Thoughts and Sentiments* that may strike readers as ungrammatical, repetitive, imitative, and lacking in narrative force may be explained by approaching the text from the African oral and Christian homiletic traditions, as well as the written tradition in which critics have placed it. *Thoughts and Sentiments* belongs primarily to the genre of the jeremiad, or political sermon, named after the Old Testament prophet Jeremiah, who denounced the sins of the Hebrew community and warned of divine retribution should the evil behavior continue. Recognizing Cugoano's work to be a jeremiad helps to account for his pervasive use of biblical and quasi-biblical diction, as well as for his invocations of biblical precedents in his argument against slavery. Since the Middle Ages, Christian preachers had employed jeremiads to rebuke the com-

munal or national backsliding of their congregations and countries, especially in times of public distress such as the duration and
aftermath of the American Revolution, when explanations for the
recent national calamity were sought. As Hannah More, who
would herself soon oppose the African slave trade, remarked in
1780, it was "the fashion to make the most lamentable *Jeremiades*
on the badness of times."

The jeremiad was especially appropriate for Cugoano's times
because, in response to increasing opposition, defenders of slavery
and the slave trade sought to justify their actions with religious and
economic arguments, pointing out that slavery had a very long history. Although Cugoano concedes that "slavery was an ancient
custom," he adds that it was "never lawful." Speaking in 1763 to
his biographer, James Boswell, on "the cause of some part of
mankind being black," before so-called scientific racism was developed to justify slavery, Samuel Johnson succinctly described the
state of knowledge on the subject before the abolitionist movement: "It has been accounted for in three ways: either by supposing that they are the posterity of Ham, who was cursed; or that
God at first created two kinds of men, one black and another
white; or that by the heat of the sun the skin is scorched, and so
gets the sooty hue. This matter has been much canvassed among
naturalists, but has never been brought to any certain issue." Some
apologists for slavery argued that Black Africans were doomed to
slavery by the biblical curses on either Cain or the descendants of
Ham and his son Canaan, the son and grandson of Noah, and that
Blackness was the sign of the curse. The Bible, however, offers no
evidence of such a curse. Other apologists contended that the visible physical differences among ethnic groups on the various conti-
nents resulted from the polygenetic origins of humans—the
different groups had different ancestors. Orthodox religious belief
maintained that all people shared a monogenetic origin in the common ancestors Adam and Eve. To the apologists for slavery, variations in complexion reflected variations in humanity; to the
orthodox, such variations in color were often attributed to climate
or accident rather than interpreted as indicators of inferiority. To
the apologists, the economic rewards of African slavery proved the
validity of the biblically based arguments they devised to defend it.

Cugoano's radical stance on slavery might seem to suggest that he had assimilated British values less fully than either Sancho or Equiano. More obviously concerned than Cugoano with not offending their White audiences by their critical comments on the slave trade and slavery, Sancho and Equiano appear to have more fully adopted British cultural assumptions than the outspoken Cugoano. But in a fundamental way, he is arguably more assimilated than either. Cugoano speaks from the very core of European culture because he frequently uses the persona of an Old Testament prophet to address his audiences, which include both the English public and his fellow Africans, to castigate everyone actively and passively involved in the perpetuation of slavery. To signify his assumed rhetorical identity, his last biblical quotation in the text is from Jeremiah 16:18: "And first, saith the Lord, I will recompence their iniquity, and their sin double; because they have defiled my land, they have filled mine inheritance with the carcases of their detestable and abominable things." Though he embraces Christianity, his Christianity has a strongly Old Testament tone, stressing justice far more often than mercy—a point he underscores by combining passages from Numbers and Matthew to form his epigraph. Like the Old Testament prophets he cites, quotes, and imitates in his quasi-biblical diction, Cugoano rhetorically positions himself at the edge of the society in which he finds himself.

From this position, Cugoano can more easily appropriate traditional ways in which the British saw themselves and then redefine those ways to support his argument. For example, to underscore his argument that by trading in slaves Britain was resisting the divine plan to establish her as "the Queen of nations," Cugoano uses the ambivalent post-Reformation tradition of likening the English to the Old Testament Jews, who were God's chosen yet were headstrong and often disobedient people who had not yet embraced Christianity. In one of his many reversals in his work of received opinions, Cugoano says that slavery, rather than being the result of a curse, will cause Britain to be cursed. At one point, Cugoano cleverly accepts the belief that the offspring of Canaan were cursed: he invokes the legend that Canaanites settled in Cornwall on the west coast of England to suggest that, "for anything that can be known to the contrary, there may be some of the descendants of that wicked generation still subsisting among the slaveholders in the West-Indies." Cugoano also inverts Britain's definition of itself as a virtuous imperial power in contrast to what was known as the "black legend" of Portuguese and Spanish colonial misrule developed in England and Holland during the Protestant propaganda campaign against the Roman Catholic Church and Spain. Cugoano argues that the British slave trade is simply a historical extension of the Iberian trade, and he reminds his readers that the British had become the major conductors of the trade. "The French and English," he says, have "joined hand in hand with the Portuguese and Spanish to rob and pillage Africa" and "have infested the inhabitants with some of the vilest combinations of fraudulent and treacherous villains." Similarly, Cugoano uses conventional Protestant polemics against Roman Catholics and Muslims demonizing the Pope and Muhammad as servants of the Antichrist, to argue that the shared institution of slavery rendered Britain morally akin to its political and religious opponents.

More consistently and fully than either Sancho or Equiano, Cugoano uses his marginal status as an African in England to regard Europeans with the innocent but angry eye of a participant observer. At times in *Thoughts and Sentiments*, Cugoano writes to his readers directly in the voice of the African: "And we that are particularly concerned would humbly join with all the rest of our brethren and countrymen in complexion [in] imploring and earnestly entreating the most respectful and generous people of Great Britain." Sancho and Equiano also take advantage of the perspective of the stranger in a strange land who innocently—naively—records the sins and follies of the natives he observes. But from Cugoano's moral vantage point of not sharing the behavior of the sinners he excoriates, even Sancho and Equiano would be complicit in the sins of the land. As a free man, Equiano had been a slave driver on a plantation in Central America in 1776; as a Westminster grocer, much of Sancho's income depended on the sale of sugar and tobacco, the primary products of West Indian slavery. Cugoano repeatedly points out that the economic and political effects of slavery are so pervasive that all members of society, including the monarch, bear responsibility by their passive or active behavior for the continuation of the evil. Indeed, "kings and great men [are] considered as more particularly guilty."

In Cugoano's prophetic persona in *Thoughts and Sentiments*, we find little explicit reference to the double consciousness of being Black in Britain that Sancho and Equiano frequently express. In his public and private letters, however, Cugoano uses both his African and British identities. As if to underscore his morally privileged status as a resident alien, he signs letters to the press with both names; at times combining his identities to become Ottobah Cugoana [*sic*] Steward. In most of his private letters he signs himself simply John Stuart. In his 1787 letter to the Prince of Wales, whom he no doubt met while in Cosway's employ, he makes clear that his African identity is being revealed for the first time to someone who had known him only by his British name: "None can wish it more than He whose African Name is the title of the book." And in 1789 he subscribed to *The Interesting Narrative* of Equiano, another binomial Black author, as "Ottobah Cugoano, or John Stewart." For reasons unknown, he did not reveal his full African name, Quobna Ottobah Cugoano, until the publication of his abridged work in 1791.

Cugoano derives his authority, his right and power to write, from his combined African and British identities, as well as from the biblical prophetic tradition. He is the first self-authorized Afro-British writer; Equiano is the second. Unlike Marrant, Gronniosaw, Sancho, and Phillis Wheatley, Cugoano published his works without any authenticating documentation or mediation by White authorities implying that his words had been supervised by others before publication. Although he briefly displays a conventionally humble pose early in *Thoughts and Sentiments*, Cugoano quickly takes a more confrontational stance toward his opponents, a stance authorized by both his "complexion" and the prophetic tradition: "In this little undertaking, I must humbly hope the impartial reader will excuse such defects as may arise from want of better education; and as to the resentment of those who can lay their cruel lash upon the backs of thousands, for a thousand times less crimes than writing against their enormous wickedness and brutal avarice, is what I may be sure to meet with." And he acknowledges that physical enslavement has para-

doxically been a fortunate fall into emancipation from spiritual enslavement through his exposure to Christianity: "One great duty I
owe to Almighty God . . . that, although I have been brought
away from my native country, in that torrent of robbery and
wickedness, thanks be to God for his good providence towards
me. . . . I am highly indebted to many of the good people of England for learning and principles unknown to the people of my
native country." Anticipating Equiano's use of autobiography to
establish his credibility through his personal experience of enslavement, Cugoano rapidly moves from introductory statements
in his *Thoughts and Sentiments* to a brief narrative account of his
early life, which he follows with a lengthy treatment of the evils of
slavery and the price that enslavers must pay. His account of the
horrors of slavery culminates with the figure of "the inhuman
monster of a captain" of the *Zong*, who had gone unpunished after
having thrown 133 enslaved Africans overboard in 1781 in an attempt to claim the insurance on his lost "cargo."

Cugoano's emphasis on the evils of slavery and the anger of his
voice almost overwhelm the more positive structural frame of
Thoughts and Sentiments. He opens his work with an expression
of gratitude to his White countrymen for their writings and actions against the slave trade. And he acknowledges that in the new
United States "some mitigation of slavery has been obtained in
some respective districts of America, though not in proportion to
their own vaunted claims of freedom." Unfortunately, his hope
"that they will yet go to make a further and greater reformation"
would not be realized until the American Civil War. Cugoano also
closes his work on a positive note, again imitating the common
structure of a jeremiad, in which mercy often came after justice, a
new covenant after reproval and punishment. Cugoano offers a
tripartite program of redemption and regeneration to Britain's
better self, calling the country "the Queen of nations," "this fair
land of liberty," and its inhabitants "the noble Britons." Embrac-
ing his program of reform by designating days of mourning and
fasting for past sins, immediately abolishing slavery and emanci-
pating all slaves, and acting to end the slave trade by other European countries, "the temperate climes of Great-Britain [might] be
seen to vie with the rich land of Canaan of old, which is now, be-

cause of the wickedness of its inhabitants, in comparison of what it was, as only a barren desert." In effect, Cugoano transforms the curse of Canaan from one of color to one of behavior, and the recipients of the curse from the enslaved to the enslavers. Like a new Moses, he offers the wayward British a path back to the promised land.

Though he does not entirely cast off his Old Testament persona, as his text continues Cugoano increasingly speaks as one Christian to others. He addresses his readers as "O beloved," just as the apostles John and Jude addressed their fellow newly converted Christians in the New Testament. By the penultimate paragraph of the work, he has assumed the sacerdotal role of the Anglican priest catechizing the neophyte with a call-and-response; however, by that point in the text the whole nation has become his corporate catechumen as he rewrites the liturgy to use the significance of naming and its relationship to identity to erase the boundaries between Africans and Europeans: "And Christianity does not require that we should be deprived of our own personal name, or the name of our ancestors; but it may very fitly add another name unto us, Christian, or one anointed. And it may as well be answered so to that question in the English liturgy, *What is your name?*—A Christian." Cugoano's interest in naming is reflected in his use of his binomial identity: he is literally Afro-British, neither simply Cugoano nor Stuart. Although he publicly reveals his African identity in print in 1787 and his full African name in 1791, he keeps his English name and British identity as well. When he writes on public issues to correspondents who knew him in his private capacity as Cosway's servant, he uses both names. The name "Christian" not only enables him to transcend his own dual identities but also allows him and his readers to replace ethnic difference with religious likeness, ending what remains a surprisingly radical and angry call for action with the possibility for reconciliation, harmony, and hope.

ACKNOWLEDGMENTS

I thank Michael Millman, Joseph F. Marcey, Jr., and Penguin Putnam for having offered me the opportunity to publish the edited works of Olaudah Equiano, Ignatius Sancho, and Quobna Ottobah Cugoano. Anyone who writes on Cugoano or his *Thoughts and Sentiments* is indebted to Paul Edwards for his facsimile reproduction of the first edition, with its introduction and notes.

I am very grateful to the staffs and collections of the following institutions: the Annandale (Virginia) Family History Center of the Church of Jesus Christ of Latter-day Saints; the British Library; the British Museum; the City of Westminster Archives Centre; Cornell University; the Family Records Centre (London); the Folger Shakespeare Library (Washington, D.C.); the Gloucestershire Record Office; the Institute of Historical Research at the University of London; the Library of Congress; the London Metropolitan Archive; the McKeldin Library and the Interlibrary Loan Office of the University of Maryland; the Northamptonshire Record Office for permission to reproduce Cugoano's letter to Sir William Dolben; the Public Record Office (London); the Sheffield City Library; the Society of Genealogists (London); and the University of London.

I thank Mr. Charles Lloyd-Baker for his kind permission to reproduce the letters from Cugoano to George III, the Prince of Wales, and Granville Sharp.

For questions, comments, and answers I thank Gerald Barnett, Brycchan Carey, Lillian Carretta, Michael Crump, Leigh Anna Eicke, Susan Essman, Christopher Fyfe, Judith Jennings, Reyahn King, Stephen Lloyd, Paula McDowell, J. R. Oldfield, and Arthur Torrington.

The University of Maryland provided financial support for my research through a sabbatical leave and an award from the Committee on Africa and the Americas.

Following Paul Edwards, I assume that the British Library copy of *Thoughts and Sentiments*, T 111 (4), in which a short list of "ERRATA" is added after the "GENERAL CONTENTS," is the original of at least three 1787 issues of the only known edition of Cugoano's first book. This first issue is the copy-text for the Penguin edition. Cugoano's corrections and revisions are incorporated into the text and identified in the notes of the Penguin edition.

The British Library also has the few extant pages of what I assume was another issue, T 700 (6), bearing the imprint, "Sold by T[homas] *BECKET*, Bookseller, *Pall-Mall*; also by Mr. [William] *HALL*, at No. 25, *Princes-Street, Soho*; Mr. [James] *PHILLIPS*, *George-Yard, Lombard-Street*; and also by the AUTHOR, at Mr. [Richard] *COSWAY*'s, No. 88, *Pall-Mall*." Its title page bears the place and date "London, July 1787" and misprints "submited" and "OTTABAH" in the title. All that remains of this issue are the title page, "GENERAL CONTENTS," and "*N[ota] B[ene]*."

The issue of *Thoughts and Sentiments* in the Porteus Library of the University of London, after the "GENERAL CONTENTS," has pasted in "London, July 1787" and the following imprint: "to be had of Mr. HALL, at No. 25, *Princes-Street, Soho*; Mr. PHILLIPS, *George-Yard, Lombard-Street*; or of the AUTHOR, at Mr. COSWAY's, No. 88, *Pall-Mall*." Also pasted in is the "*N[ota] B[ene]*," which is included in a note to the Penguin edition.

Spelling (including the various spellings of proper names, such as the interchangeable use of "I" and "J") and punctuation have not been modernized unless the original usage would confuse or mislead a twentieth-century reader. The eighteenth-century long "s" has been replaced throughout. Obvious errors in printing, such as dropped or inverted letters, have been silently corrected.

A French translation of *Thoughts and Sentiments* was published in Paris in 1788.

ILLUSTRATIONS

Isaac Cruikshank (1764–1811), *The Abolition of the Slave Trade*, 10 April 1792. Engraving reproduced by courtesy of the Library of Congress.

Cruikshank's print was occasioned by William Wilberforce's speech in the House of Commons, 2 April 1792, denouncing Captain John Kimber's brutal murder of an enslaved African girl who had refused to dance at his command. In Cruikshank's design, an attractive young woman is raised by her ankle from the ship's deck by a rope on a pulley. The sailor who lifts her remarks, "Dam me if I like it I have a good mind to let go." Two sailors walk away on the right. One says, "My eyes Jack our Girles at Wapping [an area on the Thames near London frequented by seamen and prostitutes] are never flogged for their modesty." The other responds, "By G-d that's too bad if he had taken her to bed to him it would be well enough, Split me I'm almost sick of this Black Business." On the viewer's left, laughing and looming large, is captain Kimber, whip in hand. On the deck beneath the suspended victim are two scourges; other slaves are seated behind her. Under the print's title we read, "Or the Inhumanity of Dealers in human flesh exemplified in Capt[ai]n Kimber's treatment of a Young Negro Girl of 15 for her Virgen [*sic*] Modesty." When Kimber was brought before the Admiralty on a charge of murder in the case and tried on the evidence of the ship's surgeon and mate, he was acquitted and his accusers committed for perjury.

As Cugoano demonstrates several times in *Thoughts and Sentiments*, including in his discussion of the *Zong* atrocity, by the 1780s the figure of the evil captain had become a stock figure in attacks on the slave trade. Opponents of the trade often argued that it dehumanized the enslaver as well as the enslaved. Cugoano was one of many who frequently used visual and verbal images of mistreated women and children to underscore the horrors of the trade.

Mr. and Mrs. Cosway. Etching by Richard Cosway, inscribed "Cosway 1784." Reproduced by permission of Whitworth Art Gallery, University of Manchester.

Cugoano is almost certainly the servant depicted in this etching. Gerald Barnett, biographer of Richard and Maria Cosway, and Christopher Fyfe, historian of Sierra Leone, believe that Cugoano, not Equiano, is the subject of the portrait reproduced on the cover of the Penguin edition of Equiano's writings, a portrait that Barnett believes was done by Richard Cosway.

The title page of *Thoughts and Sentiments on the Evil and Wicked Traffic of the Slavery and Commerce of the Human Species, Humbly Submitted to the Inhabitants of Great-Britain, by Ottobah Cugoano, a Native of Africa* (London, 1787) is reproduced courtesy of the British Library.

The title page of *Thoughts and Sentiments on the Evil of Slavery; or, the Nature of Servitude as Admitted by the Law of God, Compared to the Modern Slavery of the Africans in the West-Indies; In an Answer to the Advocates for Slavery and Oppression. Addressed to the Sons of Africa, by a Native* (London: 1791) is reproduced courtesy of the Cornell University Library.

SUGGESTIONS FOR FURTHER READING

EDITION

Thoughts and Sentiments on the Evil and Wicked Traffic of the Slavery and Commerce of the Human Species, Humbly Submitted to the Inhabitants of Great-Britain, by Ottobah Cugoano, a Native of Africa. London, 1787; facsimile of the first edition, with an Introduction and Notes by Paul Edwards. London: Dawsons of Pall Mall, 1969.

CRITICISM AND SCHOLARSHIP

Braidwood, Stephen J. *Black Poor and White Philanthropists: London's Blacks and the Foundation of the Sierra Leone Settlement 1786-1791.* Liverpool: Liverpool University Press, 1994.

Carretta, Vincent. *Unchained Voices: An Anthology of Black Authors in the English-Speaking World of the Eighteenth Century.* Lexington: University Press of Kentucky, 1996.

Costanzo, Angelo. *Surprizing Narrative: Olaudah Equiano and the Beginnings of Black Autobiography.* New York: Greenwood Press, 1987.

Davis, Charles T., and Gates, Henry Louis, Jr. *The Slave's Narrative.* New York: Oxford University Press, 1985.

Davis, David Brion. *The Problem of Slavery in Western Culture.* New York: Oxford University Press, 1966.

———. *The Problem of Slavery in the Age of Revolution 1770–1823.* Ithaca: Cornell University Press, 1975.

Drescher, Seymour. *Capitalism and Antislavery: British Mobilization in Comparative Perspective.* London: Macmillan, 1986.

Edwards, Paul, and David Dabydeen, eds. *Black Writers in Britain, 1760–1890.* Edinburgh: Edinburgh University Press, 1991.

Edwards, Paul, and James Walvin, eds. *Black Personalities in the Era of the Slave Trade.* London: Macmillan, 1983.

Fryer, Peter. *Staying Power: The History of Black People in Britain.* London: Pluto Press, 1984.

Gates, Henry Louis, Jr. *The Signifying Monkey: A Theory of African-American Literary Criticism.* New York: Oxford University Press, 1988.

Hogg, Peter C. *The African Slave Trade and Its Suppression: A Classified and Annotated Bibliography of Books, Pamphlets and Periodical Articles.* London: Frank Cass, 1973.

Jennings, Judith. *The Business of Abolishing the British Slave Trade 1783–1807.* London: Frank Cass, 1997.

Jordan, Winthrop D. *White over Black: American Attitudes toward the Negro, 1550–1812.* New York: Norton, 1968.

Ogude, S. E. *Genius in Bondage: A Study of the Origins of African Literature in English.* Ile-Ife, Nigeria: University of Ife Press, 1983.

Sandiford, Keith. *Measuring the Moment: Strategies of Protest in Eighteenth-Century Afro-English Writing.* London: Associated University Press, 1988.

Shyllon, Folarin. *Black People in Britain 1555–1833.* London: Oxford University Press, 1977.

Walvin, James. *Black Ivory: A History of British Slavery.* London: Fontana Press, 1992.

THOUGHTS AND SENTIMENTS

ON THE

EVIL AND WICKED TRAFFIC

OF THE

SLAVERY AND COMMERCE

OF THE

HUMAN SPECIES,

HUMBLY SUBMITTED TO

The INHABITANTS of *GREAT-BRITAIN*,

BY

OTTOBAH CUGOANO,

A NATIVE of *AFRICA*.

He that stealeth a man and selleth him, or maketh merchan-
dize of him, or if he be found in his hand: then that thief
shall die.   LAW OF GOD.

LONDON:

PRINTED IN THE YEAR

M.DCC.LXXXVII.

GENERAL CONTENTS

N.B. Since these Thoughts and Sentiments have been read by some, I find a general Approbation has been given, and that the things pointed out thereby might be more effectually taken into consideration, I was requested by some friends to add this information concerning myself:—When I was kidnapped and brought away from Africa, I was then about 13 years of age, in the year of the Christian aera 1770; and being about nine or ten months in the slave-gang at Grenada, and about one year at different places in the West-Indies, with Alexander Campbell, Esq; who brought me to England in the end of the year 1772,[2] I was advised by some good people to get myself baptized, that I might not be carried away and sold again.[3]—I was called Stewart by my master, but in order that I might embrace this ordinance, I was called John Stewart, and I went several times to Dr. Skinner,[4] who instructed me, and I was baptized by him, and registered at St. James's Church in the year 1773.[5] Some of my fellow-servants, who assisted me in this, got themselves turned away for it; I have only put my African name to the title of the book.—When I was brought away from Africa, my father and relations were then chief men in the kingdom of Agimaque and Assinee; but what they may be now, or whether dead or alive, I know not. I wish to go back as soon as I can hear any proper security and safe conveyance can be found; and I wait to hear how it fares with the Black People sent to Sierra Leona.[6] But it is my highest wish and earnest prayer to God, that some encouragement could be given to send able school masters, and intelligent ministers, who would be faithful and able to teach the Christian religion. This would be doing great good to the Africans, and be a kind restitution for the great injuries that they have suffered. But still I fear no good can be done near any of the European settlements, while such a horrible and infernal traffic of slavery is carried on by them.[7] Wherever the foot of man can go, at the forts and garrisons it would seem to be wrote with these words—

O earth! O sea! cover not thou the blood of the poor negro slaves.[8]

Thoughts and Sentiments on the Evil of Slavery

> One law, and one manner shall be for you, and
> for the stranger that sojourneth with you; and
> therefore, all things whatsoever ye would that
> men should do to you, do ye even so to them.
> NUMB[ERS] XV.16., MATTHEW VII.12.

AS SEVERAL LEARNED GENTLEMEN of distinguished abilities, as
well as eminent for their great humanity, liberality and candour,
have written various essays against that infamous traffic of the
African Slave Trade, carried on with the West-India planters and
merchants, to the great shame and disgrace of all Christian nations
wherever it is admitted in any of their territories, or place or situation amongst them; it cannot be amiss that I should thankfully
acknowledge these truly worthy and humane gentlemen with the
warmest sense of gratitude, for their beneficent and laudable endeavours towards a total suppression of that infamous and iniquitous traffic of stealing, kid-napping, buying, selling, and cruelly
enslaving men!

Those who have endeavoured to restore to their fellow-
creatures the common rights of nature, of which especially the unfortunate Black People have been so unjustly deprived, cannot fail
in meeting with the applause of all good men, and the approbation
of that which will for ever redound to their honor; they have the
warrant of that which is divine: *Open thy mouth, judge righteously, plead the cause of the poor and needy; for the liberal deviseth liberal things, and by liberal things shall stand.*[9] And they
can say with the pious Job, *Did not I weep for him that was in
trouble; was not my soul grieved for the poor?*[10]

The kind exertions of many benevolent and humane gentlemen,
against the iniquitous traffic of slavery and oppression, has been
attended with much good to many, and must redound with great
honor to themselves, to humanity and their country; their laudable endeavours have been productive of the most beneficent ef-

fects in preventing that savage barbarity from taking place in free countries at home. In this, as well as in many other respects, there is one class of people (whose virtues of probity and humanity are well known) who are worthy of universal approbation and imitation, because, like men of honor and humanity, they have jointly agreed to carry on no slavery and savage barbarity among them;[11] and, since the last war, some mitigation of slavery has been obtained in some respective districts of America, though not in proportion to their own vaunted claims of freedom; but it is to be hoped, that they will yet go on to make a further and greater reformation.[12] However, notwithstanding all that has been done and written against it, that brutish barbarity, and unparalleled injustice, is still carried on to a very great extent in the colonies, and with an avidity as insidious, cruel and oppressive as ever. The longer that men continue in the practice of evil and wickedness, they grow the more abandoned; for nothing in history can equal the barbarity and cruelty of the tortures and murders committed under various pretences in modern slavery, except the annals of the Inquisition[13] and the bloody edicts of Popish massacres.[14]

It is therefore manifest, that something else ought yet to be done; and what is required, is evidently the incumbent duty of all men of enlightened understanding, and of every man that has any claim or affinity to the name of Christian, that the base treatment which the African Slaves undergo, ought to be abolished; and it is moreover evident, that the whole, or any part of that iniquitous traffic of slavery, can no where, or in any degree, be admitted, but among those who must eventually resign their own claim to any degree of sensibility and humanity, for that of barbarians and ruffians.

But it would be needless to arrange an history of all the base treatment which the African Slaves are subjected to, in order to shew the exceeding wickedness and evil of that insidious traffic, as the whole may easily appear in every part, and at every view, to be wholly and totally inimical to every idea of justice, equity, reason and humanity. What I intend to advance against that evil, criminal and wicked traffic of enslaving men, are only some Thoughts and Sentiments which occur to me, as being obvious from the Scriptures of Divine Truth, or such arguments as are chiefly deduced from thence, with other such observations as I have been able to collect. Some of these observations may lead into a larger field of consideration, than that of the African Slave Trade alone; but those causes from wherever they originate, and become the production of slavery, the evil effects produced by it, must shew that its origin and source is of a wicked and criminal nature.

No necessity, or any situation of men, however poor, pitiful and wretched they may be, can warrant them to rob others, or oblige them to become thieves, because they are poor, miserable and wretched: But the robbers of men, the kid-nappers, ensnarers and slave-holders, who take away the common rights and privileges of others to support and enrich themselves, are universally those pitiful and detestable wretches; for the ensnarings of others, and taking away their liberty by slavery and oppression, is the worst kind of robbery, as most opposite to every precept and injunction of the Divine Law, and contrary to that command which enjoins that *all men should love their neighbours as themselves*, and *that they should do unto others, as they would that men should do to them*.[15] As to any other laws that slave-holders may make among themselves, as respecting slaves, they can be of no better kind, nor give them any better character, than what is implied in the common report—that there may be some honesty among thieves. This may seem a harsh comparison, but the parallel is so coincident that, I must say, I can find no other way of expressing my Thoughts and Sentiments, without making use of some harsh words and comparisons against the carriers on of such abandoned wickedness. But, in this little undertaking, I must humbly hope the impartial reader will excuse such defects as may arise from want of better education; and as to the resentment of those who can lay their cruel lash upon the backs of thousands, for a thousand times less crimes than writing against their enormous wickedness and brutal avarice, is what I may be sure to meet with.

However, it cannot but be very discouraging to a man of my complexion in such an attempt as this, to meet with the evil aspersions of some men, who say, "That an African is not entitled to any competent degree of knowledge, or capable of imbibing any sentiments of probity; and that nature designed him for some infe-

rior link in the chain,[16] fitted only to be a slave."[17] But when I
meet with those who make no scruple to deal with the human
species, as with the beasts of the earth, I must think them not only
brutish, but wicked and base; and that their aspersions are insidious and false: And if such men can boast of greater degrees of
knowledge, than any African is entitled to, I shall let them enjoy
all the advantages of it unenvied, as I fear it consists only in greater
share of infidelity, and that of a blacker kind than only skin deep.
And if their complexion be not what I may suppose, it is at least
the nearest in resemblance to an infernal hue. A good man will
neither speak nor do as a bad man will; but if a man is bad, it
makes no difference whether he be a black or a white devil.

By some of such complexion, as whether black or white it matters not, I was early snatched away from my native country, with
about eighteen or twenty more boys and girls, as we were playing
in a field. We lived but a few days journey from the coast where
we were kid-napped, and as we were decoyed and drove along, we
were soon conducted to a factory,[18] and from thence, in the fashionable way of traffic, consigned to Grenada. Perhaps it may not
be amiss to give a few remarks, as some account of myself, in this
transposition of captivity.

I was born in the city of Agimaque, on the coast of Fantyn; my
father was a companion to the chief in that part of the country of
Fantee, and when the old king died I was left in his house with his
family; soon after I was sent for by his nephew, Ambro Accasa,
who succeeded the old king in the chiefdom of that part of Fantee
known by the name of Agimaque and Assinee.[19] I lived with his
children, enjoying peace and tranquillity, about twenty moons,
which, according to their way of reckoning time, is two years. I
was sent for to visit an uncle, who lived at a considerable distance
from Agimaque. The first day after we set out we arrived at Assinee, and the third day at my uncle's habitation, where I lived
about three months, and was then thinking of returning to my father and young companion at Agimaque; but by this time I had
got well acquainted with some of the children of my uncle's hundreds of relations, and we were some days too venturesome in going into the woods to gather fruit and catch birds, and such
amusements as pleased us. One day I refused to go with the rest,

being rather apprehensive that something might happen to us; till one of my play-fellows said to me, because you belong to the great men, you are afraid to venture your carcase, or else of the *bounsam*, which is the devil. This enraged me so much, that I set a resolution to join the rest, and we went into the woods as usual; but we had not been above two hours before our troubles began, when several great ruffians came upon us suddenly, and said we had committed a fault against their lord, and we must go and answer for it ourselves before him.

Some of us attempted in vain to run away, but pistols and cutlasses were soon introduced, threatening, that if we offered to stir we should all lie dead on the spot. One of them pretended to be more friendly than the rest, and said, that he would speak to their lord to get us clear, and desired that we should follow him; we were then immediately divided into different parties, and drove after him. We were soon led out of the way which we knew, and towards the evening, as we came in sight of a town, they told us that this great man of theirs lived there, but pretended it was too late to go and see him that night. Next morning there came three other men, whose language differed from ours, and spoke to some of those who watched us all the night, but he that pretended to be our friend with the great man, and some others, were gone away. We asked our keepers what these men had been saying to them, and they answered, that they had been asking them, and us together, to go and feast with them that day, and that we must put off seeing the great man till after; little thinking that our doom was so nigh, or that these villains meant to feast on us as their prey. We went with them again about half a day's journey, and came to a great multitude of people, having different music playing; and all the day after we got there, we were very merry with the music, dancing and singing. Towards the evening, we were again persuaded that we could not get back to where the great man lived till next day; and when bedtime came, we were separated into different houses with different people. When the next morning came, I asked for the men that brought me there, and for the rest of my companions; and I was told that they were gone to the sea side to bring home some rum, guns and powder, and that some of my companions were gone with them, and that some were gone to the fields to do something or other. This gave me strong suspicion that there was some treachery in the case, and I began to think that my hopes of returning home again were all over. I soon became very uneasy, not knowing what to do, and refused to eat or drink for whole days together, till the man of the house told me that he would do all in his power to get me back to my uncle; then I eat[20] a little fruit with him, and had some thoughts that I should be sought after, as I would be then missing at home about five or six days. I enquired every day if the men had come back, and for the rest of my companions, but could get no answer of any satisfaction. I was kept about six days at this man's house, and in the evening there was another man came and talked with him a good while, and I heard the one say to the other he must go, and the other said the sooner the better; that man came out and told me that he knew my relations at Agimaque, and that we must set out to-morrow morning, and he would convey me there. Accordingly we set out next day, and travelled till dark, when we came to a place where we had some supper and slept. He carried a large bag with some gold dust, which he said he had to buy some goods at the sea side to take with him to Agimaque. Next day we travelled on, and in the evening came to a town, where I saw several white people, which made me afraid that they would eat me, according to our notion as children in the inland parts of the country. This made me rest very uneasy all the night, and next morning I had some victuals brought, desiring me to eat and make haste, as my guide and kid-napper told me that he had to go to the castle with some company that were going there, as he had told me before, to get some goods. After I was ordered out, the horrors I soon saw and felt, cannot be well described; I saw many of my miserable countrymen chained two and two, some hand-cuffed, and some with their hands tied behind. We were conducted along by a guard, and when we arrived at the castle, I asked my guide what I was brought there for, he told me to learn the ways of the *brow-sow*, that is the white faced people. I saw him take a gun, a piece of cloth, and some lead for me, and then he told me that he must now leave me there, and went off. This made me cry bitterly, but I was soon conducted to a prison, for three days, where I heard the groans and cries of many, and saw some of my fellow-captives.

But when a vessel arrived to conduct us away to the ship, it was a most horrible scene; there was nothing to be heard but rattling of chains, smacking of whips, and the groans and cries of our fellow-men. Some would not stir from the ground, when they were lashed and beat in the most horrible manner. I have forgot the name of this infernal fort; but we were taken in the ship that came for us, to another that was ready to sail from Cape Coast. When we were put into the ship, we saw several black merchants coming on board, but we were all drove into our holes, and not suffered to speak to any of them. In this situation we continued several days in sight of our native land; but I could find no good person to give any information of my situation to Accasa at Agimaque. And when we found ourselves at last taken away, death was more preferable than life, and a plan was concerted amongst us, that we might burn and blow up the ship, and to perish all together in the flames; but we were betrayed by one of our own countrywomen, who slept with some of the head men of the ship, for it was common for the dirty filthy sailors to take the African women and lie upon their bodies; but the men were chained and pent up in holes. It was the women and boys which were to burn the ship, with the approbation and groans of the rest; though that was prevented, the discovery was likewise a cruel bloody scene

But it would be needless to give a description of all the horrible scenes which we saw, and the base treatment which we met with in this dreadful captive situation, as the similar cases of thousands, which suffer by this infernal traffic, are well known. Let it suffice to say, that I was thus lost to my dear indulgent parents and relations, and they to me. All my help was cries and tears, and these could not avail; nor suffered long, till one succeeding woe, and dread, swelled up another. Brought from a state of innocence and freedom, and, in a barbarous and cruel manner, conveyed to a state of horror and slavery: This abandoned situation may be easier conceived than described. From the time that I was kid-napped and conducted to a factory, and from thence in the brutish, base, but fashionable way of traffic, consigned to Grenada, the grievous thoughts which I then felt, still pant in my heart; though my fears and tears have long since subsided. And yet it is still grievous to think that thousands more have suffered in similar and greater distress, under the hands of barbarous robbers, and merciless task-masters; and that many even now are suffering in all the extreme bitterness of grief and woe, that no language can describe. The cries of some, and the sight of their misery, may be seen and heard afar; but the deep sounding groans of thousands, and the great sadness of their misery and woe, under the heavy load of oppressions and calamities inflicted upon them, are such as can only be distinctly known to the ears of Jehovah Sabaoth.[21]

This Lord of Hosts, in his good[22] Providence, and in great mercy to me, made a way for my deliverance from Grenada.—Being in this dreadful captivity and horrible slavery, without any hope of deliverance, for about eight or nine months, beholding the most dreadful scenes of misery and cruelty, and seeing my miserable companions often cruelly lashed, and as it were cut to pieces, for the most trifling faults; this made me often tremble and weep, but I escaped better than many of them. For eating a piece of sugarcane, some were cruelly lashed, or struck over the face to knock their teeth out. Some of the stouter ones,[23] I suppose often reproved, and grown hardened and stupid with many cruel beatings and lashings, or perhaps faint and pressed with hunger and hard labour, were often committing trespasses of this kind, and when detected, they met with exemplary punishment. Some told me they had their teeth pulled out to deter others, and to prevent them from eating any cane in future. Thus seeing my miserable companions and countrymen in this pitiful, distressed and horrible situation, with all the brutish baseness and barbarity attending it, could not but fill my little mind with horror and indignation. But I must own, to the shame of my own countrymen, that I was first kid-napped and betrayed by some of my own complexion, who were the first cause of my exile and slavery; but if there were no buyers there would be no sellers. So far as I can remember, some of the Africans in my country keep slaves, which they take in war, or for debt; but those which they keep are well fed, and good care taken of them, and treated well; and, as to their cloathing, they differ according to the custom of the country. But I may safely say, that all the poverty and misery that any of the inhabitants of Africa meet with among themselves, is far inferior to those inhospitable regions of misery which they meet with in the

West-Indies, where their hard-hearted overseers have neither regard to the laws of God, nor the life of their fellow-men.

Thanks be to God, I was delivered from Grenada, and that horrid brutal slavery.—A gentleman coming to England,[24] took me
for his servant, and brought me away, where I soon found my situation become more agreeable. After coming to England, and seeing others write and read, I had a strong desire to learn, and
getting what assistance I could, I applied myself to learn reading
and writing, which soon became my recreation, pleasure, and delight; and when my master perceived that I could write some, he
sent me to a proper school for that purpose to learn. Since, I have
endeavoured to improve my mind in reading, and have sought to
get all the intelligence I could, in my situation of life, towards the
state of my brethren and countrymen in complexion, and of the
miserable situation of those who are barbarously sold into captivity, and unlawfully held in slavery.

But, among other observations, one great duty I owe to
Almighty God, (the thankful acknowledgement I would not omit
for any consideration) that, although I have been brought away
from my native country, in that torrent of robbery and wickedness, thanks be to God for his good providence towards me; I
have both obtained liberty, and acquired the great advantages of
some little learning, in being able to read and write, and, what is
still infinitely of greater advantage, I trust, to know something of
HIM *who is that God whose providence rules over all, and who is
the only Potent One that rules in the nations over the children of
men. It is unto Him, who is the Prince of the Kings of the earth,*[25]
that I would give all thanks. And, in some manner, I may say with
Joseph, as he did with respect to the evil intention of his brethren,
when they sold him into Egypt, that whatever evil intentions and
bad motives those insidious robbers had in carrying me away
from my native country and friends, I trust, was what the Lord intended for my good.[26] In this respect, I am highly indebted to
many of the good people of England for learning and principles
unknown to the people of my native country. But, above all, what
have I obtained from the Lord God of Hosts, the God of the
Christians! in that divine revelation of the only true God, and the
Saviour of men, what a treasure of wisdom and blessings are in-

volved? How wonderful is the divine goodness displayed in those invaluable books the Old and New Testaments, that inestimable compilation of books, the Bible? And, O what a treasure to have, and one of the greatest advantages to be able to read therein, and a divine blessing to understand![27]

But, to return to my subject, I begin with the Cursory Remarker.[28] This man stiles himself a friend to the West-India colonies and their inhabitants, like Demetrius,[29] the silversmith, a man of some considerable abilities, seeing their craft in danger, a craft, however, not so innocent and justifiable as the making of shrines for Diana,[30] though that was base and wicked enough to enslave the minds of men with superstition and idolatry; but his craft, and the gain of those craftsmen, consists in the enslaving both soul and body to the cruel idolatry, and most abominable service and slavery, to the idol of cursed avarice: And as he finds some discoveries of their wicked traffic held up in a light where truth and facts are so clearly seen, as none but the most desperate villain would dare to obstruct or oppose, he therefore sallies forth with all the desperation of an Utopian assailant, to tell lies by a virulent contradiction of facts, and with false aspersions endeavour to calumniate the worthy and judicious essayist of that discovery, a man, whose character is irreproachable. By thus artfully supposing, if he could bring the reputation of the author, who has discovered so much of their iniquitous traffic, into dispute, his work would fall and be less regarded. However, this virulent craftsman has done no great merit to his cause and the credit of that infamous craft; at the appearance of truth, his understanding has got the better of his avarice and infidelity, so far, as to draw the following concession: "I shall not be so far misunderstood, by the candid and judicious part of mankind, as to be ranked among the advocates of slavery, as I most sincerely join Mr. Ramsay, and every other man of sensibility, in hoping the blessings of freedom will, in due time, be equally diffused over the whole globe."[31]

By this, it would seem that he was a little ashamed of his craftsmen, and would not like to be ranked or appear amongst them. But as long as there are any hopes of gain to be made by that insidious craft, he can join with them well enough, and endeavour to justify them in that most abandoned traffic of buying, selling, and enslaving men. He finds fault with a plan for punishing robbers, thieves and vagabonds, who distress their neighbours by their thrift, robbery and plunder, without regarding any laws human or divine, except the rules of their own fraternity, and in that case, according to the proverb, there may be some honor among thieves; but these are the only people in the world that ought to suffer some punishment, imprisonment or slavery; their external complexion, whether black or white, should be no excuse for them to do evil. Being aware of this, perhaps he was afraid that some of his friends, the great and opulent banditti of slaveholders in the western part of the world, might be found guilty of more atrocious and complicated crimes, than even those of the highwaymen, the robberies and the petty larcenies committed in England. Therefore, to make the best of this sad dilemma, he brings in a ludicrous invective comparison that it would be "an event which would undoubtedly furnish a new and pleasant compartment to that well known and most delectable print, call'd, *The world turn'd up side down*, in which the cook is roasted by the pig, the man saddled by the horse," &c.[32] If he means that the complicated banditties of pirates, thieves, robbers, oppressors and enslavers of men, are those cooks and men that would be roasted and saddled, it certainly would be no unpleasant sight to see them well roasted, saddled and bridled too; and no matter by whom, whether he terms them pigs, horses or asses. But there is not much likelihood of this silly monkeyish comparison as yet being verified, in bringing the opulent pirates and thieves to condign punishment, so that he could very well bring it in to turn it off with a grin. However, to make use of his words, it would be a most delectable sight, when thieves and robbers get the upper side of the world, to see them turned down; and I should not interrupt his mirth, to see him laugh at his own invective monkeyish comparison as long as he pleases.

But again, when he draws a comparison of the many hardships that the poor in Great-Britain and Ireland labour under, as well as many of those in other countries; that their various distresses are worse than the West India slaves—It may be true, in part, that some of them suffer greater hardships than many of the slaves; but, bad as it is, the poorest in England would not change their situation for that of slaves. And there may be some masters, under various circumstances, worse off than their servants; but they would not change their own situation for theirs: Nor as little would a rich man wish to change his situation of affluence, for that of a beggar: and so, likewise, no freeman, however poor and distressing his situation may be, would resign his liberty for that of a slave, in the situation of a horse or a dog. The case of the poor, whatever their hardships may be, in free countries, is widely different from that of the West-India slaves. For the slaves, like animals, are bought and sold, and dealt with as their capricious owners may think fit, even in torturing and tearing them to pieces, and wearing them out with hard labour, hunger and oppression; and should the death of a slave ensue by some other more violent way than that which is commonly the death of thousands, and tens of thousands in the end, the haughty tyrant, in that case, has only to pay a small fine for the murder and death of his slave. The brute creation in general may fare better than man, and some dogs may refuse the crumbs that the distressed poor would be glad of; but the nature and situation of man is far superior to that of beasts; and, in like manner, whatever circumstances poor freemen may be in, their situation is much superior, beyond any proportion, to that of the hardships and cruelty of modern slavery. But where can the situation of any freeman be so bad as that of a slave; or, could such be found, or even worse, as he would have it, what would the comparison amount to? Would it plead for his craft of slavery and oppression? Or, rather, would it not cry aloud for some redress, and what every well regulated society of men ought to hear and consider, that none should suffer want or be oppressed among them? And this seems to be pointed out by the circumstances which he describes; that it is the great duty, and ought to be the highest ambition of all governors, to order and establish such policy, and in such a wise manner, that every thing should be so managed, as to be conducive to the moral, temporal and eternal welfare of every individual from the lowest degree to the highest; and the consequence of this would be, the harmony, happiness and good prosperity of the whole community.

But this crafty author has also, in defence of his own or his employer's craft in the British West-India slavery, given sundry comparisons and descriptions of the treatment of slaves in the French islands and settlements in the West-Indies and America. And, contrary to what is the true case, he would have it supposed that the treatment of the slaves in the former, is milder than the latter; but even in this, unwarily for his own craft of slavery, all that he has advanced, can only add matter for its confutation, and serve to heighten the ardour and wish of every generous mind, that the whole should be abolished. An equal degree of enormity found in one place, cannot justify crimes of as great or greater enormity committed in another. The various depredations committed by robbers and plunderers, on different parts of the globe, may not be all equally alike bad, but their evil and malignancy, in every appearance and shape, can only hold up to view the just observation, that

> Virtue herself hath such peculiar mein,
> Vice, to be hated, needs but to be seen.[33]

The farther and wider that the discovery and knowledge of such an enormous evil, as the base and villainous treatment and slavery which the poor unfortunate Black People meet with, is spread and made known, the cry for justice, even virtue lifting up her voice, must rise the louder and higher, for the scale of equity and justice to be lifted up in their defence. And doth not wisdom cry, and understanding put forth her voice? But who will regard the voice and hearken to the cry? Not the sneaking advocates for slavery, though a little ashamed of their craft; like the monstrous crocodile weeping over their prey with fine concessions (while gorging their own rapacious appetite) to hope for universal freedom taking place over the globe. Not those inebriated with avarice and infidelity, who hold in defiance every regard due to the divine law, and who endeavour all they can to destroy and take away the natural and common rights and privileges of men. Not the insolent and crafty author for slavery and oppression, who would have us to believe, that the benign command of God in appointing the seventh day for a sabbath of rest for the good purposes of our present and eternal welfare, is not to be regarded. He will exclaim against the teachers of obedience to it; and tells us, that the poor, and the oppressed, and the heavy burdened slave, should not lay down his load that day, but appropriate these hours of sacred rest to labour in some bit of useful ground. His own words are, "to dedicate the unappropriated hours of Sunday to the cultivation of this useful spot, he is brought up to believe would be the worst of sins, and that the sabbath is a day of absolute and universal rest is a truth he hears frequently inculcated by the curate of the parish,"[34] &c. But after bringing it about in this round-about way and manner, whatever the curate has to say of it as a truth, he would have us by no means to regard. This may serve as a specimen of his crafty and detestable production, where infidelity, false aspersions, virulent calumnies, and lying contradictions abound throughout. I shall only refer him to that description which he meant for another, as most applicable and best suited for himself; and so long as he does not renounce his craft, as well as to be somewhat ashamed of his craftsmen and their insensibility, he may thus stand as described by himself: "A man of warm imagination (but strange infatuated unfeeling sensibility) to paint things not as they really are, but as his rooted prejudices represent them, and even to shut his eyes against the convictions afforded him by his own senses."[35]

But such is the insensibility of men, when their own craft of gain is advanced by the slavery and oppression of others, that after all the laudable exertions of the truly virtuous and humane, towards extending the beneficence of liberty and freedom to the much degraded and unfortunate Africans, which is the common right and privilege of all men, in every thing that is just, lawful and consistent, we find the principles of justice and equity, not only opposed, and every duty in religion and humanity left unregarded; but that unlawful traffic of dealing with our fellow-creatures, as with the beasts of the earth, still carried on with as great assiduity as ever; and that the insidious piracy of procuring and holding slaves is countenanced and supported by the government of sundry Christian nations. This seems to be the fashionable way of getting riches, but very dishonourable; in doing this, the slave-holders are meaner and baser than the African slaves, for while they subject and reduce them to a degree with brutes, they seduce themselves to a degree with devils.

"Some pretend that the Africans, in general, are a set of poor, ignorant, dispersed, unsociable people; and that they think it no crime to sell one another, and even their own wives and children; therefore they bring them away to a situation where many of them may arrive to a better state than ever they could obtain in their own native country."[36] This specious pretence is without any shadow of justice and truth, and, if the argument was even true, it could afford no just and warrantable matter for any society of men to hold slaves. But the argument is false; there can be no ignorance, dispersion, or unsociableness so found among them, which can be made better by bringing them away to a state of a degree equal to that of a cow or a horse.

But let their ignorance in some things (in which the Europeans have greatly the advantage of them) be what it will, it is not the intention of those who bring them away to make them better by it; nor is the design of slave-holders of any other intention, but that they may serve them as a kind of engines and beasts of burden; that their own ease and profit may be advanced, by a set of poor helpless men and women, whom they despise and rank with brutes, and keep them in perpetual slavery, both themselves and children, and merciful death is the only release from their toil. By the benevolence of some, a few may get their liberty, and by their own industry and ingenuity, may acquire some learning, mechanical trades, or useful business; and some may be brought away by different gentlemen to free countries, where they get their liberty, but no thanks to slave-holders for it. But amongst those who get their liberty, like all other ignorant men, are generally more corrupt in their morals, than they possibly could have been amongst their own people in Africa; for, being mostly amongst the wicked and apostate Christians, they sooner learn their oaths and blasphemies, and their evil ways, than any thing else. Some few, indeed, may eventually arrive at some knowledge of the Christian religion, and the great advantages of it. Such was the case of Ukawsaw Groniosaw,[37] an African prince, who lived in England. He was a long time in a state of great poverty and distress, and must have died at one time for want, if a good and charitable attorney had not supported him. He was long after in a very poor state, but he would not have given his faith in the Christian religion, in exchange for all the kingdoms of Africa, if they could have been given to him, in place of his poverty, for it. And such was

A. Morrant in America.[38] When a boy, he could stroll away into a desart, and prefer the society of wild beasts to the absurd Christianity of his mother's house. He was conducted to the king of the Cherokees, who, in a miraculous manner, was induced by him to embrace the Christian faith. This Morrant was in the British service last war, and his royal convert, the king of the Cherokee Indians, accompanied General Clinton at the siege of Charles Town.

These, and all such, I hope thousands, as meet with the knowledge and grace of the Divine clemency, are brought forth quite contrary to the end and intention of all slavery, and, in general, of all slave holders too. And should it please the Divine goodness to visit some of the poor dark Africans, even in the brutal stall of slavery, and from thence to instal them among the princes of his grace, and to invest them with a robe of honor that will hang about their necks for ever; but who can then suppose, that it will be well pleasing unto him to find them subjected there in that dejected state? Or can the slave-holders think that the Universal Father and Sovereign of Mankind will be well pleased with them, for the brutal transgression of his law, in bowing down the necks of those to the yoke of their cruel bondage? Sovereign goodness may eventually visit some men even in a state of slavery, but their slavery is not a cause of that event and benignity; and therefore, should some event of good ever happen to some men subjected to slavery, that can plead nothing for men to do evil that good may come; and should it apparently happen from thence, it is neither sought for nor designed by the enslavers of men. But the whole business of slavery is an evil of the first magnitude, and a most horrible iniquity to traffic with slaves and souls of men; and an evil. [S]orry I am, that it still subsists, and more astonishing to think, that it is an iniquity committed amongst Christians, and contrary to all the genuine principles of Christianity, and yet carried on by men denominated thereby.

In a Christian aera, in a land where Christianity is planted, where every one might expect to behold the flourishing growth of every virtue, extending their harmonious branches with universal philanthropy wherever they came; but, on the contrary, almost nothing else is to be seen abroad but the bramble of ruffians, barbarians and slave-holders, grown up to a powerful luxuriance in wickedness. I cannot but wish, for the honor of Christianity, that the bramble grown up amongst them, was known to the heathen nations by a different name, for sure the depredators, robbers and ensnarers of men can never be Christians, but ought to be held as the abhorrence of all men, and the abomination of all mankind, whether Christians or heathens. Every man of any sensibility, whether he be a Christian or an heathen, if he has any discernment at all, must think, that for any man, or any class of men, to deal with their fellow-creatures as with the beasts of the field; or to account them as such, however ignorant they may be, and in whatever situation, or wherever they may find them, and whatever country or complexion they may be of, that those men, that are the procurers and holders of slaves, are the greatest villains in the world. And surely those men must be lost to all sensibility themselves, who can think that the stealing, robbing, enslaving, and murdering of men can be no crimes; but the holders of men in slavery are at the head of all these oppressions and crimes. And, therefore, however unsensible they may be of it now, and however long they may laugh at the calamity of others, if they do not repent of their evil way, and the wickedness of their doings by keeping and holding their fellow-creatures in slavery, and trafficking with them as with the brute creation, and to give up and surrender that evil traffic, with an awful abhorrence of it, that this may be averred, if they do not, and if they can think, they must and cannot otherwise but expect in one day at last, to meet with the full stroke of the long suspended vengeance of heaven, when death will cut them down to a state as mean as that of the most abjected slave, and to a very eminent danger of a more dreadful fate hereafter, when they have the just reward of their iniquities to meet with.

And now, as to the Africans being dispersed and unsociable, if it was so, that could be no warrant for the Europeans to enslave them; and even though they may have many different feuds and bad practices among them, the continent of Africa is of vast extent, and the numerous inhabitants are divided into several kingdoms and principalities, which are governed by their respective kings and princes, and those are absolutely maintained by their free subjects. Very few nations make slaves of any of those under their government; but such as are taken prisoners of war from their neighbours, are generally kept in that state, until they can exchange and dispose of them otherwise; and towards the west coast they are generally procured for the European market, and sold. They have a great aversion to murder, or even in taking away the lives of those which they judge guilty of crimes; and, therefore, they prefer disposing of them otherwise better than killing them.[39] This gives their merchants and procurers of slaves a power to travel a great way into the interior parts of the country to buy such as are wanted to be disposed of. These slave-procurers are a set of as great villains as any in the world. They often steal and kidnap many more than they buy at first, if they can meet with them by the way; and they have only their certain boundaries to go to, and sell them from one to another; so that if they are sought after and detected, the thieves are seldom found, and the others only plead that they bought them so and so. These kid-nappers and slave-procurers, called merchants, are a species of African villains, which are greatly corrupted, and even viciated by their intercourse with the Europeans; but, wicked and barbarous as they certainly are, I can hardly think, if they knew what horrible barbarity they were sending their fellow-creatures to, that they would do it. But the artful Europeans have so deceived them, that they are bought by their inventions of merchandize, and beguiled into it by their artifice; for the Europeans, at their factories, in some various manner, have always kept some as servants to them, and with gaudy cloaths, in a gay manner, as decoy ducks to deceive others, and to tell them that they want many more to go over the sea, and be as they are. So in that respect, wherein it may be said that they will sell one another, they are only ensnared and enlisted to be servants, kept like some of those which they see at the factories, which, for some gewgaws,[40] as presents given to themselves and friends, they are thereby enticed to go; and something after the same manner that East-India soldiers are procured in Britain; and the inhabitants here, just as much sell themselves, and one another, as they do; and the kid-nappers here, and the slave-procurers in Africa, are much alike. But many other barbarous methods are made use of by the vile instigators, procurers and ensnarers of men; and some of the wicked and profligate princes and chiefs of Africa accept of presents, from the Europeans, to procure a certain number of slaves; and thereby they are wickedly instigated to go to war with one another on purpose to get them, which produces many terrible depredations; and sometimes when those engagements are entered into, and they find themselves defeated of their purpose, it has happened that some of their own people have fallen a sacrifice to their avarice and cruelty. And it may be said of the Europeans, that they have made use of every insidious method to procure slaves whenever they can, and in whatever manner they can lay hold of them, and that their forts and factories are the avowed dens of thieves for robbers, plunderers and depredators.

But again, as to the Africans selling their own wives and children, nothing can be more opposite to every thing they hold dear and valuable; and nothing can distress them more, than to part with any of their relations and friends. Such are the tender feelings of parents for their children, that, for the loss of a child, they seldom can be rendered happy, even with the intercourse and enjoyment of their friends, for years. For any man to think that it should be otherwise, when he may see a thousand instances of a natural instinct, even in the brute creation, where they have a sympathetic feeling for their offspring; it must be great want of consideration not to think, that much more than meerly what is natural to animals, should in a higher degree be implanted in the breast of every part of the rational creation of man. And what man of feeling can help lamenting the loss of parents, friends, liberty, and perhaps property and other valuable and dear connections. Those people annually brought away from Guinea, are born as free, and are brought up with as great a predilection for their own country, freedom and liberty, as the sons and daughters of fair Britain. Their free subjects are trained up to a kind of military service, not so much by the desire of the chief, as by their own voluntary inclination. It is looked upon as the greatest respect they can shew to their king, to stand up for his and their own defence in time of need. Their different chieftains, which bear a reliance on the great chief, or king, exercise a kind of government something like that feudal institution which prevailed some time in Scotland. In this respect, though the common people are free, they often suffer by the villainy of their different chieftains, and by the wars and feuds which happen among them. Nevertheless their freedom and rights are as dear to them, as those privileges are to other people. And it may be said that freedom, and the liberty of enjoying their own privileges, burns with as much zeal and fervour in the breast of an Æthiopian,[41] as in the breast of any inhabitant on the globe.

But the supporters and favourers of slavery make other things a pretence and an excuse in their own defence; such as, that they find that it was admitted under the Divine institution by Moses, as well as the long continued practice of different nations for ages; and that the Africans are peculiarly marked out by some signal prediction in nature and complexion for that purpose.

This seems to be the greatest bulwark of defence which the advocates and favourers of slavery can advance, and what is generally talked of in their favour by those who do not understand it. I shall consider it in that view, whereby it will appear, that they deceive themselves and mislead others. Men are never more liable to be drawn into error, than when truth is made use of in a guileful manner to seduce them. Those who do not believe the scriptures to be a Divine revelation, cannot, consistently with themselves, make the law of Moses, or any mark or prediction they can find respecting any particular set of men, as found in the sacred writings, any reason that one class of men should enslave another. In that respect, all that they have to enquire into should be whether it be right, or wrong, that any part of the human species should enslave another; and when that is the case, the Africans, though not so learned, are just as wise as the Europeans; and when the matter is left to human wisdom, they are both liable to err. But what the light of nature, and the dictates of reason, when rightly considered, teach, is, that no man ought to enslave another; and some, who have been rightly guided thereby, have made noble defences for the universal natural rights and privileges of all men. But in this case, when the learned take neither revelation nor reason for their guide, they fall into as great, and worse errors, than the unlearned; for they only make use of that system of Divine wisdom, which should guide them into truth, when they can find or pick out any thing that will suit their purpose, or that they can pervert

to such—the very means of leading themselves and others into error. And, in consequence thereof, the pretences that some men
make use of for holding of slaves, must be evidently the grossest
perversion of reason, as well as an inconsistent and diabolical use
of the sacred writings. For it must be a strange perversion of reason, and a wrong use or disbelief of the sacred writings, when any
thing found there is so perverted by them, and set up as a precedent and rule for men to commit wickedness. They had better
have no reason, and no belief in the scriptures, and make no use of
them at all, than only to believe, and make use of that which leads
them into the most abominable evil and wickedness of dealing unjustly with their fellow men.

But this will appear evident to all men that believe the scriptures, that every reason necessary is given that they should be believed; and, in this case, that they afford us this information: "That
all mankind did spring from one original, and that there are no
different species among men. For God who made the world, hath
made of one blood all the nations of men that dwell on all the face
of the earth."[42] Wherefore we may justly infer, as there are no inferior species, but all of one blood and of one nature, that there
does not an inferiority subsist, or depend, on their colour, features
or form, whereby some men make a pretence to enslave others;
and consequently, as they have all one creator, one original, made
of one blood, and all brethren descended from one father, it never
could be lawful and just for any nation, or people, to oppress and
enslave another.

And again, as all the present inhabitants of the world sprang
from the family of Noah, and were then all of one complexion,
there is no doubt, but the difference which we now find, took its
rise very rapidly after they became dispersed and settled on the
different parts of the globe. There seems to be a tendency to this,
in many instances, among children of the same parents, having different colour of hair and features from one another. And God
alone who established the course of nature, can bring about and
establish what variety he pleases; and it is not in the power of man
to make one hair white or black. But among the variety which it
hath pleased God to establish and caused to take place, we may
meet with some analogy in nature, that as the bodies of men are

tempered with a different degree to enable them to endure the respective climates of their habitations, so their colours vary, in some degree, in a regular gradation from the equator towards either of the poles. However, there are other incidental causes arising from time and place, which constitute the most distinguishing variety of colour, form, appearance and features, as peculiar to the inhabitants of one tract of country, and differing in something from those in another, even in the same latitudes, as well as from those in different climates. Long custom and the different way of living among the several inhabitants of the different parts of the earth, has a very great effect in distinguishing them by a difference of features and complexion. These effects are easy to be seen; as to the causes, it is sufficient for us to know, that all is the work of an Almighty hand. Therefore, as we find the distribution of the human species inhabiting the barren, as well as the most fruitful parts of the earth, and the cold as well as the most hot, differing from one another in complexion according to their situation; it may be reasonably, as well as religiously, inferred, that He who placed them in their various situations, hath extended equally his care and protection to all; and from thence, that it becometh unlawful to counteract his benignity, by reducing others of different complexions to undeserved bondage.

According, as we find that the difference of colour among men is only incidental, and equally natural to all, and agreeable to the place of their habitation; and that if nothing else be different or contrary among them, but that of features and complexion, in that respect, they are all equally alike entitled to the enjoyment of every mercy and blessing of God. But there are some men of that complexion, because they are not black, whose ignorance and insolence leads them to think, that those who are black, were marked out in that manner by some signal interdiction or curse, as originally descending from their progenitors. To those I must say, that the only mark which we read of, as generally alluded to, and by them applied wrongfully, is that mark or sign which God gave to Cain,[43] to assure him that he should not be destroyed. Cain understood by the nature of the crime he had committed, that the law required death, or cutting off, as the punishment thereof. But God in his providence doth not always punish the wicked in this life according to their enormous crimes, (we are told, by a sacred poet, that he saw the wicked flourishing like a green bay tree)[44] though he generally marks them out by some signal token of his vengeance; and that is a sure token of it, when men become long hardened in their wickedness. The denunciation that passed upon Cain was, that he should be a fugitive and a vagabond on the earth, bearing the curse and reproach of his iniquity; and the rest of men were prohibited as much from meddling with him, or defiling their hands by him, as it naturally is, not to pull down the dead carcase of an atrocious criminal, hung up in chains by the laws of his country. But allow the mark set upon Cain to have consisted in a black skin, still no conclusion can be drawn at all, that any of the black people are of that descent, as the whole posterity of Cain were destroyed in the universal deluge.

Only Noah, a righteous and just man, who found grace in the sight of God, and his three sons, Japheth, Shem and Ham, and their wives, eight persons, were preserved from the universal deluge, in the ark which Noah was directed to build.[45] The three sons of Noah had each children born after the flood, from whom all the present world of men descended. But it came to pass, in the days of Noah, that an interdiction, or curse, took place in the family of Ham, and that the descendants of one of his sons should become the servants of servants to their brethren, the descendants of Shem and Japheth. This affords a grand pretence for the supporters of the African slavery to build a false notion upon, as it is found by history that Africa, in general, was peopled by the descendants of Ham; but they forget, that the prediction has already been fulfilled as far as it can go.

There can be no doubt, that there was a shameful misconduct in Ham himself, by what is related of him; but the fault, according to the prediction and curse, descended only to the families of the descendants of his youngest son, Canaan. The occasion was, that Noah, his father, had drank wine, and (perhaps unawares) became inebriated by it, and fell asleep in his tent. It seems that Ham was greatly deficient of that filial virtue as either becoming a father or a son, went into his father's tent, and, it may be supposed, in an undecent manner, he had suffered his own son, Canaan, so to meddle with, or uncover, his father, that he saw his nakedness; for which he did not check the audacious rudeness of Canaan, but went and told his brethren without in ridicule of his aged parent. This rude audacious behaviour of Canaan, and the obloquy of his father Ham, brought on him the curse of his grandfather, Noah, but he blessed Shem and Japheth for their decent and filial virtues, and denounced, in the spirit of prophecy, that Canaan should be their servant, and should serve them.[46]

It may be observed, that it is a great misfortune for children, when their parents are not endowed with that wisdom and prudence which is necessary for the early initiation of their offspring in the paths of virtue and righteousness. Ham was guilty of the offence as well as his son; he did not pity the weakness of his father, who was overcome with wine in that day wherein, it is likely, he had some solemn work to do. But the prediction and curse rested wholly upon the offspring of Canaan, who settled in the land known by his name, in the west of Asia, as is evident from the sacred writings. The Canaanites became an exceeding wicked people, and were visited with many calamities, according to the prediction of Noah, for their abominable wickedness and idolatry.

Chedorlaomer,[47] a descendant of Shem, reduced the Canaanitish kingdoms to a tributary subjection; and some time after, upon their revolt, invaded and pillaged their country. Not long after Sodom, Gomorrah, Admah and Zeboim, four kingdoms of the Canaanites were overthrown for their great wickedness, and utterly destroyed by fire and brimstone from heaven. The Hebrews, chiefly under Moses, Joshua and Barak, as they were directed by God, cut off most of the other Canaanitish kingdoms, and reduced many of them to subjection and vassalage. Those who settled in the north-west of Canaan, and formed the once flourishing states of Tyre and Sidon, were by the Assyrians, the Chaldeans, and the Persians successively reduced to great misery and bondage; but chiefly by the Greeks, the Romans, and the Saracens, and lastly by the Turks, they were compleatly and totally ruined, and have no more since been a distinct people among the different nations. Many of the Canaanites who fled away in the Time of Joshua, became mingled with the different nations, and some historians think that some of them came to England, and settled about Cornwall, as far back as that time;[48] so that, for any thing that can be known to the contrary, there may be some of the descendants of that wicked generation still subsisting among the slave-holders in the West-Indies. For if the curse of God ever rested upon them, or upon any other men, the only visible mark thereof was always upon those who committed the most outrageous acts of violence and oppression. But colour and complexion has nothing to do with that mark; every wicked man, and the enslavers of others, bear the stamp of their own iniquity, and that mark which was set upon Cain.

Now, the descendants of the other three sons of Ham, were not included under the curse of his father, and as they dispersed and settled on the different parts of the earth, they became also sundry distinct and very formidable nations.[49] Cush, the oldest, settled in the south-west of Arabia, and his descendants were anciently known to the Hebrews by the name of Cushites, or Cushie; one of his sons, Nimrod, founded the kingdom of Babylon, in Asia; and the others made their descent southward, by the Red Sea, and came over to Abyssinia and Ethiopia, and, likely, dispersed themselves throughout all the southern and interior parts of Africa; and as they lived mostly under the torrid zone, or near the tropics, they became black, as being natural to the inhabitants of those sultry hot climates; and, in that case, their complexion bears the signification of the name of their original progenitor, Cush, as known to[50] the Hebrews by that name, both on the east and on the west, beyond the Red Sea; but the Greeks called them Ethiopians, or black faced people.[51] The Egyptians and Philistines were the descendants of Mizraim, and the country which they inhabited was called the land of Mizraim, and Africa, in general, was anciently called the whole land of Ham. Phut, another of his sons, also settled on the west of Egypt, and as the youngest were obliged to emigrate farthest, afterwards dispersed themselves chiefly up the south of the Mediterranean sea, towards Lybia and Mauritania, and might early mingle with some of the Cushites on the more southern, and, chiefly, on the western parts of Africa. But all these might be followed by some other families and tribes from Asia; and some think that Africa got its name from the King of Lybia marrying a daughter of Aphra, one of the descendants of Abraham, by Keturah.[52]

But it may be reasonably supposed, that the most part of the black people in Africa, are the descendants of the Cushites, towards the east, the south, and interior parts, and chiefly of the Phutians towards the west; and the various revolutions and changes which have happened among them have rather been local than universal; so that whoever their original progenitors were, as descending from one generation to another, in a long continuance, it becomes natural for the inhabitants of that tract of country to be a dark black, in general. The learned and thinking part of men, who can refer to history, must know, that nothing with respect to colour, nor any mark or curse from any original prediction, can in anywise be more particularly ascribed to the Africans than to any other people of the human species, so as to afford any pretence why they should be more evil treated, persecuted and enslaved, than any other. Nothing but ignorance, and the dreams of a viciated imagination, arising from the general countenance given to the evil practice of wicked men, to strengthen their hands in wickedness, could ever make any person to fancy otherwise, or ever to think that the stealing, kid-napping, enslaving, persecuting or killing a black man, is in any way and manner less criminal, than the same evil treatment of any other man of another complexion.

But again, in answer to another part of the pretence which the favourers of slavery make use of in their defence, that slavery was an ancient custom, and that it became the prevalent and universal practice of many different barbarous nations for ages: This must be granted; but not because it was right, or any thing like right and equity. A lawful servitude was always necessary, and became contingent with the very nature of human society. But when the laws of civilization were broken through, and when the rights and properties of others were invaded, that brought the oppressed into a kind of compulsive servitude, though often not compelled to it by those whom they were obliged to serve. This arose from the different depredations and robberies which were committed upon one another; the helpless were obliged to seek protection from such as could support them, and to give unto them their service, in order to preserve themselves from want, and to deliver them from the injury either of men or beasts. For while civil society continued in a rude state, even among the establishers of kingdoms, when they became powerful and proud, as they wanted to enlarge their territories, they drove and expelled others from their peaceable habitations, who were not so powerful as themselves. This made those who were robbed of their substance, and drove from the place of their abode, make their escape to such as could and would help them; but when such a relief could not be found, they were obliged to submit to the yoke of their oppressors, who, in many cases, would not yield them any protection upon any terms. Wherefore, when their lives were in danger otherwise, and they could not find any help, they were obliged to sell themselves for bond servants to such as would buy them, when they could not get a service that was better. But as soon as buyers could be found, robbers began their traffic to ensnare others, and such as fell into their hands were carried captive by them, and were obliged to submit to their being sold by them into the hands of other robbers, for there are few buyers of men, who intend thereby to make them free, and such as they buy are generally subjected to hard labour and bondage. Therefore at all times, while a man is a slave, he is still in captivity, and under the jurisdiction of robbers; and every man who keeps a slave, is a robber, whenever he compels him to his service without giving him a just reward. The barely supplying his slave with some necessary things, to keep him in life, is no reward at all, that is only for his own sake and benefit; and the very nature of compulsion and taking away the liberty of others, as well as their property, is robbery; and that kind of service which subjects men to a state of slavery, must at all times, and in every circumstance, be a barbarous, inhuman and unjust dealing with our fellow men. A voluntary service, and slavery, are quite different things; but in ancient times, in whatever degree slavery was admitted, and whatever hardships they were, in general, subjected to, it was not nearly so bad as the modern barbarous and cruel West-India slavery.

Now, in respect to that kind of servitude which was admitted into the law of Moses, that was not contrary to the natural liberties of men, but a state of equity and justice, according as the nature and circumstances of the times required. There was no more harm in entering into a covenant with another man as a bond-servant,[53] than there is for two men to enter into partnership the one with the other; and sometimes the nature of the case may be, and their business require it, that the one may find money and live at a distance and ease, and the other manage the business for him: So a bond-servant was generally the steward in a man's house, and sometimes his heir. There was no harm in buying a man who was in a state of captivity and bondage by others, and keeping him in servitude till such time as his purchase was redeemed by his labour and service. And there could be no harm in paying a man's debts, and keeping him in servitude until such time as an equitable agreement of composition was paid by him. And so, in general, whether they had been bought or sold in order to pay their just debts when they became poor, or were bought from such as held them in an unlawful captivity, the state of bondage which they and their children fell under, among the Israelites, was into that of a vassalage state, which rather might be termed a deliverance from debt and captivity, than a state of slavery.[54] In that vassalage state which they were reduced to, they had a tax of some service to pay, which might only be reckoned equivalent to a poor man in England paying rent for his cottage. In this fair land of liberty, there are many thousands of the inhabitants who have no right to so much land as an inch of ground to set their foot upon, so as to take up their residence upon it, without paying a lawful and reasonable vassalage of rent for it—and yet the whole community is free from slavery.[55] And so, likewise, those who were reduced to a state of servitude, or vassalage, in the land of Israel, were not negociable like chattels and goods; nor could they be disposed of like cattle and beasts of burden, or ever transferred or disposed of without their own consent; and perhaps not one man in all the land of Israel would buy another man, unless that man was willing to serve him. And when any man had gotten such a servant, as he had entered into a covenant of agreement with, as a bond-servant, if the man liked his master and his service, he could not oblige him to go away; and it sometimes happened, that they refused to go out free when the year of jubilee came.[56] But even that state of servitude which the Canaanites were reduced to, among those who survived the general overthrow of their country, was nothing worse, in many respects, than that of poor labouring people in any free country.

Their being made hewers of wood and drawers of water,[57] were laborious employments; but they were paid for it in such a manner as the nature of their service required, and were supplied with abundance of such necessaries of life as they and their families had need of; and they were at liberty, if they chose, to go away, there was no restriction laid on them. They were not hunted after, and a reward offered for their heads, as it is the case in the West-Indies for any that can find a strayed slave; and he who can bring such a head warm reeking with his blood, as a token that he had murdered him—inhuman and shocking to think!—he is paid for it; and, cruel and dreadful as it is, that law is still in force in some of the British colonies.[58]

But the Canaanites, although they were predicted to be reduced to a state of servitude, and bondage to that poor and menial employment, fared better than the West-India slaves; for when they were brought into that state of servitude, they were often employed in an honourable service. The Nethenims, and others, were to assist in the sacred solemnities and worship of God at the Temple of Jerusalem.[59] They had the same laws and immunities respecting the solemn days and sabbaths, as their masters the Israelites, and they were to keep and observe them. But they were not suffered, much less required, to labour in their own spots of useful ground on the days of sacred rest from worldly employment; and that, if they did not improve the culture of it, in these times and seasons, they might otherwise perish for hunger and want; as it is the case of the West-India slaves, by their inhuman, infidel, hard-hearted masters. And, therefore, this may be justly said, that whatever servitude that was, or by whatever name it may be called, that the service which was required by the people of Israel in old time, was of a far milder nature, than that which became the prevalent practice of other different and barbarous nations; and, if compared with modern slavery, it might be called liberty, equity, and felicity, in respect to that abominable, mean, beastly, cruel, bloody slavery carried on by the inhuman, barbarous Europeans, against the poor unfortunate Black Africans.

But again, this may be averred, that the servitude which took place under the sanction of the divine law, in the time of Moses, and what was enjoined as the civil and religious polity of the people of Israel, was in nothing contrary to the natural rights and common liberties of men, though it had an appearance as such for great and wise ends. The Divine Law Giver, in his good providence, for great and wise purposes intended by it, has always admitted into the world riches and poverty, prosperity and adversity, high and low, rich and poor; and in such manner, as in all their variety and difference, mutation and change, there is nothing set forth in the written law, by Moses, contrary, unbecoming, or inconsistent with that goodness of himself, as the wise and righteous Governor of the Universe. Those things admitted into the law, that had a seeming appearance contrary to the natural liberties of men, were only so admitted for a local time, to point out, and to establish, and to give instruction thereby, in an analogous allusion to other things.

And therefore, so far as I have been able to consult the law written by Moses, concerning that kind of servitude admitted by it, I can find nothing imported thereby, in the least degree, to warrant the modern practice of slavery. But, on the contrary, and what was principally intended thereby, and in the most particular manner, as respecting Christians, that it contains the strongest prohibition against it. And every Christian man, that can read his Bible, may find that which is of the greatest importance for himself to know, implied even under the very institution of bond-servants; and that the state of bondage which the law denounces and describes, was thereby so intended to point out something necessary, as well as similar to all the other ritual and ceremonial services; and that the whole is set forth in such a manner, as containing the very essence and foundation of the Christian religion. And, moreover, that it must appear evident to any Christian believer, that it was necessary that all these things should take place, and as the most beautiful fabric of Divine goodness, that in all their variety, and in all their forms, they should stand recorded under the sanction of the Divine law.

And this must be observed, that it hath so pleased the Almighty Creator, to establish all the variety of things in nature, different complexions and other circumstances among men, and to record the various transactions of his own providence, with all the ceremonial economy written in the books of Moses, as more particularly respecting and enjoined to the Israelitish nation and people, for the use of sacred language, in order to convey wisdom to the fallen apostate human race. Wherefore, all the various things established, admitted and recorded, whether natural, moral, typical or ceremonial, with all the various things in nature referred to, were so ordered and admitted, as figures, types and emblems, and other symbolical representations, to bring forward, usher in, hold forth and illustrate that most amazing transaction, and the things concerning it, of all things the most wonderful that ever could take place amongst the universe of intelligent beings; as in that, and the things concerning it, of the salvation of apostate men, and the wonderful benignity of their Almighty Redeemer.

Whoever will give a serious and unprejudiced attention to the various things alluded to in the language of sacred writ, must see reason to believe that they imply a purpose and design far more glorious and important, than what seems generally to be understood by them; and to point to objects and events far more extensive and interesting, than what is generally ascribed to them. But as the grand eligibility and importance of those things, implied and pointed out in sacred writ, and the right understanding thereof, belongs to the sublime science of metaphysics and theology to enforce, illustrate and explain, I shall only select a few instances, which I think have a relation to my subject in hand.

Among other things it may be considered, that the different colours and complexions among men were intended for another purpose and design, than that of being only eligible in the variety of the scale of nature. And, accordingly, had it been otherwise, and if there had never been any black people among the children of men, nor any spotted leopards among the beasts of the earth, such an instructive question, by the prophet, could not have been proposed, as this, *Can the Ethiopian change his skin, or the leopard his spots? Then, may ye also do good, that are accustomed to do evil.* Jer[emiah] xiii. 23. The instruction intended by this is evident, that it was a convincing and forcible argument to shew, that none among the fallen and apostate race of men, can by any effort of their own, change their nature from the blackness and guilt of the sable dye of sin and pollution, or alter their way accustomed to do evil, from the variegated spots of their iniquity; and that such a change is as impossible to be totally and radically effected by them, as it is for a black man to change the colour of his skin, or the leopard to alter his spots. But these differences of a natural variety amongst the things themselves, is in every respect equally innocent, and what they cannot alter or change, was made to be so, and in the most eligible and primary design, were so intended for the very purposes of instructive language to men. And by these extreme differences of colour, it was intended to point out and shew to the white man, that there is a sinful blackness in his own nature, which he can no more change, than the external blackness which he sees in another can be rendered otherwise; and it likewise holds out to the black man, that the sinful blackness of his own nature is such, that he can no more alter, than the outward appearance of his colour can be brought to that of another. And this is imported by it, that there is an inherent evil in every man, contrary to that which is good; and that all men are like Ethiopians (even God's elect)[60] in a state of nature and unregeneracy, they are black with original sin, and spotted with actual transgression, which they cannot reverse. But to this truth, asserted of blackness, I must add another glorious one. All thanks and eternal praise be to God! His infinite wisdom and goodness has found out a way of renovation, and has opened a fountain through the blood of Jesus, for sin and for uncleanness, wherein all the stains and blackest dyes of sin and pollution can be washed away for ever, and the darkest sinner be made to shine as the brightest angel in heaven. And for that end and purpose, God alone has appointed all the channels of conveyance of the everlasting Gospel for these healing and purifying streams of the water of life to run in, and to bring life and salvation, with light and gladness to men; but he denounces woe to those who do not receive it themselves, but hinder and debar others who would, from coming to those salutary streams for life: Yet not alone confined to these, nor hindered in his purpose by any opposers, HE, who can open the eyes of the blind, and make the deaf to hear, can open streams in the desart, and make his benignity to flow, and his salvation to visit, even the meanest and most ignorant man, in the darkest shades of nature, as well as the most learned on the earth; and he usually carries on his own gracious work of quickening and redeeming grace, in a secret,

sovereign manner. To this I must again observe, and what I chiefly
intended by this similitude, that the external blackness of the
Ethiopians, is as innocent and natural, as spots in the leopards;
and that the difference of colour and complexion, which it hath
pleased God to appoint among men, are no more unbecoming
unto either of them, than the different shades of the rainbow are
unseemly to the whole, or unbecoming to any part of that apparent arch. It does not alter the nature and quality of a man, whether
he wears a black or a white coat, whether he puts it on or strips it
off, he is still the same man. And so likewise, when a man comes
to die, it makes no difference whether he was black or white,
whether he was male or female, whether he was great or small, or
whether he was old or young; none of these differences alter the
essentiality of the man, any more than he had wore a black or a
white coat and thrown it off for ever.

Another form of instruction for the same purpose, may be
taken from the slavery and oppression which men have committed
upon one another, as well as that kind of bondage and servitude
which was admitted under the sanction of the Divine law. But
there is nothing set forth in the law as a rule, or any thing recorded
therein that can stand as a precedent, or make it lawful, for men to
practice slavery; nor can any laws in favour of slavery be deduced
from thence, for to enslave men, be otherwise, than as unwarrantable, as it would be unnecessary and wrong, to order and
command the sacrifices of beasts to be still continued. Now the
great thing imported by it, and what is chiefly to be deduced from
it in this respect, is, that so far as the law concerning bond-
servants, and that establishment of servitude, as admitted in the
Mosaical institution, was set forth, it was thereby intended to prefigure and point out, that spiritual subjection and bondage to sin,
that all mankind, by their original transgression, were fallen into.
All men in their fallen depraved state, being under a spirit of
bondage, sunk into a nature of brutish carnality, and by the lusts
thereof, they are carried captive and enslaved; and the consequence is, that they are sold under sin and in bondage to iniquity,
and carried captive by the devil at his will. This being the case, the
thing proves itself; for if there had been no evil and sin amongst
men, there never would have been any kind of bondage, slavery

and oppression found amongst them; and if there was none of these things to be found, the great cause of it could not, in the present situation of men, be pointed out to them in that eligible manner as it is. Wherefore it was necessary that something of that bondage and servitude should be admitted into the ritual law for a figurative use, which, in all other respects and circumstances, was, in itself, contrary to the whole tenure of the law, and naturally in itself unlawful for men to practice.

Nothing but heavenly wisdom, and heavenly grace, can teach men to understand. The most deplorable of all things is, that the dreadful situation of our universal depraved state, which all mankind lyeth under, is such, that those who are not redeemed in time, must for ever continue to be the subjects of eternal bondage and misery. Blessed be God! he hath appointed and set up a deliverance, and the Saviour of Men is an Almighty Redeemer. When God, the Almighty Redeemer and Saviour of his people, brought his Israel out of Egypt and temporal bondage, it was intended and designed thereby, to set up an emblematical representation of their deliverance from the power and captivity of sin, and from the dominion of that evil and malignant spirit, who had with exquisite subtilty and guile at first seduced the original progenitors of mankind. And when they were brought to the promised land, and had gotten deliverance, and subdued their enemies under them, they were to reign over them; and their laws respecting bond-servants, and other things of that nature, were to denote, that they were to keep under and in subjection the whole body of their evil affections and lusts. This is so declared by the Apostle, that the law is spiritual,[61] and intended for spiritual uses. The general state of slavery which took place in the world, among other enormous crimes of wicked men might have served for an emblem and similitude of our spiritual bondage and slavery to sin; but, unless it had been admitted into the spiritual and divine law, it could not have stood and become an emblem that there was any spiritual restoration and deliverance afforded to us. By that which is evil in captivity and slavery among men, we are thereby so represented to be under a like subjection to sin; but by what is instituted in the law by Moses, in that respect we are thereby represented as Israel to have dominion over sin, and to rule over and keep in subjection all

our spiritual enemies. And, therefore, any thing which had a seeming appearance in favour of slavery, so far as it was admitted into
the law, was to shew that it was not natural and innocent, like that
of different colours among men, but as necessary to be made an
emblem of what was intended by it, and, consequently, as it stands
enjoined among other typical representations, was to shew that
every thing of any evil appearance of it was to be removed, and to
end with the other typical and ceremonial injunctions, when the
time of that dispensation was over. This must appear evident to all
Christian believers; and since therefore all these things are fulfilled
in the establishment of Christianity, there is now nothing remaining in the law for a rule of practice to men, but the ever abiding
obligations, and ever binding injunctions of moral rectitude, justice, equity and righteousness. All the other things in the Divine
law, are for spiritual uses and similitudes, for giving instruction
to the wise, and understanding to the upright in heart, that the
man of God may be perfect, thoroughly furnished unto all good
works.

Among other things also, the wars of the Israelites, and the extirpation of the Canaanites, and other circumstances as recorded
in sacred history, were intended to give instruction to men, but
have often been perverted to the most flagrant abuse, and even inverted to the most notorious purposes, for men to embolden
themselves to commit wickedness. Every possession that men enjoy upon earth are the gifts of God, and he who gives them, may
either take them away again from men, or he may take men away
themselves from the earth, as it pleaseth him. But who dare, even
with Lucifer, the malignant devourer of the world, think to imitate
the most High? The extirpation of the Canaanites out of their
land, was so ordered, not only to punish them for their idolatry
and abominable wickedness, but also to shew forth the honour of
his power, and the sovereignty of him who is the only potent one
that reigneth over the nations; that all men at that time might learn
to fear and know him who is Jehovah; and ever since that it might
continue a standing memorial of him, and a standard of honor
unto him who doth according to his will among the armies of
heaven, and whatever pleaseth him with the inhabitants of the
earth. And, in general, these transactions stand recorded for an

emblematical use and similitude, in the spiritual warfare of every true Israelite throughout all the ages of time. Every real believer and valiant champion in the knowledge and faith of their Omnipotent Saviour and Almighty Deliverer, as the very nature of Christianity requires and enjoins, knoweth the use of these things, *and they know how to endure hardness as good soldiers of Jesus Christ.*[62] They have many battles to fight with their unbelief, the perverseness of their nature, evil tempers and besetting sins, these Canaanites which still dwell in their land. They are so surrounded with adversaries, that they have need always to be upon their guard, and to have all their armour on. They are *commanded to cast off the works of darkness, and to put on the whole armour of righteousness and light; and that they may be strong in the Lord, and in the power of his might.*[63] For it is required *that they should be able to stand against the wiles of the devil, the powers of the rulers of the darkness of this world, against spiritual wickedness in high places.*[64] And as their foes are *mighty and tall like the Anakims,*[65] *and fenced up to heaven,* they must be mighty warriors, *men of renown, valiant for the truth, strong in the faith, fighting the Lord's battles, and overcoming all their enemies, through the dear might of the Great Captain of their salvation.*[66] In this warfare, should they meet with some mighty *Agag,*[67] some strong corruption, or besetting sin, they are commanded *to cut it down,* and with the sword of Samuel *to hew it to pieces before the Lord.*[68] This, in its literal sense, may seem harsh, as if Samuel had been cruel; and so will our sins, and other sinners insinuate and tell us not to mind such things as the perfect law of God requires. But if we consider that the Lord God who breathed into man the breath of life, can suspend and take it away when he pleaseth, and that there is not a moment we have to exist, wherein that life may not be suspended before the next: it was therefore of an indifferent matter for that man Agag, when the Lord, who hath the breath and life of every man in his hand, had appointed him at that time to die, for his great wickedness and the murders committed by him, whether he was slain by Samuel or any other means. But what Samuel, the servant of the Lord, did in that instance, was in obedience to his voice, and in itself a righteous deed, and a just judgment upon Agag. And the matter imported by it, was also intended to shew, that all our Amalekite sins, and even the chief and darling of them, the avaricious and covetous Agags, should be cut off for ever. But if we spare them, and leave them to remain alive in stubborn disobedience to the law and commandments of God, we should in that case, be like Saul,[69] cut off ourselves from the kingdom of his grace. According to this view, it may suffice to shew (and what infinite wisdom intended, no doubt) that a wise and righteous use may be made of those very things, which otherwise are generally perverted to wrong purposes.

And now, as to these few instances which I have collected from that sacred hypothesis, whereby it is shewn, that other things are implied and to be understood by the various incidents as recorded in sacred writ, with a variety of other things in nature, bearing an analogous allusion to things of the greatest importance for every Christian man to know and understand; and that the whole of the ritual law, though these things themselves are not to be again repeated, is of that nature and use as never to be forgot. And therefore to suppose, or for any Christians to say, that they have nothing to do with those things now in the right use thereof, and what was intended and imported thereby respecting themselves, would be equally as absurd as to hear them speaking in the language of devils; and they might as well say as they did, when speaking out of the demoniac, that they have nothing to do with Christ.

Having thus endeavoured to shew, and what, I think, must appear evident and obvious, that none of all these grand pretensions, as generally made use of by the favourers of slavery, to encourage and embolden them, in that iniquitous traffic, can have any foundation or shadow of truth to support them; and that there is nothing in nature, reason, and scripture can be found, in any manner or way, to warrant the enslaving of black people more than others.

But I am aware that some of these arguments will weigh nothing against such men as do not believe the scriptures themselves, nor care to understand; but let them be aware not to make use of these things against us which they do not believe, or whatever pretence they may have for committing violence against us. Any property taken away from others, whether by stealth, fraud, or violence, must be wrong; but to take away men themselves, and keep them in slavery, must be worse. *Skin for skin, all that a man hath would he give for his life;*[70] and would rather lose his property to any amount whatever, than to have his liberty taken away, and be kept as a slave. It must be an inconceivable fallacy to think otherwise: none but the inconsiderate, most obdurate and stubborn, could ever think that it was right to enslave others. *But the way of the wicked is brutish: his own iniquity shall take the wicked himself, and he shall be holden with the cords of his sins: he shall die without instruction, and in the greatness of his folly he shall go astray.*[71]

Among the various species of men that commit rapine, and violence, and murders, and theft, upon their fellow-creatures, like the ravenous beasts of the night, prowling for their prey, there are also those that set out their heads in the open day, opposing all the obligations of civilization among men, and breaking through all the laws of justice and equity to them, and making even the very things which are analogous to the obligations, which ought to warn and prohibit them, a pretence for their iniquity and injustice. Such are the insidious merchants and pirates that gladen their oars with the carnage and captivity of men, and the vile negociators and enslavers of the human species. The prohibitions against them are so strong, that, in order to break through and to commit the most notorious and flagrant crimes with impunity, they are obliged to oil their poisonous pretences with various perversions of sundry transactions of things even in sacred writ, that the acrimonious points of their arsenic may be swallowed down the better, and the evil effects of their crimes appear the less. In this respect, instead of *the sacred history of the Israelitish nation being made profitable to them, for doctrine, for reproof, for correction, and for instruction in righteousness,*[72] as it was intended, *and given to men* for that purpose; but, instead thereof, the wars of the Israelites, the extirpation and subjection of the Canaanites, and other transactions of that kind, are generally made use of by wicked men as precedents and pretences to encourage and embolden themselves to commit cruelty and slavery on their fellow-creatures: and the merciless depredators, negociators, and enslavers of men, revert to the very ritual law of Moses as a precedent for their barbarity, cruelty, and injustice; which law, though devoid of any iniquity, as bearing a parallel allusion to other things signified thereby, can afford no precedent for their evil way, in any shape or view: what was intended by it is fulfilled, and in no respect, or any thing like it, can be repeated again, without transgressing and breaking through every other injunction, precept, and command of the just and tremendous law of God.

The consequence of their apostacy from God, and disobedience to his law, became a snare to those men in times of old, who departed from it; and because of their disobedience and wickedness, the several nations, which went astray after their own abominations, were visited with many dreadful calamities and judgments. But to set up the ways of the wicked for an example, and to make the laws respecting their suppression, and the judgments that were inflicted upon them for their iniquity, and even the written word of God, and the transactions of his providence, to be reversed and become precedents and pretences for men to commit depredations and extirpations, and for enslaving and negociating or merchandizing the human species, must be horrible wickedness indeed, and sinning with a high hand. And it cannot be thought otherwise, but that the abandoned aggressors, among the learned nations will, in due time, as the just reward of their aggravated iniquity, be visited with some more dreadful and tremendous judgments of the righteous vengeance of God, than what even befel to the Canaanites of old.

And it may be considered further, that to draw any inferences in favour of extirpation, slavery, and negociation of men, from the written word of God, or from any thing else in the history and customs of different nations, as a precedent to embolden wicked men in their wickedness; cannot be more wicked, ridiculous, and absurd to shew any favour to these insidious negociators and enslavers, than it would be to stand and laugh, and look on with a brutal and savage impunity, at beholding the following supposition transacted. Suppose two or three half-witted foolish fellows happened to come past a crowd of people, gazing at one which they had hung up by the neck on a tree, as a victim suffering for breaking the laws of his country; and suppose these foolish fellows went on a little way in a bye path, and found some innocent person, not suffering any harm till taken hold of by them, and

could not deliver himself from them, and just because they had
seen among the crowd of people which they came past, that there
had been a man hung by the neck, they took it into their foolish
wicked heads to hang up the poor innocent man on the next tree,
and just did as they had seen others do, to please their own fancy
and base foolishness, to see how he would swing. Now if any of
the other people happened to come up to them, and saw what they
had done, would they hesitate a moment to determine between
themselves and these foolish rascals which had done wickedness? Surely not; they would immediately take hold of such
stupid wicked wretches, if it was in their power, and for their
brutish foolishness, have them chained in a Bedlam,[73] or hung on a
gibbet. But what would these base foolish wretches say for themselves? That they saw others do so, and they thought there had
been no harm in it, and they only did as they had seen the crowd
of people do before. A poor foolish, base, rascally excuse indeed!
But not a better excuse than this, can the brutish enslavers and negociators of men find in all the annals of history. The ensnarers,
negociators, and oppressors of men, have only to become more
abandoned in wickedness than these supposed wretches could be;
and to pass on in the most abominable bye paths of wickedness,
and make, every thing that they can see an example for their brutal
barbarity; and whether it be a man hanged for his crimes, or an innocent man for the wretched wickedness of others; right or wrong
it makes no difference to them, if they can only satisfy their own
wretched and brutal avarice. Whether it be the Israelites subjecting
the Canaanites for their crimes, or the Canaanites subjecting the
Israelites, to gratify their own wickedness, it makes no difference
to them. When they see some base wretches like themselves ensnaring, enslaving, oppressing, whipping, starving with hunger,
and cruelly torturing and murdering some of the poor helpless
part of mankind, they would think no harm in it, they would do
the same. Perhaps the Greeks and Romans, and other crowds of
barbarous nations have done so before; they can make that a
precedent, and think no harm in it, they would still do the same,
and worse than any barbarous nations ever did before; and if they
look backwards and forwards they can find no better precedent,
ancient or modern, than that which is wicked, mean, brutish, and

base. To practise such abominable parallels of wickedness of ensnaring, negociating, and enslaving men, is the scandal and shame
of mankind; And what must we think of their crimes? Let the
groans and cries of the murdered, and the cruel slavery of the
Africans tell!

They that can stand and look on and behold no evil in the infamous traffic of slavery must be sunk to a wonderful degree of insensibility; but surely those that can delight in that evil way for
their gain, and be pleased with the wickedness of the wicked, and
see no harm in subjecting their fellow-creatures to slavery, and
keeping them in a state of bondage and subjection as a brute, must
be wretchedly brutish indeed. But so bewitched are the general
part of mankind with some sottish or selfish principle, that they
care nothing about what is right or wrong, any farther than their
own interest leads them to; and when avarice leads them on they
can plead a thousand excuses for doing wrong, or letting others do
wickedly, so as they have any advantage by it, to their own gratifi-
cation and use. That sottish and selfish principle, without concern
and discernment among men is such, that if they can only prosper
themselves, they care nothing about the miserable situation of
others: and hence it is, that even those who are elevated to high
rank of power and affluence, and as becoming their eminent stations, have opportunity of extending their views afar, yet they can
shut their eyes at this enormous evil of the slavery and commerce
of the human species; and, contrary to all the boasted accomplishments, and fine virtues of the civilized and enlightened nations,
they can sit still and let the torrent of robbery, slavery, and oppression roll on.

*There is a way which seemeth good unto a man, but the end
thereof are the ways of death.*[74] Should the enslavers of men think
to justify themselves in their evil way, or that it can in any possible
way be right for them to subject others to slavery; it is but charitable to evince and declare unto them, that they are those who have
gone into that evil way of brutish stupidity as well as wickedness,
that they can behold nothing of moral rectitude and equity among
men but in the gloomy darkness of their own hemisphere, like
the owls and night-hawks, who can see nothing but mist and darkness in the meridian blaze of day. When men forsake the paths of

virtue, righteousness, justice, and mercy, and become vitiated in
any evil way, all their pretended virtues, sensibility, and prudence
among men, however high they may shine in their own, and of
others estimation, will only appear to be but specious villainy at
last. That virtue which will ever do men any good in the end, is as
far from that which some men call such, as the gaudy appearance
of a glow-worm in the dark is to the intrinsic value and lustre of
a diamond: for if a man hath not love in his heart to his fellow-
creatures, with a generous philanthropy diffused throughout his
whole soul, all his other virtues are not worth a straw.

The whole law of God is founded upon love, and the two grand
branches of it are these: *Thou shalt love the Lord thy God with all
thy heart and with all thy soul; and thou shalt love thy neighbour
as thyself.*[75] And so it was when man was first created and made:
they were created male and female, and pronounced to be in the
image of God, and, as his representative, to have dominion over
the lower creation: and their Maker, who is love, and the intellectual Father of Spirits, blessed them, and commanded them to arise
in a bond of union of nature and of blood, each being a brother
and a sister together, and each the lover and the loved of one another. But when they were envied and invaded by the grand enslaver of men, all their jarring inconsistency arose, and those who
adhered to their pernicious usurper soon became envious, hateful,
and hating one another. And those who go on to injure, ensnare,
oppress, and enslave their fellow-creatures, manifest their hatred
to men, and maintain their own infamous dignity and vassalage, as
the servants of sin and the devil: but the man who has any honour
as a man scorns their ignominious dignity: the noble philan-
thropist looks up to his God and Father as his only sovereign; and
he looks around on his fellow men as his brethren and friends; and
in every situation and case, however mean and contemptible they
may seem, he endeavours to do them good: and should he meet
with one in the desert, whom he never saw before, he would hail
him my brother! my sister! my friend! how fares it with thee?
And if he can do any of them any good it would gladden every
nerve of his soul.

But as there is but *one law and one manner* prescribed universally for all mankind, *for you, and for the stranger that sojourneth*

with you,[76] and wheresoever they may be scattered throughout the face of the whole earth, the difference of superiority and inferiority which are found subsisting amongst them is no way incompatible with the universal law of love, honor, righteousness, and equity; so that a free, voluntary, and sociable servitude, which is the very basis of human society, either civil or religious, whereby we serve one another that we may be served, or do good that good may be done unto us, is in all things requisite and agreeable to all law and justice. But the taking away the natural liberties of men, and compelling them to any involuntary slavery or compulsory service, is an injury and robbery contrary to all law, civilization, reason, justice, equity, and humanity: therefore when men break through the laws of God, and the rules of civilization among men, and go forth to steal, to rob, to plunder, to oppress and to enslave, and to destroy their fellow-creatures, the laws of God and man require that they should be suppressed, and deprived of their liberty, or perhaps their lives.

But justice and equity does not always reside among men, even where some considerable degree of civilization is maintained; if it had, that most infamous reservoir of public and abandoned merchandizers and enslavers of men would not have been suffered so long, nor the poor unfortunate Africans, that never would have crossed the Atlantic to rob them, would not have become their prey. But it is just as great and as heinous a transgression of the law of God to steal, kidnap, buy, sell, and enslave any one of the Africans, as it would be to ensnare any other man in the same manner, let him be who he will. And suppose that some of the African pirates had been as dextrous as the Europeans, and that they had made excursions on the coast of Great-Britain or elsewhere, and though even assisted by some of your own insidious neighbours, for there may be some men even among you vile enough to do such a thing if they could get money by it; and that they should carry off your sons and your daughters, and your wives and friends, to a perpetual and barbarous slavery, you would certainly think that those African pirates were justly deserving of any punishment that could be put upon them. But the European pirates and merchandizers of the human species, let them belong to what nation they will, are equally as bad; and they have no better right to steal, kidnap, buy, and carry away and sell the Africans, than the Africans would have to carry away any of the Europeans in the same barbarous and unlawful manner.

But again, let us follow the European piracy to the West-Indies, or any where among Christians, and this law of the *Lord Christ* must stare every infidel slave-holder in the face, *And as ye would that men should do to you, do ye also to them likewise.*[77] But there is no slave-holder would like to have himself enslaved, and to be treated as a dog, and sold like a beast; and therefore the slave-holders, and merchandizers of men, transgress this plain law, and they commit a greater violation against it, and act more contrary unto it, than it would be for a parcel of slaves to assume authority over their masters, and compel them to slavery under them; for, if that was not doing as they would wish to be done to, it would be doing, at least, as others do to them, in a way equally as much and more wrong. But our Divine Lord and *Master Christ* also teacheth men to *forgive one another their trespasses,*[78] and that we are not to do evil because others do so, and to revenge injuries done unto us, Wherefore it is better, and more our duty, to suffer ourselves to be lashed and cruelly treated, than to take up the task of their barbarity. The just law of God requires an equal retaliation and restoration for every injury that men may do to others, to shew the greatness of the crime; but the law of forbearance, righteousness and forgiveness, forbids the retaliation to be sought after, when it would be doing as great an injury to them, without any reparation or benefit to ourselves. For what man can restore an eye that he may have deprived another of, and if even a double punishment was to pass upon him, and that he was to lose both his eyes for the crime, that would make no reparation to the other man whom he had deprived of one eye. And so, likewise, when a man is carried captive and enslaved, and maimed and cruelly treated, that would make no adequate reparation and restitution for the injuries he had received, if he was even to get the person who had ensnared him to be taken captive and treated in the same manner. What he is to seek after is a deliverance and protection for himself, and not a revenge upon others. Wherefore the honest and upright, like the just Bethlehem Joseph,[79] cannot think of doing evil, nor require an equal retaliation for such injuries done to them, so as to revenge themselves upon others, for that which would do them no manner of good. Such vengeance belongeth unto the Lord, and he will render vengeance and recompence to his enemies and the violaters of his law.[80]

But thus saith the law of God: *If a man be found stealing any of his neighbours, or he that stealeth a man (let him be who he will) and selleth him, or that maketh merchandize of him, or if he be found in his hand, then that thief shall die.*[81] However, in all modern slavery among Christians, who ought to know this law, they have not had any regard to it. Surely if any law among them admits of death as a punishment for robbing or defrauding others of their money or goods, it ought to be double death, if it was possible, when a man is robbed of himself, and sold into captivity and cruel slavery. But because of his own goodness, and because of the universal depravity of men, the Sovereign Judge of all has introduced a law of forbearance, to spare such transgressors, where in many cases the law denounces death as the punishment for their crimes, unless for those founded upon murder, or such abominations as cannot be forborn with in any civilizations among men. but this law of forbearance is no alteration of the law itself; it is only a respite in order to spare such as will fly to him for refuge and forgiveness for all their crimes, and for all their iniquities, who is the righteous fulfiller of the law,[82] and the surety and representative of men before God: and if they do not repent of their iniquity, and reform to a life of new obedience, as being under greater obligations to the law, but go on in their evil way, they must at last for ever lie under the curse and every penalty of the just and holy law of the Most High. This seems to be determined so by that Great Judge of the law, when the accusers of a woman, taken in adultery, brought her before him, he stooped down as a man and wrote, we may suppose, the crimes of her accusers in the dust, and as the God of all intelligence painted them in their consciences, wherefore they fled away one by one, and the woman was left alone before him; and as there was none of her accusers in that case righteous enough to throw the first stone, and to execute the law upon her, she was, Bid to go and sin no more.[83] But it is manifest that every crime that men may commit, where death is mentioned as the penalty thereof in the righteous law of God, it

denotes a very great offence and a heinous transgression; and although, in many cases, it may meet with some mitigation in the
punishment, because of the forbearance of God, and the unright-
eousness of men, it cannot thereby be thought the less criminal in
itself. But it also supposes, where strict severities are made use of
in the laws of civilization, that the doers of the law, and the judges
of it, ought to be very righteous themselves. And with great regard
to that law of men-stealers, merchandizers, and of slaves found in
their hands, that whatever mitigation and forbearance such offenders ought to meet with, their crimes denote a very heinous offence, and a great violation of the law of God; they ought, therefore, to be punished according to their trespasses, which, in some
cases, should be death, if the person so robbed and stole should
die in consequence thereof, or should not be restored and brought
back; and even then to be liable to every damage and penalty that
the judges should think proper: for so it is annexed to this law and
required, *that men should put away evil from among them.*[84] But
this cannot now extend to the West-India slavery: what should
rather be required of them, in their present case of infatuation, is
to surrender and give it up, and heal the stripes that they have
wounded, and to pour the healing balm of Christianity into the
bleeding wounds of Heathen barbarity and cruelty.

All the criminal laws of civilization seem to be founded upon
that law of God which was published to Noah and his sons; and,
consequently, as it is again and again repeated, it becomes irre-
versible, and universal to all mankind. *And surely your blood of
your lives will I require: at the hand of every beast will I require it;
and at the hand of man, at the hand of every man's brother, will I
require the life of man. Whoso sheddeth man's blood, by man shall
his blood be shed: for in the image of God made he man.*[85] If this
law of God had not been given to men, murder itself would not
have been any crime; and those who punished it with death would
just have been as guilty as the other. But the law of God is just,
righteous and holy, and ought to be regarded and revered above all
the laws of men; and this is added unto it: *What thing soever I
command you, observe to do it: thou shalt not add thereto, nor diminish from it.*[86] But it is an exceeding impious thing for men ever
to presume, or think, as some will say, that they would make it

death as a punishment for such a thing, and such a trespass; or that they can make any criminal laws of civilization as binding with a penalty of death for any thing just what they please. No such thing can be supposed; no man upon earth ever had, or ever can have, a right to make laws where a penalty of cutting off by death is required as the punishment for the transgression thereof: what is required of men is to be the doers of the law, and some of them to be judges of it; and if they judge wrongfully in taking away the lives of their fellow-creatures contrary to the law of God, they commit murder.

The reason why a man suffers death for breaking the laws of his country is, because he transgresseth the law of God in that community he belongs to; and the laws of civilization are binding to put that law in force, and to point out and shew a sufficient warrant wherefore he should suffer, according as the just law of God requires for his trespass; and then it is just and right that he should die for his crime. And as murder is irreversibly to be punished with death, sometimes when it is not done, or only implied or eventually intended, it even then requires death; and in this sense it becomes right to face our enemies in the field of battle, and to cut them off. And when spies and incendiaries rise up, or when rebellions break forth, and the lives of the Sovereign and others, and the good of the community is not safe while such pretenders and their chief supporters are suffered to live; then it may be lawful, in some cases, that they should die; but in cases of this kind there is generally more cowardice and cruelty than justice and mercy regarded, and more discretionary power left for men to use their authority in, and to establish criminal laws or precedents than in any thing else. Hence we may find many of the different chiefs and kings in different parts of the world, in all ages, wading through a sea of blood to their thrones, or supporting themselves upon it, by desolating and destroying others; and we may find good and bad in all ages setting up wretched examples for men to be guided by; and herein we may find a David,[87] a Solomon,[88] a Cromwell,[89] committing murder and death, and a Charles the Second[90] committing a greater carnage upon more innocent people than those who suffered in the reign of a bloody Queen Mary;[91] and even in a late rebellion there were many suffered in Britain,[92] which, if they had been preserved to this mild reign, they would have been as good neighbours, and as faithful subjects, as any other. But among all pretences for taking away the lives of men by any form of law, that for religion is the most unwarrantable: it is the command of God to suppress idolatry, and to break down the images and external pomp of gross superstition, but not to destroy men themselves: that persecution is murder if it takes away the lives of men for their religion, for it has nothing to do with what men may think with respect to their duty; and if a man is foolish enough to make an image of wood or stone, and to worship it, or even to adore a picture, if he keeps it to himself, persecution has nothing to do with him.

The law of God forbids all manner of covetousness and theft: but when any thing is taken away by stealth, it is not like those injuries which cannot be restored, as the cutting off or wounding any of the members of the body; but it admits of a possible restoration, whether the violators can restore it or not as the law requires, so if a man owes a just debt it is not the less due by him if he has got nothing to pay it with; such transgressors ought to be punished according to their trespasses, but not with death: for the law of God is, "If a thief be found breaking up, and he be smitten that he die, if it was in the night there shall be no blood shed for him; but if the sun be risen upon him, there was blood required for him if he was killed; for saith the law it required only he should make full restitution; and if he had nothing, then he should be sold for his theft. And if any manner of theft be found in a man's hand, the law requires a retaliation and restoration; that is, that he should restore double; but if it be sold or made away with, it was then to be four-fold, and, in some cases, five, six or seven times as much."[93] According to this law, when the property of others is taken away, either by stealth, fraud, or violence, the aggressors should be subjected to such bondage and hard labour, (and especially when the trespass is great, and they have nothing to pay) as would be requisite to make restitution to the injured, and to bring about a reformation to themselves. And if they have committed violence either by threats or force, they ought to suffer bodily punishment, and the severity of it according to their crimes, and the stubbornness of their obduracy; and all such punishments as are necessary should be inflicted upon them without pitying or sparing them, though perhaps not to be continued forever in the brutal manner that the West-India slaves suffer for almost no crimes.

But whereas the robbing of others in any manner of their property is often attended with such cruelty and violence, and a severe loss to the sufferers, it may, in some cases, be thought that the law of God sufficiently warrants the taking away the lives of the aggressors; for the taking away of a man's property in general may be considered as taking away his life, or at least the means of his support, and then the punishing the aggressors with death can only in that case be reckoned a constructive murder. Wherefore the transgressors ought to be punished severely; but never with any laws of civilization where death is concerned, without regard to the law of God. And when the law of God admits of a forbearance, and a kind of forgiveness in many things, it ought to be the grand law of civilization to seek out such rules of punishment as are best calculated to prevent injuries of every kind, and to reclaim the transgressors; and it is best, if it can be done, to punish with a less degree of severity than their crimes deserve. But all the laws of civilization must jar greatly when the law of God is screwed up in the greatest severity to punish men for their crimes on the one hand, and on the other to be totally disregarded.[94] When the Divine law points out a theft, where the thief should make restitution for his trespass, the laws of civilization say, he must die for his crime: and when the law tells us, that he who stealeth or maketh merchandize of men, that such a thief shall surely die, the laws of civilization say, in many cases, that it is no crime. In this the ways of men are not equal; but let the wise and just determine whether the laws of God or the laws of men are right.

Amongst some of the greatest transgressors of the laws of civilization, those that defraud the public by forgery, or by substituting or falsifying any of the current specie,[95] ought to have their lives or their liberties taken away; for although they may not do any personal injury, they commit the greatest robbery and theft, both to individuals and the whole community. But even in the suppression of those, men have no right to add or diminish any thing to the law of God, with respect to taking away their lives.

Wherefore, if the law of God does not so clearly warrant, that they should die for their theft, it, at least, fully warrants that they should be sold into slavery for their crimes; and the laws of civilization may justly bind them, and hold them in perpetual bondage, because they have sold themselves to work iniquity; but not that they should be sold to the heathen, or to such as would not instruct them: for there might be hope, that if good instruction was properly administered unto them, there might be a possible reformation wrought upon some of them. Some, by their ingenious assiduity, have tamed the most savage wild beasts; it is cer-tainly more laudable to tame the most brutish and savage men, and, in time, there might be some Onesimus's found amongst them, that would become useful to reclaim others.[96] Those that break the laws of civilization, in any flagrant manner, are the only species of men that others have a right to enslave; and such ought to be sold to the community, with every thing that can be found belonging to them, to make a commutation of restitution as far as could be; and they should be kept at some useful and labourious employment, and it might be at some embankation, or recovering of waste ground, as there might be land recovered on rivers and shores, worth all the expence, for the benefit of the community they belonged to. The continuance of that criminal slavery and bondage, ought to be according to the nature of their crimes, with a reference to their good behaviour, either to be continued or protracted. Such as were condemned for life, when their crimes were great, and themselves stubborn, might be so marked as to render their getting away impossible without being discovered, and that the very sight of one of them might deter others from committing their crimes, as much as hanging perhaps a dozen of them; and it might be made so severe unto them, that it would render their own society in bondage, almost the only preferable one that they could enjoy among men. The manner of confining them would not be so impracticable as some may be apt to think; and all these severities come under the laws of men to punish others for their crimes, but they should not go beyond the just law of God; and neither should his laws be suspended, where greater trespasses are committed.

In this sense every free community might keep slaves, or criminal prisoners in bondage; and should they be sold to any other, it should not be to strangers, nor without their own consent; and if any were sold for a term of years, they would naturally become free as soon as their purchase could be paid. But if any man should buy another man without his own consent, and compel him to his service and slavery without any agreement of that man to serve him, the enslaver is a robber, and a defrauder of that man every day. Wherefore it is as much the duty of a man who is robbed in that manner to get out of the hands of his enslaver, as it is for an honest community of men to get out of the hands of rogues and villains. And however much is required of men to forgive one another their trespasses in one respect, it is also manifest, and what we are commanded, as noble, to resist evil in another, in order to prevent others doing evil, and to keep ourselves from harm. Therefore, if there was no other way to deliver a man from slavery, but by enslaving his master, it would be lawful for him to do so if he was able, for this would be doing justice to himself, and be justice as the law requires, to chastise his master for enslaving of him wrongfully.

Thence this general and grand duty should be observed by every man, not to follow the multitude to do evil, neither to recompence evil for evil; and yet, so that a man may lawfully defend himself, and endeavour to secure himself, and others, as far as he can, from injuries of every kind. Wherefore all along, in the history of mankind, the various depredations committed in the world, by enslaving, extirpating and destroying men, were always contrary to the laws of God, and what he had strictly forbidden and commanded not to be done. But insolent, proud, wicked men, in all ages, and in all places, are alike; they disregard the laws of the Most High, and stop at no evil in their power, that they can contrive with any pretence of consistency in doing mischief to others, so as it may tend to promote their own profit and ambition. Such are all the depredators, kidnappers, merchandizers and enslavers of men; they do not care, nor consider, how much they injure others, if they can make any advantage to themselves by it. But whenever these things were committed by wicked men, a retaliation was sought after, as the only way of deliverance; for he who leadeth into captivity, should be carried captive; and he which de-

stroyeth with the sword, should die with the sword.[97] And as it
became necessary to punish those that wronged others, when the
punishers went beyond the bounds of a just retaliation, and fell
into the same crimes of the oppressors, not to prevent themselves
from harm, and to deliver the oppressed and the captive, but to
oppress and enslave others, as much as they before them had done,
the consequence is plain, that an impending overthrow must still
fall upon them likewise. In that respect, so far as conquerors are
permitted to become a judgment and a scourge to others, for their
enormous transgressions, they are themselves not a bit more safe,
for what they do, they often do wickedly for their own purpose;
and when the purpose of Divine Providence, who raised them up,
is fulfilled by them, in the punishment of others for their crimes;
the next wave thereof will be to visit them also according to their
wickedness with some dreadful overthrow, and to swallow them
up in the sea of destruction and oblivion.

History affords us many examples of severe retaliations, revolutions and dreadful overthrows; and of many crying under the
heavy load of subjection and oppression, seeking for deliverance.
And methinks I hear now, many of my countrymen, in complexion, crying and groaning under the heavy yoke of slavery and
bondage, and praying to be delivered; and the word of the Lord is
thus speaking for them, while they are bemoaning themselves under the grievous bonds of their misery and woe, saying, *Woe is me!*
alas Africa! for I am as the last gleanings of the summer fruit, as
the grape gleanings of the vintage, where no cluster is to eat. The
good are perished out of the earth, and there is none upright
among men; they all lie in wait for blood; they hunt every man
his brother with a net. That they may do evil with both hands
earnestly, the prince asketh, and the judge asketh for a reward; and
the great man he uttereth his mischievous desire: so they wrap it
up. Among *the best* in Africa, we have found them *sharp as a*
briar; among *the most upright,* we have found them *sharper than a*
thorn-hedge in the West-Indies. Yet, O Africa! yet, poor slave!
The day of thy watchmen cometh, and thy visitation draweth nigh,
that shall be their perplexity. Therefore I will look unto the Lord; I
will wait for the God of my salvation; my God will hear me. Re-
joice not against me, O mine enemy; though I be fallen, I shall yet

arise; though I sit in darkness, the Lord shall yet be a light unto me. I will bear the indignation of the Lord, because I have sinned against him, until he plead my cause, and execute judgment for me, and I shall behold his righteousness. Then mine enemies shall see it, and shame shall cover them which said unto me, Where is the Lord thy God, that regardeth thee: *Mine eyes shall behold them trodden down as the mire of the streets. In that day that thy walls* of deliverance *are to be built, in that day shall the decree* of slavery *be far removed.*[98]

What revolution the end of that predominant evil of slavery and oppression may produce, whether the wise and considerate will surrender and give it up, and make restitution for the injuries that they have already done, as far as they can; or whether the force of their wickedness, and the iniquity of their power, will lead them on until some universal calamity burst forth against the abandoned carriers of it on, and against the criminal nations in confederacy with them, is not for me to determine? But this must appear evident, that for any man to carry on a traffic in the merchandize of slaves, and to keep them in slavery; or for any nation to oppress, extirpate and destroy others; that these are crimes of the greatest magnitude, and a most daring violation of the laws and commandments of the Most High, and which, at last, will be evidenced in the destruction and overthrow of all the transgressors. And nothing else can be expected for such violations of taking away the natural rights and liberties of men, but that those who are the doers of it will meet with some awful visitation of the righteous judgment of God, and in such a manner as it cannot be thought that his just vengeance for their iniquity will be the less tremendous because his judgments are long delayed.

None but men of the most brutish and depraved nature, led on by the invidious influence of infernal wickedness, could have made their settlements in the different parts of the world discovered by them, and have treated the various Indian nations, in the manner that the barbarous inhuman Europeans have done; and their establishing and carrying on that most dishonest, unjust and diabolical traffic of buying and selling, and of enslaving men, is such a monstrous, audacious and unparalleled wickedness, that the very idea of it is shocking, and the whole nature of it is horrible

and infernal. It may be said with confidence as a certain general
fact, that all their foreign settlements and colonies were founded
on murders and devastations, and that they have continued their
depredations in cruel slavery and oppression to this day: for where
such predominant wickedness as the African slave-trade, and the
West Indian slavery, is admitted, tolerated and supported by them,
and carried on in their colonies, the nations and people who are
the supporters and encouragers thereof must be not only guilty
themselves of that shameful and abandoned evil and wickedness,
so very disgraceful to human nature, but even partakers in those
crimes of the most vile combinations of various pirates, kidnappers, robbers and thieves, the ruffians and stealers of men, that
ever made their appearance in the world.

Soon after Columbus had discovered America, that great navi-
gator was himself greatly embarrassed and treated unjustly, and
his best designs counteracted by the wicked baseness of those
whom he led to that discovery. The infernal conduct of his Spanish competitors, whose leading motives were covetousness, avarice
and fanaticism, soon made their appearance, and became cruel
and dreadful. At Hispaniola the base perfidy and bloody treachery
of the Spaniards, led on by the perfidious Ovando, in seizing the
peaceable Queen Anacoana and her attendants, burning her
palace, putting all to destruction, and the innocent Queen and
her people to a cruel death, is truly horrible and lamentable.[99]
And led on by the treacherous Cortes,[100] the fate of the great
Montezuma[101] was dreadful and shocking; how that American
monarch was treated, betrayed and destroyed, and his vast extensive empire of the Mexicans brought to ruin and devastation, no
man of sensibility and feeling can read the history without pity
and resentment. And looking over another page of that history,
sensibility would kindle into horror and indignation, to see the
base treacherous bastard Pizarra at the head of the Spanish banditti of miscreant depredators, leading them on, and overturning
one of the most extensive empires in the world. To recite a little of
this as a specimen of the rest: It seems Pizarra,[102] with his company of depredators, had artfully penetrated into the Peruvian empire, and pretended an embassy of peace from a great monarch,[103]
and demanded an audience of the noble Atahualpa,[104] the great

Inca or Lord of that empire, that the terms of their embassy might be explained, and the reason of their coming into the territories of that monarch. Atahualpa fearing the menaces of those terrible invaders, and thinking to appease them by complying with their request, relied on Pizzara's feigned pretensions of friendship; accordingly the day was appointed, and Atahualpa made his appearance with the greatest decency and splendor he could, to meet such superior beings as the Americans conceived their invaders to be, with four hundred men in an uniform dress, as harbingers to clear the way before him, and himself sitting on a throne or couch, adorned with plumes of various colours, and almost covered with plates of gold and silver, enriched with precious stones, and was carried on the shoulders of his principal attendants. As he approached near the Spanish quarters the arch fanatic Father Vincent Valverde, chaplain to the expedition,[105] advanced with a crucifix in one hand and a breviary in the other, and began with a long discourse, pretending to explain some of the general doctrines of Christianity, together with the fabulous notion of St. Peter's viceregency, and the transmission of his apostolic power continued in the succession of the Popes;[106] and that the then Pope, Alexander, by donation, had invested their master as the sole Monarch of all the New World.[107] In consequence of this, Atahualpa was instantly required to embrace the Christian religion, acknowledge the jurisdiction of the Pope, and submit to the Great Monarch of Castile; but if he should refuse an immediate compliance with these requisitions, they were to declare war against him, and that he might expect the dreadful effects of their vengeance. This strange harangue, unfolding deep mysteries, and alluding to such unknown facts, of which no power of eloquence could translate, and convey, at once, a distinct idea to an American, that its general tenor was altogether incomprehensible to Atahualpa. Some parts in it, as more obvious that the rest, filled him with astonishment and indignation. His reply, however, was temperate, and as suitable as could be well expected. He observed that he was Lord of the domains over which he reigned by hereditary succession; and, said, that he could not conceive how a foreign priest should pretend to dispose of territories which did not belong to him, and that if such a preposterous grant had been made, he, who was the rightful possessor, refused to confirm it; that he had no inclination to renounce the religious institutions established by his ancestors; nor would he forsake the service of the Sun, the immortal divinity whom he and his people revered, in order to worship the God of the Spaniards, who was subject to death; and that with respect to other matters, he had never heard of them before, and did not then understand their meaning. And he desired to know where Valverde had learned things so extraordinary. In this book, replied the fanatic Monk, reaching out his breviary. The Inca opened it eagerly, and turning over the leaves, lifted it to his ear: This, says he, is silent; it tells me nothing; and threw it with disdain to the ground.[108] The enraged father of ruffians, turning towards his countrymen, the assassinators, cried out, To arms, Christians, to arms; the word of God is insulted; avenge this profanation on these impious dogs.

At this the Christian desperadoes impatient in delay, as soon as the signal of assault was given their martial music began to play, and their attack was rapid, rushing suddenly upon the Peruvians, and with their hell-invented enginery of thunder, fire and smoke,[109] they soon put them to flight and destruction. The Inca, though his nobles crouded around him with officious zeal, and fell in numbers at his feet, while they vied with one another in sacrificing their own lives that they might cover the sacred person of their Sovereign, was soon penetrated to by the assassinators, dragged from his throne, and carried to the Spanish quarters. The fate of the Monarch increased the precipitate flight of his followers; the plains being covered with upwards of thirty thousand men, were pursued by the ferocious Spaniards towards every quarter, who, with deliberate and unrelenting barbarity, continued to slaughter the wretched fugitives till the close of the day, that never had once offered at any resistance. Pizarra had contrived this daring and perfidious plan on purpose to get hold of the Inca, notwithstanding his assumed character of an ambassador from a powerful monarch to court an alliance with that prince, and in violation of all the repeated offers of his own friendship. The noble Inca thus found himself betrayed and shut up in the Spanish quarters, though scarce aware at first of the vast carnage and destruction of his people; but soon conceiving the destructive consequences that attended his confinement, and by beholding the vast treasures of spoil that the Spaniards had so eagerly gathered up, he learned something of their covetous disposition: and he offered as a ransom what astonished the Spaniards, even after all they now knew concerning the opulence of his kingdom: the apartment in which he was confined was twenty-two feet in length and sixteen in breadth, he undertook to fill it with vessels of gold as high as he could reach. This tempting proposal was eagerly agreed to by Pizarra, and a line was drawn upon the walls of the chamber to mark the stipulated height to which the treasure was to rise. The gold was accordingly collected from various parts with the greatest expedition by the Inca's obedient and loving subjects, who thought nothing too much for his ransom and life; but, after all, poor Atahualpa was cruelly murdered, and his body burnt by a military inquisition, and his extensive and rich dominions devoted to destruction and ruin by these merciless depredators.

The history of those dreadfully perfidious methods of forming settlements, and acquiring riches and territory, would make humanity tremble, and even recoil, at the enjoyment of such acquisitions and become reverted into rage and indignation at such horrible injustice and barbarous cruelty, "It is said by the Peruvians, that their Incas, or Monarchs, had uniformly extended their power with attention to the good of their subjects, that they might diffuse the blessings of civilization, and the knowledge of the arts which they possessed, among the people that embraced their protection; and during a succession of twelve monarchs, not one had deviated from this beneficent character."[110] Their sensibility of such nobleness of character would give them the most poignant dislike to their new terrible invaders that had desolated and laid waste their country. The character of their monarchs would seem to vie with as great virtues as any King in Europe can boast of. Had the Peruvians been visited by men of honesty, knowledge, and enlightened understanding, to teach them, by patient instruction and the blessing of God, they might have been induced to embrace the doctrines and faith of Christianity, and to abandon their errors of superstition and idolatry. Had Christians, that deserve the name thereof, been sent among them, the many useful things that they would have taught them, together with their own

pious example, would have captivated their hearts; and the knowledge of the truth would have made it a very desirous thing for the
Americans to have those who taught them to settle among them.
Had that been the case the Americans, in various parts, would
have been as eager to have the Europeans come there as they
would have been to go, so that the Europeans might have found
settlements enough, in a friendly alliance with the inhabitants,
without destroying and enslaving them. And had that been the
case it might be supposed, that Europe and America, long before
now, would both, with a growing luxuriancy, have been flourishing with affluence and peace, and their long extended and fruitful
branches, loaden with benefits to each other, reaching over the
ocean, might have been more extensive, and greater advantages
have been expected, for the good of both than what has yet appeared. But, alas! at that time there [were] no Christians to send,
(and very few now), these were obliged to hide themselves in the
obscure places of the earth; that was, according to Sir Isaac Newton,[111] to mix in obscurity among the meanest of the people, having no power and authority; and it seems at that time there was no
power among Christians on earth to have sent such as would have
been useful to the Americans; and if there had they would have
sent after the depredators, and rescued the innocent.

But as I said before, it is surely to the great shame and scandal
of Christianity among all the Heathen nations, that those robbers,
plunderers, destroyers and enslavers of men should call themselves Christians, and exercise their power under any Christian
government and authority. I would have my African countrymen
to know and understand, that the destroyers and enslavers of men
can be no Christians; for Christianity is the system of benignity
and love, and all its votaries are devoted to honesty, justice, humanity, meekness, peace and good-will to all men. But whatever
title or claim some may assume to call themselves by it, without
possessing any of its virtues, can only manifest them to be the
more abominable liars, and the greatest enemies unto it, and as belonging to the synagogue of Satan, and not the adherers to Christ.
For the enslavers and oppressors of men, among those that have
obtained the name of Christians, they are still acting as its greatest
enemies, and contrary to all its genuine principles; they should

therefore be called by its opposite, the Antichrist. Such are fitly belonging to that most dissolute sorceress of all religion in the world: "With whom the kings of the earth have lived deliciously; and the inhabitants of the earth have been made drunk with the wine of her abominations; and the merchants of the earth are waxed rich through the abundance of her delicacies, by their traffic in various things, and in slaves and souls of men!"[112] It was not enough for the malignant destroyer of the world to set up his hydra-headed kingdom of evil and wickedness among the kingdom of men; but also to cause an image to be made unto him, by something imported in the only true religion that ever was given to men; and that image of iniquity is described as arising up out of the earth, having two horns like a lamb, which, by its votaries and adherents, has been long established and supported. One of its umbrageous horns of apostacy and delusion is founded, in a more particular respect, on a grand perversion of the Old Testament dispensations, which has extended itself over all the Mahometan nations in the East; and the other horn of apostacy, bearing an allusion and professional respect to that of the new, has extended itself over all the Christian nations in the West.[113] That grand umbrageous shadow and image of evil and wickedness, has spread its malignant influence over all the nations of the earth, and has, by its power of delusion, given countenance and support to all the power of evil and wickedness done among men; and all the adherents and supporters of that delusion, and all the carriers on of wickedness, are fitly called Antichrist. But all the nations have drunk of the wine of that iniquity, and become drunk with the wine of the wrath of her fornication, whose name, by every mark and feature, is the Antichrist; and every dealer in slaves, and those that hold them in slavery, whatever else they may call themselves, or whatever else they may profess. And likewise, those nations whose governments support that evil and wicked traffic of slavery, however remote the situation where it is carried on may be, are, in that respect, as much Antichristian as any thing in the world can be. No man will ever rob another unless he be a villain: nor will any nation or people ever enslave and oppress others, unless themselves be base and wicked men, and who act and do contrary and against every duty in Christianity.

The learned and ingenious author of Britannia Libera, as chiefly alluding to Great-Britain alone, gives some account of that great evil and wickedness carried on by the Christian nations, respecting the direful effects of the great devastations committed in foreign parts, whereby it would appear that the ancient and native inhabitants have been drenched in blood and oppression by their merciless visitors (which have formed colonies and settlements among them) the avaricious depredators, plunderers and destroyers of nations. As some estimate of it, "to destroy eleven million, and distress many more in America, to starve and oppress twelve million in Asia, and the great number destroyed, is not the way to promote the dignity, strength and safety of empire, but to draw down the Divine vengeance on the offenders, for depriving so many of their fellow-creatures of life, or the common blessings of the earth: whereas by observing the humane principles of preservation with felicitation, the proper principles of all rulers, their empire might have received all reasonable benefit, with the encrease of future glory."[114] But should it be asked, what advantages Great-Britain has gained by all its extensive territories abroad, the devastations committed, and the abominable slavery and oppression carried on in its colonies? It may be answered according to the old proverb,

> It seldom is the grand-child's lot,
> To share of wealth unjustly got.

This seems to be verified too much in their present situation: for however wide they have extended their territories abroad, they have sunk into a world of debt at home, which must ever remain an impending burden upon the inhabitants. And it is not likely, by any plan as yet adopted, to be ever paid, or any part of it, without a long continued heavy annual load of taxes.[115] Perhaps, great as it is some other plan, more equitable for the good of the whole community, if it was wanted to be done, and without any additional taxes, might be so made use of to pay it all off in twenty or thirty years time, and in such manner as whatever emergencies might happen, as never to need to borrow any money at interest. The national debt casts a sluggish deadness over the whole realm, greatly stops ingenuity and improvements, promotes idleness and wickedness, clogs all the wheels of commerce, and drains the money out of the nation. If a foreigner buys stock, in the course of years that the interest amounts to the principal, he gets it all back; and in an equitable time the same sum ever after, and in course must take that money to foreign parts. And those who hold stock at home, are a kind of idle drones, as a burden to the rest of the community: whereas if there were no funds, those who have money would be obliged to occupy it in some improvements themselves, or lend it to other manufacturers or merchants, and by that means useful employments, ingenuity and commerce would flourish. But all stock-jobbing, lotteries, and useless business,[116] has a tendency to slavery and oppression; for as the greater any idle part of the community is, there must be the greater labour and hardships resting upon the industrious part who support the rest; as all men are allotted in some degree to eat their bread with the sweat of their brow; *but it is evil with any people when the rich grind the face of the poor.*[117] Lotteries must be nearly as bad a way of getting money for the good of a nation, as it is for an individual when he is poor, and obliged to pawn his goods to increase his poverty, already poor. On the reverse, if a nation was to keep a bank to lend money to merchants and others, that nation might flourish, and its support to those in need might be attended with advantage to the whole; but that nation which is obliged to borrow money from others, must be in a poor and wretched situation, and the inhabitants, who have to bear the load of its taxes, must be greatly burdened, and perhaps many of those employed in its service (as soldiers and others) poorly paid. It was otherwise with *the people of Israel of old;* it was the promise and blessing of God to them, *That they should lend unto many nations, but should not borrow.*[118]

But when a nation or people do wickedly, and commit cruelties and devastations upon others, and enslave them, it cannot be expected that they should be attended with the blessings of God, neither to eschew evil. They often become infatuated to do evil unawares; and those employed under their service sometimes lead them into debt, error and wickedness, in order to enrich themselves by their plunder, in committing the most barbarous cruel-

ties, under pretences of war, wherein they were the first aggressors, and which is generally the case in all unnatural and destructive disputes of war. In this business money is wanted, the national
debt becomes increased, and new loans and other sums must be
added to the funds. The plunderers abroad send home their cash as
fast as they can, and by one means and another the sums wanted
to borrow, are soon made up. At last when the wars subside, or
other business calls them home, laden with the spoils of the East
or elsewhere, they have then the grand part of their business to
negotiate, in buying up bank stock, and lodging their plunder and
ill-got wealth in the British or other funds. Thus the nation is
loaded with more debt, and with an annual addition of more interest to pay, to the further advantage of those who often occasioned
it by their villainy; who, if they had their deserts, like the Popish
inquisitors, are almost the only people in the world who deserve
to be hung on the rack.

But so it happens in general, that men of activity and affluence,
by whatever way they are possessed of riches, or have acquired a
greatness of such property, they are always preferred to take the
lead in matters of government, so that the greatest depredators,
warriors, contracting companies of merchants, and rich slave-
holders, always endeavour to push themselves on to get power
and interest in their favour; that whatever crimes any of them
commit they are seldom brought to a just punishment. Unless that
something of this kind had been the case, 'tis impossible to conceive how such an enormous evil as the slave-trade could have
been established and carried on under any Christian government:
and from hence that motly system of government, which hath so
sprung up and established itself, may be accounted for, and as being evident and universal depravity of one of the finest consti-
tutions in the world; and it may be feared if these unconstitutional
laws, reaching from Great-Britain to her colonies, be long continued in and supported, to the carrying on that horrible and wicked
traffic of slavery, must at last mark out the whole of the British
constitution with ruin and destruction; and that the most generous
and tenacious people in the world for liberty, may also at last be
reduced to slaves. And an Ethiopian may venture to assert, that so
long as slavery is continued in any part of the British dominions,

that more than one-half of the legislature are the virtual supporters
and encouragers of a traffic which ought to be abolished, as it cannot be carried on but by some of the most abandoned and profligate men upon earth.

However, the partizans of such a class of men are generally too
many and numerous, whose viciated principles from time to time
have led the whole nation into debt, error and disgrace; and by
their magnetic influence there is a general support given to despo-
tism, oppression and cruelty. For many have acquired great riches
by some insidious traffic or illegal gain; and as these become often
leading men in governments, vast multitudes by sea and land pursue the same course, and support the same measures; like adventurers in the lottery, each grasping for the highest prize; or as
much enamoured with any infamous way of getting riches, as the
Spaniards were with the Peruvian vessels of gold. And when ambi-
tious and wicked men are bent upon avarice and covetousness, it
leads them on to commit terrible cruelties, and their hearts become hardened in wickedness; so that even their enormous crimes
sink in their own estimation, and soften into trivial matters. The
housebreakers and highwaymen, petty depredators, think nothing
of any mischief or cruelty that they can do, so as they can gain
their end and come off safe; but their villainy and crimes appear to
other men as they ought to do, and if they can be detected, and
taken hold of, they will meet with such punishment as they justly
deserve for their crimes. But it is otherwise with the Colonians,[119]
the great depredators, pirates, kidnappers, robbers, oppressors and
enslavers of men. The laws as reaching from Great-Britain to the
West-Indies, do not detect them, but protect the opulent slave-
holders; though their opulence and protection by any law, or any
government whatsoever, cannot make them less criminal than violators of the common rights and liberties of men. They do not take
away a man's property, like other robbers; but they take a man
himself, and subject him to their service and bondage, which is a
greater robbery, and a greater crime, than taking away any property from men whatsoever. And, therefore, with respect to them,
there is very much wanted for regulating the natural rights of
mankind, and very much wrong in the present forms of government, as well as much abuse of that which is right.

The Spaniards began their settlements in the West Indies and
America, by depredations of rapine, injustice, treachery and murder; and they have continued in the barbarous practice of devastation, cruelty, and oppression ever since: and their principles and
maxims in planting colonies have been adopted, in some measure,
by every other nation in Europe. This guiltful method of colonization must undoubtedly and imperceptibly have hardened
men's hearts, and led them on from one degree of barbarity and
cruelty to another: for when they had destroyed, wasted and desolated the native inhabitants, and when many of their own people,
enriched with plunder, had retired, or returned home to enjoy
their ill-gotten wealth, other resources for men to labour and cul-
tivate the ground, and such other laborious employments were
wanted. Vast territories and large possessions, without getting inhabitants to labour for them, were of no use. A general part of
what remained of the wretched fugitives, who had the best native
right to those possessions, were obliged to make their escape to
places more remote, and such as could not, were obliged to submit
to the hard labour and bondage of their invaders; but as they had
not been used to such harsh treatment and laborious employment
as they were then subjected to, they were soon wasted away and
became few. Their proud invaders found the advantage of having
their labour done for nothing, and it became their general practice
to pick up the unfortunate strangers that fell in their way, when
they thought they could make use of them in their service. That
base traffic of kidnapping and stealing men was begun by the Portuguese on the coast of Africa,[120] and as they found the benefit of
it for their own wicked purposes, they soon went on to commit
greater depredations. The Spaniards followed their infamous example,[121] and the African slave-trade was thought most advanta-
geous for them, to enable themselves to live in ease and affluence
by the cruel subjection and slavery of others. The French and
English, and some other nations in Europe, as they founded settlements and colonies in the West Indies, or in America, went on in
the same manner, and joined hand in hand with the Portuguese
and Spaniards, to rob and pillage Africa, as well as to waste and
desolate the inhabitants of the western continent. But the European depredators and pirates have not only robbed and pillaged

the people of Africa themselves; but, by their instigation, they have infested the inhabitants with some of the vilest combinations of fraudulent and treacherous villains, even among their own people; and have set up their forts and factories as a reservoir of public and abandoned thieves, and as a den of desperadoes, where they may ensnare, entrap and catch men. So that Africa has been robbed of its inhabitants; its free-born sons and daughters have been stole, and kidnapped, and violently taken away, and carried into captivity and cruel bondage. And it may be said, in respect to that diabolical traffic which is still carried on by the European depredators, that Africa has suffered as much and more than any other quarter of the globe. O merciful God! when will the wickedness of man have an end?

The Royal African Company (as it is called, ought rather to be reversed as unworthy of the name) was incorporated 14th Charles II, and impowered to trade from Salle in South Barbary to the Cape of Good Hope,[122] and to erect forts and factories on the western coast of Africa for that purpose. But this trade was laid open by an act of parliament, Anno 1697,[123] and every private merchant permitted to trade thither, upon paying the sum of ten pounds towards maintaining the forts and garrisons. This Company, for securing their commerce, erected several factories on the coast; the most remarkable are these, viz.[124] on the North part of Guinea, James Fort, upon an island in the River Gambia, Sierra Leona, and Sherbro; and on the South part of Guinea, viz. on the Gold Coast, Dick's Cove, Succunda, Commenda, Cape Coast Castle, Fort Royal, Queen Anne's Point, Charles Fort, Annamabo, Winebah, Shidoe, Acra, &c.[125] In all these places it is their grand business to traffic in the human species; and dreadful and shocking as it is to think, it has even been established by royal authority, and is still supported and carried on under a Christian government; and this must evidently appear thereby, that the learned, the civilized, and even the enlightened nations are become as truly barbarous and brutish as the unlearned.

To give any just conception of the barbarous traffic carried on at those factories, it would be out of my power to describe the miserable situation of the poor exiled Africans, which by the craft of wicked men daily become their prey, though I have seen enough of their misery as well as read; no description can give an adequate idea of the horror of their feelings, and the dreadful calamities they undergo. The treacherous, perfidious and cruel methods made use of in procuring them, are horrible and shocking. The bringing them to the ships and factories, and subjecting them to brutal examinations stripped naked and markings, is barbarous and base. The stowing them in the holds of the ships like goods of burden, with closeness and stench, is deplorable; and, what makes addition to this deplorable situation, they are often treated in the most barbarous and inhuman manner by the unfeeling monsters of Captains. And when they arrive at the destined port in the colonies, they are again stripped naked for the brutal examination of their purchasers to view them, which, to many, must add shame and grief to their other woe, as may be evidently seen with sorrow, melancholy and despair marked upon their countenances. Here again another scene of grief and lamentation arises;—friends and near relations must be parted never to meet again, nor knowing to whence they go. Here daughters are clinging to their mothers, and mothers to their daughters, bedewing each others naked breasts with tears;[126] here fathers, mothers, and children, locked in each others arms, are begging never to be separated; here the husband will be pleading for his wife, and the wife praying for her children, and entreating, enough to melt the most obdurate heart, not to be torn from them, and taken away from her husband; and some will be still weeping for their native shore, and their dear relations and friends, and other endearing connections which they have left behind, and have been barbarously tore away from, and all are bemoaning themselves with grief and lamentation at the prospect of their wretched fate. And when sold and delivered up to their inhuman purchasers, a more heart-piercing scene cannot well take place. The last embrace of the beloved husband and wife may be seen, taking their dear offspring in their arms, and with the most parental fondness, bathing their cheeks with a final parting endearment. But on this occasion they are not permitted to continue long, they are soon torn away by their unfeeling masters, entirely destitute of a hope of ever seeing each other again; and no consolation is afforded to them in this sorrowful and truly pitiable situation. Should any of them still linger, and cling together a little longer, and not part as readily as their owners would have them, the flogger is called on, and they are soon drove away with the bloody commiseration of the cutting fangs of the whip lashing their naked bodies. This last exercise of the bloody whip, with many other cruel punishments, generally becomes an appendage of their miserable fate, until their wretched lives be wore out with hunger, nakedness, hard labour, dejection and despair. Alas! alas! poor unhappy mortal! to experience such treatment from men that take upon themselves the sacred name of Christians!

In such a vast extended, hideous and predominant slavery, as the Europeans carry on in their Colonies, some indeed may fall into better hands, and meet with some commiseration and better treatment than others, and a few may become free, and get themselves liberated from that cruel and galling yoke of bondage; but what are these to the whole, even hundreds of thousands, held and perpetrated in all the prevalent and intolerable calamities of that state of bondage and exile. The emancipation of a few, while ever that evil and predominant business of slavery is continued, cannot make that horrible traffic one bit the less criminal.[127] For, according to the methods of procuring slaves in Africa, there must be great robberies and murders committed before any emancipation can take place, and before any lenitive favours can be shewn to any of them, even by the generous and humane. This must evidence that the whole of that base traffic is an enormous evil and wicked thing, which cries aloud for redress, and that an immediate end and stop should be put to it.

The worthy and judicious author of the Historical account of Guinea,[128] and others, have given some very striking estimates of the exceeding evil occasioned by that wicked diabolical traffic of the African slave-trade; wherein it seems, of late years, the English have taken the lead, or the greatest part of it, in carrying it on.[129] They have computed that the ships from Liverpool, Bristol and London have exported from the coast of Africa upwards of one hundred thousand slaves annually; and that among other evils attending this barbarous inhuman traffic, it is also computed that the numbers which are killed by the treacherous and barbarous methods of procuring them, together with those that perish in the voyage, and die in the seasoning,[130] amount to at least an hundred thousand, which perish in every yearly attempt to supply the colonies, before any of the wretched survivors, reduced to about sixty thousand, annually required as an additional stock can be made useful. But as the great severities and oppressions loaded upon the wretched survivors are such that they are continually wearing out, and a new annual supply wanted; that the vast carnage, and the great multitude of human souls that are actually deprived of life by carrying on that iniquitous business, may be supposed to be even more than one hundred thousand that perish annually; or supposing that to be greatly less than it is, still it is so great that the very idea is shocking to conceive, at the thought of it sensibility would blush, and feeling nature absolutely turn pale.

"Gracious God! how wicked, how beyond all example impious, must be that servitude which cannot be carried on without the continual murder of so many innocent persons. What punishment is not to be expected from such monstrous and unparalleled barbarity? For if the blood of one man unjustly shed cries with so loud a voice for the Divine vengeance, how shall the cries and groans of an hundred thousand men annually murdered ascend the celestial mansions, and bring down that punishment such enormities deserve?"[131] As this enormous iniquity is not conjecture, but an obvious fact, occasioned by that dreadful and wicked business of slavery, were the inhabitants of Great-Britain to hear tell of any other nation that murdered one hundred thousand innocent people annually, they would think them an exceeding inhuman, barbarous, and wicked people indeed, and that they would be surely punished by some signal judgment of Almighty God. But surely law and liberty, justice and equity, which are the proper foundations of the British government, and humanity the most amiable characteristic of the people, must be entirely fled from their land, if they can think a less punishment due to themselves, for supporting and carrying on such enormous wickedness, if they do not speedily relinquish and give it up. The very nature of that wickedness of enslaving of men is such, that were the traffic, which European nations carry on in it, a thousand times less than it is, it would be what no righteous nation would admit of for the sake of any gain whatsoever. Wherefore as it is, what ought to be done? If there is any righteousness, any wisdom, any justice, or any humanity to be found, ought not the whole of it, and all the branches of such exceeding evil and wicked traffic, and all the iniquity of it to be relinquished, and root and branches to be speedily given up and put an end to?

"For while such monstrous iniquity, such deliberate barbarity and cruelty is carried on, whether it be considered as the crime of individuals,[132] or as patronized and encouraged by the laws of the land, it holds forth an equal degree of enormity. And a crime founded in such a dreadful pre-eminence in wickedness, both of individuals and the nation, must some time draw down upon them the heaviest judgments of Almighty God."[133]—"On this occasion there seems already to be an interference of Divine Providence, though the obdurate and impenitent part of mankind may not regard it.[134] The violent and supernatural agitations of all the elements, which for a series of years have prevailed in those European settlements where the unfortunate Africans are retained in a state of slavery, and which have brought unspeakable calamities to the inhabitants, and public losses to the states to which they severally belong, are so many awful visitations of God for this inhuman violation of his laws. And it is not perhaps unworthy of remark, but as the subjects of Great-Britain have two-thirds of this impious commerce in their own hands, so they have suffered in the same proportion, or more severely than the rest. How far these misfortunes may appear to be acts of Providence, and to create an alarm to those who have been accustomed to refer every effect to its apparent cause; who have been habituated to stop there, and to overlook the finger of God, because it is slightly covered under the veil of secondary laws, we will not pretend to determine; but this we will assert with confidence, that the Europeans have richly deserved them all: the fear of sympathy that can hardly be restrained on other melancholy occasions, seems to forget to flow at the relation of these; and that we can never, with any shadow of justice, wish prosperity to the undertakers of those whose success must be at the expence of the happiness of millions of their fellow-creatures."[135]

For though this world is not the place of final retribution, yet there is an evidence maintained in the course of Divine Provi-

dence, that verily there is a God that judgeth in the earth. That nations may continue long, with a considerable degree of worldly
prosperity, and without seeming to be distinguished by remarkable calamities, when their wickedness is become very great and
prevalent; yet it is no way inconsistent to assert, (and what sacred
history warrant[s] us to conclude) that their judgment slumbereth
not. Had one been among the Canaanites a few years before the
Israelites entered their country, or in Babylon a little before Cyrus
encamped against it,[136] he would have beheld a people in a state of
great worldly prosperity, and in much security, notwithstanding
that the judgments of God were ready to seize upon them. Great
and destructive wars are kindled up from time to time, whereby
multitudes of mankind are swept away from the face of the
earth, and the wealth of nations are exhausted. Famine, pestilence
and earthquakes have often spread terror, desolation and misery
among the inhabitants of the world. Nor are there wanting instances of remarkable national distresses as a judgment for their
wickedness, by a variety of other causes. Though men cannot easily be prevailed with to regard these as the operation of the hand
of God, the scriptures, which contain the rules and history of Divine Providence, represent these as inflicted for the sins of nations,
and not merely as casual things, for which no account can be
given. And therefore some of these causes which may seem natural, and which have begun to make their appearance, and the annual destructions thereof, which are constantly heard of in some
part or other, may be considered as tokens of God's judgments
against the British empire, and a variety of them might be named;
such as loss of territory and destructive wars, earthquakes and
dreadful thunders, storms and hurricanes, blastings and destructive insects, inclement and unfruitful seasons, national debt and
oppressions, poverty and distresses of individuals, &c. *For his own
iniquity shall take the wicked himself;* and who can tell what
dreadful calamities may yet befal to a people responsible for so
great a share of iniquity as in that part which they carry on of the
African slave-trade alone. "And it is not known how soon a just
national retribution of vengeance may burst forth against it; how
soon the Almighty may think fit to recompence the British nation,
according to the work, of their hands, for the horrible oppression
of the poor Africans."[137]

"For national wickedness from the beginning of the world has generally been visited with national punishments; and surely no national wickedness can be more heinous in the sight of God than a public toleration of slavery, and sooner or later these kingdom[s] will be visited with some signal mark of his displeasure, for the notorious oppression of the poor Africans, that are harassed and continually wearing out with a most shameful involuntary servitude in the British colonies, and by a public toleration under the sanction of laws, to which the monarchs of England from time to time, by advice of their privy-counsellors, have given the royal assent, and thereby rendered themselves parties in the oppression, and it may be feared partakers in their guilt."[138]—"And every man has ample reason to fear that God will make of this nation, in proportion to the magnitude of its guilt in the slave-dealing, a tremendous example of retribution to deter other nations from offending his eternal justice, if a sincere and speedy repentance does not avert it."[139]—"For such notorious crimes the Almighty, even the Lord, hath sworn, *surely I will never forget any of these works.*" See Amos viii. But the judgments of God are often suspended and mitigated for the sake of the righteous; and nations are preserved from destruction in favour to them who remain faithful in times of general defection. Isaiah i. 9. *"Except the Lord of Hosts had left us a very small remnant, we should have been as Sodom, and we should have been like unto Gomorah."*

But while ever such a horrible business as the slavery and oppression of the Africans is carried on, there is not one man in all Great-Britain and her colonies, that knoweth any thing of it, can be innocent and safe, unless he speedily riseth up with abhorrence of it in his own judgment, and, to avert evil, declare himself against it, and all such notorious wickedness. But should the contrary be adhered to, as it has been in the most shameful manner, by men of eminence and power; according to their eminence in station, the nobles and senators, and every man in office and authority, must incur a double load of guilt, and not only that burden of guilt in the oppression of the African strangers, but also in that of an impending danger and ruin to their country; and such a double load of iniquity must rest upon those guilty heads who withhold their testimony against the crying sin of tolerating slavery.[140] The inhabitants in general who can approve of such inhuman barbari-

ties, must themselves be a species of unjust barbarians and inhuman men. But the clergy of all denominations, whom we would
consider as the devout messengers of righteousness, peace, and
good-will to all men, if we find any of them ranked with infidels
and barbarians, we must consider them as particularly responsible,
and, in some measure, guilty of the crimes of other wicked men in
the highest degree. For it is their duty to warn every man, and to
teach every man to know their errors; and if they do not, the
crimes of those under their particular charge must rest upon themselves, and upon some of them, in such a case as this, that of the
whole nation in general; and those (whatever their respective situation may be) who forbid others to assist them, must not be very
sensible of their own duty, and the great extensiveness and importance of their own charge. And as it is their great duty to teach
men righteousness and piety; this ought to be considered as sufficiently obvious unto them, and to all men, that nothing can be
more contrary unto it, than the evil and very nature of enslaving
men, and making merchandize of them like the brute creation.
"For it is evident that no custom established among men was ever
more impious; since it is contrary to reason, justice, nature, the
principles of law and government, and the whole doctrine, in
short, of natural religion, and the revealed voice of God. And,
therefore, that it is both evident and expedient, that there is an
absolute necessity to abolish the slave trade, and the West-India
slavery; and that to be in power, and to neglect even a day in en-
deavouring to put a stop to such monstrous iniquity and abandoned wickedness (as the tenure of every man's life, as well as the
time of his being in office and power is very uncertain) must nec-
essarily endanger a man's own eternal welfare, be he ever so great
in temporal dignity."[141]

The higher that any man is exalted in power and dignity, his
danger is the more eminent, though he may not live to see the evil
that may eventually be contributed to his country, because of his
disobedience to the law and commandments of God. All men in
authority, and kings in general, who are exalted to the most conspicuous offices of superiority, while they take upon themselves to
be the administrators of righteousness and justice to others, they
become equally responsible for admitting or suffering others un-

der their authority to do wrong. Wherefore the highest offices of authority among men, are not so desirable as some may be apt to conceive; it was so considered by the virtuous queen Anne,[142] when she was called to the royal dignity, as she declared to the council of the nation, that it was a heavy weight and burden brought upon her. For kings are the ministers of God, to do justice, and not to bear the sword in vain, but to revenge wrath upon them that do evil. But if they do not in such a case as this, the cruel oppressions of thousands, and the blood of the murdered Africans who are slain by the sword of cruel avarice, must rest upon their own guilty heads in as eventual and plain a sense as it was David that murdered Uriah;[143] and therefore they ought to let no companies of insidious merchants, or any guileful insinuations of wicked men, prevail upon them to establish laws of iniquity, and to carry on a trade of oppression and injustice; but they ought to consider such as the worst of foes and rebels, and greater enemies than any that can rise up against their temporal dignity. From all such enemies, good Lord, deliver them! for it is even better to lose a temporal kingdom, than only to endanger the happiness and enjoyment of an eternal one.

Nothing else can be conceived, but that the power of infernal wickedness has so reigned and pervaded over the enlightened nations, as to infatuate and lead on the great men, and the kings of Europe, to promote and establish such a horrible traffic of wickedness as the African slave trade and the West-India slavery, and thereby to bring themselves under the guilty responsibility of such awful iniquity. The kings and governors of the nations in general have power to prevent their subjects and people from enslaving and oppressing others, if they will; but if they do not endeavour to do it, even if they could not effect that good purpose, they must then be responsible for their crimes; how much more, if they make no endeavours towards it, even when they can, and where no opposition, however plausible their pretences might be, would dare to oppose them. Wherefore, if kings or nations, or any men that dealeth unjustly with their fellow-creatures, to ensnare them, to enslave them, and to oppress them, or suffer others to do so, when they have it in their power to prevent it, and yet they do not, can it ever be thought that God will be well pleased with them? For can those which have no mercy on their fellow-creatures, expect to find mercy from the gracious Father of Men? Or will it not rather be said unto them, as it is declared, *that he who leadeth into captivity, shall be carried captive, and be bound in the cords of his own iniquity: Though hand join in hand the wicked shall not go unpunished; for sin and wickedness is the destruction of any people.*[144] And should these nations, in the most obnoxious and tenacious manner, still adhere to it as they have done, and continue to carry on in their colonies such works and purposes of iniquity, in oppression and injustice against the Africans, nothing else can be expected for them at last, but to meet with the fierce wrath of Almighty God, for such a combination of wickedness, according to all the examples of his just retribution, who cannot suffer such deliberate, such monstrous iniquity to go long unpunished.

There is good reason to suppose, that it was far from the intention of Ferdinand, king of Spain, to use his new subjects in America in the brutal and barbarous manner that his people did; and happy for the credit of that nation, and the honor of mankind, even among the profligate adventurers which were sent to conquer and desolate the new world, there were some persons that retained some tincture of virtue and generosity, and some men of the greatest reputation of both gentlemen and clergy, which did not only remonstrate, but protest against their measures then carried on.[145] And since that iniquitous traffic of slavery has commenced and been carried on, many gentlemen of the most distinguished reputation, of different nations, and particularly in England, have protested and remonstrated against it. But the guileful insinuations of avaricious wicked men, which prevailed formerly, have still been continued; and to answer the purposes of their own covetousness, the different nations have been fomented with jealousy to one another, least [sic] another should have the advantage in any traffic; and while naturally emulous to promote their own ambition, they have imbrewed their hands in that infamous commerce of iniquity; and by the insidious instigation of those whose private emolument depends on it, the various profligate adventurers, from time to time, have acquired the sanction of laws to support them, and have obtained the patronage of kings in their favor to encourage them, whereby that commerce of the most notorious injustice, and open violation of the laws of God, hath been carried on exceedingly to the shame of all the Christian nations, and greatly to the disgrace of all the monarchs of Europe. The fact speaks itself: *And destruction shall be to the workers of iniquity.*[146] The bold and offensive enslavers of men, who subject their fellow-creatures to the rank of a brute, and the immolate value of a beast, are themselves the most abandoned slaves of infernal wickedness, the most obnoxious ruffians among men, the enemies of their country, and the disgrace of kings. Their iniquity is wrote in the light as with a sun-beam, and engraven on the hardest rock as with the point of a diamond, that cannot be easily wiped away: *But the wicked shall fall by their own wickedness.*[147] And, nevertheless, by the insidious instigation of those who have forsaken the amiable virtues of men, and have acquired the cruel ferocity of tygers and wild beasts, they have not only polluted themselves with their iniquity, but their base treachery has brought shame and guilt upon some of the most exalted and most amiable characters in the world. And, therefore, that no evil may happen unto those who have been so shamefully beguiled and betrayed by the vile instigations of wicked, profligate, inhuman men, and that no shame and guilt may rest upon him, who standeth in the greatest eminence of responsibility, I would ever desire to pray; let all the prayers of the wise and pious be heard for the king, and for his wise counsellors, and the great men that stand before him; for kings and great men stand in the most perilous situation of having the crimes of others imputed to them; wherefore kings have need of all your prayers, that the counsel of the wicked may not prevail against them, for these are the worst foes, and most terrible enemies, both to yourselves and to your sovereign. *Righteousness exalteth a nation, but sin is a reproach to any people.*[148]

In this advanced æra, when the kings of Europe are become more conspicuous for their manly virtues, than any before them have been, it is to be hoped that they will not any longer suffer themselves to be imposed upon, and be beguiled, and brought into guilt and shame, by any instigations of the cunning craftiness and evil policy of the avaricious, and the vile profligate enslavers of men. And as their wisdom and understanding is great, and exalted as their high dignity, it is also to be hoped that they will exert themselves, in the cause of righteousness and justice, and be like the wisest and the greatest monarchs of old, to hearken to the counsel of the wise men that know the times, and to the righteous laws of God, and to deliver the oppressed, and to put an end to the iniquitous commerce and slavery of men. And as we hear tell of the kings of Europe having almost abolished, the infernal invention of the bloody tribunal of the inquisition, and the Emperor and others making some grand reformations for the happiness and good of their subjects;[149] it is to be hoped also that these exalted and liberal principles will lead them on to greater improvements in civilization and felicitation, and next to abolish that other diabolical invention of the bloody and cruel African slave-trade, and the West-Indian slavery.

But whereas the people of Great-Britain having now acquired a greater share in that iniquitous commerce than all the rest together, they are the first that ought to set an example, lest they have to repent for their wickedness when it becomes too late; lest some impending calamity should speedily burst forth against them, and lest a just retribution for their enormous crimes, and a continuance in committing similar deeds of barbarity and injustice should involve them in ruin. For we may be assured that God will certainly avenge himself of such heinous transgressors of his law, and of all those planters and merchants, and of all others, who are the authors of the Africans graves, severities, and cruel punishments, and no plea of any absolute necessity can possibly excuse them. And as the inhabitants of Great-Britain, and the inhabitants of the colonies, seem almost equally guilty of the oppression, there is great reason for both to dread the severe vengeance of Almighty God upon them, and upon all such notorious workers of wickedness; for it is evident that the legislature of Great-Britain patronises and encourages them, and shares in the infamous profits of the slavery of the Africans. It is therefore necessary that the inhabitants of the British nation should seriously consider these things for their own good and safety, as well as for our benefit and deliverance, and that they may be sensible of their own error and danger, lest they provoke the vengeance of the Almighty against them. For what wickedness was there ever risen up so monstrous, and more likely to bring a heavy rod of destruction upon a nation, than the deeds committed by the West Indian slavery, and the

African slave trade. And even in that part of it carried on by the Liverpool and Bristol merchants, the many shocking and inhuman instances of their barbarity and cruelty are such, that every one that heareth thereof has reason to tremble, and cry out, *Should not the land tremble for this, and every one mourn that dwelleth therein?*[150]

The vast carnage and murders committed by the British instigators of slavery, is attended with a very shocking, peculiar, and almost unheard of conception, according to the notion of the perpetrators of it; they either consider them as their own property, that they may do with as they please, in life or death; or that the taking away the life of a black man is of no more account than taking away the life of a beast. A very melancholy instance of this happened about the year 1780,[151] as recorded in the courts of law; a master of a vessel bound to the Western Colonies, selected 132 of the most sickly of the black slaves, and ordered them to be thrown overboard into the sea, in order to recover their value from the insurers, as he had perceived that he was too late to get a good market for them in the West-Indies. On the trial, by the counsel for the owners of the vessel against the underwriters, their argument was, that the slaves were to be considered the same as horses; and their plea for throwing them into the sea was nothing better than that it might be more necessary to throw them overboard to lighten their vessel than goods of greater value, or something to that effect. These poor creatures, it seems, were tied two and two together[152] when they were thrown into the sea, lest some of them might swim a little for the last gasp of air, and, with the animation of their approaching exit, breath[e] their souls away to the gracious Father of spirits. Some of the last parcel, when they saw the fate of their companions, made their escape from tying by jumping overboard, and one was saved by means of a rope from some in the ship. The owners of the vessel, I suppose, (inhuman connivers of robbery, slavery, murder and fraud) were rather a little defeated in this, by bringing their villainy to light in a court of law; but the inhuman monster of a captain was kept out of the way of justice from getting hold of him. Though such perpetrators of murder and fraud should have been sought after from the British Dan in the East-Indies, to her Beershebah in the West.[153]

But our lives are accounted of no value, we are hunted after as

the prey in the desart, and doomed to destruction as the beasts
that perish. And for this, should we appear to the inhabitants of
Europe, would they dare to say that they have not wronged us,
and grievously injured us, and that the blood of millions do not
cry out against them? And if we appeal to the inhabitants of
Great-Britain, can they justify the deeds of their conduct towards
us? And is it not strange to think, that they who ought to be considered as the most learned and civilized people in the world, that
they should carry on a traffic of the most barbarous cruelty and
injustice, and that many, even among them, are become so dissolute, as to think slavery, robbery and murder no crimes? But we
will answer to this, that no man can, with impunity, steal, kidnap,
buy or sell another man, without being guilty of the most atrocious villainy. And we will aver, that every slave-holder that claims
any property in slaves, or holds them in an involuntary servitude,
are the most obnoxious and dissolute robbers among men; and
that they have no more right, nor any better title to any one of
them, than the most profligate and notorious robbers and thieves
in the world, has to the goods which they have robbed and stole
from the right owners and lawful possessor thereof. But should
the slave-holders say that they buy them; their title and claim is no
better then that of the most notorious conniver, who buys goods
from other robbers, knowing them to be stole, and accordingly
gives an inferior price for them. According to the laws of England,
when such connivers are discovered, and the property of others
unlawfully found in their possession; the right owners thereof can
oblige the connivers to restore back their property, and to punish
them for their trespass. But the slave-holders, universally, are
those connivers, they do not only rob men of some of their property, but they keep men from every property belonging to them,
and compel them to their involuntary service and drudgery; and
those whom they buy from other robbers, and keep in their possession, are greatly injured by them when compared to any species
of goods whatsoever; and accordingly they give but a very inferior
price for men, as all their vast estates in the West-Indies is not sufficient to buy one of them, if the rightful possessor was to sell
himself to them in the manner that they claim possession of him.
Therefore let the inhabitants of any civilized nation determine,

whether, if they were to be treated in the same manner that the Africans are, by various pirates, kidnappers, and slave-holders, and their wives, and their sons and daughters were to be robbed from them, or themselves violently taken away to a perpetual and intolerable slavery; or whether they would not think those robbers, who only took away their property, less injurious to them than the other. If they determine it so, as reason must tell every man, that himself is of more value than his property; then the executors of the laws of civilization ought to tremble at the inconsistency of passing judgment upon those whose crimes, in many cases, are less than what the whole legislature must be guilty of, when those of a far greater is encouraged and supported by it wherever slavery is tolerated by law, and, consequently, that slavery can no where be tolerated with any consistency to civilization and the laws of justice among men; but if it can maintain its ground, to have any place at all, it must be among a society of barbarians and thieves, and where the laws of their society is, for every one to catch what he can. Then, when theft and robbery become no crimes, the man-stealer and the conniving slave-holder might possibly get free.

But the several nations of Europe that have joined in that iniquitous traffic of buying, selling and enslaving men, must in course have left their own laws of civilization to adopt those of barbarians and robbers, and that they may say to one another, *When thou sawest a thief, then thou consentest with him, and hast been partaker with all the workers of iniquity*.[154] But whereas every man, as a rational creature, is responsible for his actions, and he becomes not only guilty in doing evil himself, but in letting others rob and oppress their fellow-creatures with impunity, or in not delivering the oppressed when he has it in his power to help them. And likewise that nation which may be supposed to maintain a very considerable degree of civilization[,] justice and equity within its own jurisdiction, is not in that case innocent, while it beholds another nation or people carrying on persecution, oppression and slavery, unless it remonstrates against that wickedness of the other nation, and makes use of every effort in its power to help the oppressed, and to rescue the innocent. For so it ought to be the universal rule of duty to all men that fear God and keep his commandments, to do good to all men wherever they can; and when they find any wronged and injured by others, they should endeavour to deliver the ensnared whatever their grievances may be; and should this sometimes lead them into war they might expect the protection and blessing of heaven. How far other motives may appear eligible for men to oppose one another with hostile force, it is not my business to enquire. But I should suppose the hardy veterans who engage merely about the purposes of envying one another concerning any different advantages of commerce, or for enlarging their territories and dominions, or for the end of getting riches by their conquest; that if they fall in the combat, they must generally die, as the fool dieth, vaunting in vain glory; and many of them be like to those who go out in darkness, never to see light; and should they come off alive, what more does their honour and fame amount to, but only to be like that antediluvian conqueror, *who had slain a man to his own wounding, and a young man to his hurt.*[155] But those mighty men of renown in the days of old, because of their apostacy from God, and rebellion and wickedness to men, were at last all swallowed up by an universal deluge for their iniquity and crimes.

But again let me observe, that whatever civilization the inhabitants of Great-Britain may enjoy among themselves, they have seldom maintained their own innocence in that great duty as a Christian nation towards others; and I may say, with respect to their African neighbours, or to any other wheresoever they may go by the way of commerce, they have not regarded them at all. And when they saw others robbing the Africans, and carrying them into captivity and slavery, they have neither helped them, nor opposed their oppressors in the least. But instead thereof they have joined in combination against them with the rest of other profligate nations and people, to buy, enslave and make merchandize of them, because they found them helpless and fit to suit their own purpose, and are become the head carriers on of that iniquitous traffic. But the greater that any reformation and civilization is obtained by any nation, if they do not maintain righteousness, but carry on any course of wickedness and oppression, it makes them appear only the more inconsistent, and their tyranny and oppression the more conspicuous. Wherefore because of the great wickedness, cruelty and injustice done to the Africans, those who are greatest in the transgression give an evident and undubious warrant to all other nations beholding their tyranny and injustice to others, if those nations have any regard to their own innocence and virtue, and wish to maintain righteousness, and to remain clear of the oppression and blood of all men; it is their duty to chastize and suppress such unjust and tyrannical oppressors and enslavers of men. And should none of these be found among the enlightened and civilized nations, who maintain their own innocence and righteousness, with regard to their duty unto all men; and that there may be none to chastize the tyrannical oppressors of others; then it may be feared, as it has often been, that fierce nations of various insects, and other annoyances, may be sent as a judgment to punish the wicked nations of men. For by some way or other every criminal nation, and all their confederates, who sin and rebel against God, and against his laws of nature and nations, will each meet with some awful retribution at last, unless they repent of their iniquity. And the greater advantages of light, learning, knowledge and civilization that any people enjoy, if they do not maintain righteousness, but do wickedly, they will meet with the more severe rebuke when the visitations of God's judgment cometh upon them. And the prophecy which was given to Moses, is still as much in force against the enlightened nations now for their wickedness, in going after the abominations of heathens and barbarians, for none else would attempt to enslave and make merchandize of men, as it was when denounced against the Israelitish nation of old, when they departed, or should depart, from the laws and statutes of the Most High. *The Lord shall bring a nation against thee, from far, from the ends of the earth, as swift as the eagle flieth, a nation whose tongue thou shalt not understand,* &c. See Deut[eronomy] xxviii.

But lest any of these things should happen to the generous and respectful Britons, who are not altogether lost to virtue and consideration; let me say unto you, in the language of a wise and eminent Queen,[156] as she did when her people were sold as a prey to their enemies: That it is not all your enemies [(]for they can be reckoned nothing else), the covetous instigators and carriers on of slavery and wickedness, that can in any way countervail the dam-

age to yourselves, to your king, and to your country; nor will all
the infamous profits of the poor Africans avail you any thing if it
brings down the avenging hand of God upon you. We are not saying that we have not sinned, and that we are not deserving of the
righteous judgments of God against us. But the enemies that have
risen up against us are cruel, oppressive and unjust; and their
haughtiness of insolence, wickedness and iniquity is like to that of
Haman the son of Hammedatha; and who dare suppose, or even
presume to think, that the inhuman ruffians and ensnarers of men,
the vile negociators and merchandizers of the human species, and
the offensive combinations of slave-holders in the West have done
no evil? And should we be passive, as the suffering martyrs dying
in the flames, whose blood crieth for vengeance on their persecu-
tors and murderers; so the iniquity of our oppressors, enslavers
and murderers rise up against them. For we have been hunted after as the wild beasts of the earth, and sold to the enemies of
mankind as their prey; and should any of us have endeavoured to
get away from them, as a man would naturally fly from an enemy
that way-laid him; we have been pursued after, and, by haughty
mandates and laws of iniquity, overtaken, and murdered and slain,
and the blood of millions cries out against them. And together
with these that have been cruelly spoiled and slain, the very grievous afflictions that we have long suffered under, has been long
crying for vengeance on our oppressors; and the great distress and
wretchedness of human woe and misery, which we are yet lying
under, is still rising up before that High and Sovereign Hand of
Justice, where men, by all their oppression and cruelty, can no way
prevent; their evil treatment of others may serve to increase the
blow, but not to evade the stroke of His power, nor withhold the
bringing down that arm of vengeance on themselves, and upon all
their connivers and confederators, and the particular instigators of
such wilful murders and inhuman barbarity. The life of a black
man is of as much regard in the sight of God, as the life of any
other man; though we have been sold as a carnage to the market,
and as a prey to profligate wicked men, to torture and lash us as
they please, and as their caprice may think fit, to murder us at dis-
cretion.

And should any of the best of them plead, as they generally will

do, and tell of their humanity and charity to those whom they
have captured and enslaved, their tribute of thanks is but small; for
what is it, but a little restored to the wretched and miserable
whom they have robbed of their all; and only to be dealt with, like
the spoil of those taken in the field of battle, where the wretched
fugitives must submit to what they please. For as we have been
robbed of our natural right as men, and treated as beasts, those
who have injured us, are like to them who have robbed the widow,
the orphans, the poor and the needy of their right, and whose children are rioting on the spoils of those who are begging at their
doors for bread. And should they say, that their fathers were
thieves and connivers with ensnarers of men, and that they have
been brought up to the iniquitous practice of slavery and oppression of their fellow-creatures, and they cannot live without carrying it on, and making their gain by the unlawful merchandize and
cruel slavery of men, what is that to us, and where will it justify
them? And some will be saying, that the Black people, who are
free in the West Indies, are more miserable than the slaves;—and
well they may; for while they can get their work and drudgery
done for nothing, it is not likely that they will employ those
whom they must pay for their labour. But whatever necessity the
enslavers of men may plead for their iniquitous practice of slavery,
and the various advantages which they get by it, can only evidence
their own injustice and dishonesty. A man that is truly honest,
fears nothing so much as the very imputation of injustice; but
those men who dare not face the consequence of [not] acting up-
rightly in every case are detestable cowards, unworthy the name
of men; for it is manifest that such men are more afraid of temporal inconveniencies than they are of God: *And I say unto you, my
friends, be not afraid of them that kill the body, and after that
have no more they can do; but I will forewarn you whom you shall
fear: Fear him, who, after he hath killed, hath power to cast into
hell.* Luke xii. 4, 5.

But why should total abolition, and an universal emancipation
of slaves, and the enfranchisement of all the Black People employed in the culture of the Colonies, taking place as it ought to
do, and without any hesitation, or delay for a moment, even
though it might have some seeming appearance of loss either to

government or to individuals, be feared at all? Their labour, as
freemen, would be as useful in the sugar colonies as any other
class of men that could be found; and should it even take place in
such a manner that some individuals, at first, would suffer loss as a
just reward for their wickedness in slave-dealing, what is that to
the happiness and good of doing justice to others; and, I must say,
to the great danger, otherwise, that must eventually hang over the
whole community? It is certain, that the produce of the labour of
slaves, together with all the advantages of the West-India traffic,
bring in an immense revenue to government; but let that amount
be what it will, there might be as much or more expected from the
labour of an equal increase of free people, and without the impli-
cation of any guilt attending it, and which, otherwise, must be a
greater burden to bear, and more ruinous consequences to be
feared from it, than if the whole national debt was to sink at once,
and to rest upon the heads of all that might suffer by it. Whereas,
if a generous encouragement were to be given to a free people,
peaceable among themselves, intelligent and industrious, who by
art and labour would improve the most barren situations, and
make the most of that which is fruitful; the free and voluntary
labour of many, would soon yield to any government, many
greater advantages than any thing that slavery can produce. And
this should be expected, wherever a Christian government is extended, and the true religion is embraced, that the blessings of liberty should be extended likewise, and that it should diffuse its
influences first to fertilize the mind, and then the effects of its benignity would extend, and arise with exuberant blessings and advantages from all its operations. Was this to be the case, every
thing would increase and prosper at home and abroad, and ten
thousand times greater and greater advantages would arise to the
state, and more permanent and solid benefit to individuals from
the service of freemen, than ever they can reap, or in any possible
way enjoy, by the labour of slaves.

But why this diabolical traffic of slavery has not been abolished
before now, and why it was introduced at all, as I have already enquired, must be greatly imputed to that powerful and pervading
agency of infernal wickedness, which reigneth and prevaileth over
the nations, and to that umbrageous image of iniquity established

thereby; for had there been any truth and righteousness in that grand horn of delusion in the east, which may seem admirable to some, and be looked upon by its votaries as the fine burnished gold, and bright as the finest polished silver, then would not slavery, cruelty and oppression have been abolished wherever its influence came? And had the grand apostacy of its fellow horn, with all its lineaments been any better, and endowed with any real virtue and goodness, whom its devotees may behold as the finest polished diamond, and glistening as the finest gems, then would not slavery and barbarity have been prohibited and forbidden wherever the beams of any Christianity arose? Then might we have expected to hear tidings of good, even from those who are gone to repose in the fabulous paradise of Mahomet? Then might we have looked for it from those who are now reclined to slumber in assimulation with the old dotards of Rome, or to those who are fallen asleep and become enamoured with the scarlet couch of the abominable enchantress dyed in blood? And as well then might we not expect tenderness and compassion from those whom the goddess of avarice has so allured with her charms, that her heart-sick lovers are become reversed to the feelings of human woe; and with the great hurry and bustle of the russet slaves employed in all the drudgeries of the western isles, and maritime shores[157] in the cruel and involuntary service of her voluptuousness, having so dazzled their eyes, and bereaved them of all sensibility, that their hearts are become callous as the nether millstone, fierce as the tygers, and devoid of the natural feelings of men? From all such enchantments we would turn away, and fly from them as the ravenous beasts of prey, as from the weeping crocodiles and the devouring reptiles, and as from the hoary monsters of the deep.[158]

But we would look unto you, O ye multitude in the desert! against whom there is no enchantment, neither any divination whatever, that can prevail against you! for in your mouth there is no error or guile to be found, nor any fault before the throne of God. And what! though your dwellings be in all lands, and ye have no nation or kingdom on earth that ye can call your own, and your camp be surrounded by many enemies, yet you have a place of defence, an invincible fortress, the munitions of rocks for your refuge, and the shield of your anointed is Almighty; and be-

hold his buckler is strong, and his sceptre is exalted on high, and
the throne of his dominion and power ruleth over all. But in the
day that we shall be spoken for, if we find you a wall, we would
build upon you a palace of silver; and if you find us a door, inclose
us with boards of cedar, for we long, and would to God that we
longed more, to enter into your fortress, and follow you to your
happy retreat. Then might we, like you, stand undaunted before
our foes, and with more than heroic sullenness at all their cruel
tortures, highly disdain their rage, and boldly dare them to do
their worst. For you, O ye friends of the Most High, when you
die, when you are persecuted and slain, when you fall in the combat, when you die in the battle, it is you! only you, that come off
conquerors, and more than conquerors through him that loved
you! And should it yet be, as it has often been, that your foes
might pursue you with their usual arrogance and persecuting rage,
and cause you to die cruelly veiled in a curtain of blood, lo! your
stains are all washed away, and your wounds and scars will soon
be healed, and yourselves will be then invested with a robe of
honor that will shine in whiteness for ever new, and your blood
that was shed by the terrific rage of your foes, will testify against
them, and rise up in grandeur to you, as an enfringement of gold
floating in glory, and as his robe of honor which flames in eternal
crimson through the heavens. But we envy no man, but wish them
to do good, and not evil; and we want the prayers of the good, and
wherever they can to help us; and the blessing of God be with all
the promoters of righteousness and peace.

But wherefore, O beloved,[159] should your watchmen sit still,
when they hear tell that the enemy is invading all the out-posts
and camp of the British empire, where many of your dwellings
are? Are they all fallen asleep, and lying down to slumber in as-
similation of the workers of iniquity? Should not those who are
awake, arise, and give the alarm, that others may arise and awake
also? And should not they who feareth the name of the Lord, and
worship in his holy temples, *Let judgment to run down as waters,
and righteousness as a mighty stream?*[160] But why think ye prayers
in churches and chapels only will do ye good, if your charity do
not extend to pity and regard your fellow creatures perishing
through ignorance, under the heavy yoke of subjection and bond-

age, to the cruel and avaricious oppression of brutish profligate men; and when both the injured, and their oppressors, dwell in such a vicinity as equally to claim your regard? The injurers, oppressors, enslavers, and murderers of others, eventually bring a curse upon themselves, as far as they destroy, injure, and cruelly and basely treat those under their subjection and unlawful bondage. And where such a dreadful pre-eminence of iniquity abounds, as the admission of laws for tolerating slavery and wickedness, and the worst of robberies, not only of men's properties, but themselves; and the many inhuman murders and cruelties occasioned by it: If it meets with your approbation, it is your sin, and you are then as a conniver and confederator with those workers of wickedness; and if you give it a sanction by your passive obedience, it manifests that you have gone over to those brutish enemies of mankind, and can in no way be a true lover of your king and country.

Wherefore it ought to be the universal endeavour, and the ardent wish, of all the lovers of God and the Saviour of men, and of all that delight in his ways of righteousness, and of all the lovers of their country, and the friends of mankind, and of every real patriot in the land, and of every man and woman that dwelleth therein, and of all those that have any pretence to charity, generosity, sensibility and humanity, and whoever has any regard to innocence and virtue, to plead that slavery, with all its great and heinous magnitude of iniquity, might be abolished throughout all the British dominions; and from henceforth to hinder and prohibit the carrying on of that barbarous, brutish and inhuman traffic of the slavery and commerce of the human species, wherever the power and influence of the British empire extends. And in doing this, and always in doing righteously, let the glory and honour of it be alone ascribed unto God Most High, for his great mercy and goodness to you; and that his blessing and unbounded beneficence may shine forth upon you, and upon all the promoters of it: and that it may with great honours and advantages of peace and prosperity be ever resting upon the noble Britons, and upon their most worthy, most eminent and august Sovereign, and upon all his government and the people under it; and that the streams thereof may run down in righteousness even to us, poor, deplorable Africans.

And we that are particularly concerned would humbly join with all the rest of our brethren and countrymen in complexion, who have been grievously injured, and who jointly and separately, in all the language of grief and woe, are humbly imploring and earnestly entreating the most respectful and generous people of Great Britain, that they would consider us, and have mercy and compassion on us, and to take away that evil that your enemies, as well as our oppressors, are doing towards us, and cause them to desist from their evil treatment of the poor and despised Africans, before it be too late; and to restore that justice and liberty which is our natural right, that we have been unlawfully deprived and cruelly wronged of, and to deliver us from that captivity and bondage which we now suffer under, in our present languishing state of exile and misery. And we humbly pray that God may put it into the minds of the noble Britons, that they may have the honor and advantage of doing so great good to many, and to extend their power and influence to do good afar; and that great good in abundance may come down upon themselves, and upon all their government and the people under it, in every place belonging to the British empire. But if the people and legislature of Great-Britain altogether hold their peace at such a time as this, and even laugh at our calamity as heretofore they have been wont to do, by making merchandize of us to enrich themselves with our misery and distress: we sit like the mourning Mordecai's[161] at their gates cloathed in sackcloth; and, in this advanced aera,[162] we hope God in his Providence will rise up a deliverance for us some other way; and we have great reason to hope that the time of our deliverance is fast drawing nigh, and when the great Babylon of iniquity will fall.

And whereas we consider our case before God of the whole universe, the Gracious Father and Saviour of men; we will look unto him for help and deliverance. The cry of our affliction is already gone up before him, and he will hearken to the voice of our distress; for he hears the cries and groans of the oppressed, and professes that if they cry at all unto him, he will hearken unto them, and deliver them. *For the oppression of the poor, for the sighing of the needy, now will I arise saith Jehovah, and will set him in safety from him that puffeth at him, or that would ensnare him.* (Psa[lm] xii. 5.) *And I know that Jehovah will maintain the cause of the afflicted, and the right of the poor.* (Psa[am]. cxl. 12.) Wherefore it is our duty to look up to a greater deliverer than that of the British nation, or of any nation upon earth; for unless God gives them repentance, and peace towards him, we can expect no peace or deliverance from them. But still we shall have cause to trust, that God who made of one blood all the nations and children of men, and who gave to all equally a natural right to liberty; that he who ruleth over all the kingdoms of the earth with equal providential justice, shall then make enlargement and deliverance to arise to the grievously injured, and heavy oppressed Africans from another place.

And as we look for our help and sure deliverance to come from God Most High, should it not come in an apparent way from Great-Britain, whom we consider as the Queen of nations, let her not think to escape more than others, if she continues to carry on oppression and injustice, and such pre-eminent wickedness against us: for we are only seeking that justice may be done to us, and what every righteous nation ought to do; and if it be not done, it will be adding iniquity to iniquity against themselves. But let us not suppose that the inhabitants of the British nation will adhere to the ways of the profligate: *For such is the way of an adulterous woman; she eateth, and wipeth her mouth; and saith, I have done no wickedness.*[163] But rather let us suppose, *That whereas iniquity hath abounded, may righteousness much more abound.* For the wickedness that you have done is great, and wherever your traffic and colonies have been extended it is shameful; and the great injustice and cruelty done to the poor Africans crieth to heaven against you; and therefore that it may be forgiven unto you, it cries aloud for universal reformation and national repentance. But let it not suffice that a gracious call from the throne is inviting you, *To a religious observance of God's holy laws, as fearing, lest God's wrath and indignation, should be provoked against you;* but in your zeal for God's holy law, because of the shameful transgression thereof, every man every woman hath reason to mourn apart, and every one that dwelleth in the land ought to mourn and sigh for all the abominations done therein, and for the great wickedness carried on thereby.

And now that blessings may come instead of a curse, and that

many beneficent purposes of good might speedily arise and flow
from it, and be more readily promoted; I would hereby presume
to offer the following considerations, as some outlines of a general
reformation which ought to be established and carried on. And
first, I would propose, that there ought to be days of mourning
and fasting appointed, to make enquiry into that great and pre-
eminent evil for many years past carried on against the Heathen
nations, and the horrible iniquity of making merchandize of us,
and cruelly enslaving the poor Africans; and that you might seek
grace and repentance, and find mercy and forgiveness before God
Omnipotent; and that he may give you wisdom and understanding to devise what ought to be done.

Secondly, I would propose that a total abolition of slavery
should be made and proclaimed; and that an universal emancipation of slaves should begin from the date thereof, and be carried
on in the following manner: That a proclamation should be caused
to be made, setting forth the Antichristian unlawfulness of the
slavery and commerce of the human species; and that it should be
sent to all the courts and nations in Europe, to require their advice
and assistance, and as they may find it unlawful to carry it on, let
them whosoever will join to prohibit it. And if such a proclamation be found advisable to the British legislature, let them publish
it, and cause it to be published, throughout all the British empire,
to hinder and prohibit all men under their government to traffic
either in buying or selling men; and, to prevent it, a penalty might
be made against it of one thousand pounds, for any man either to
buy or sell another man. And that it should require all slave-
holders, upon the immediate information thereof, to mitigate the
labour of their slaves to that of a lawful servitude, without tortures
or oppression; and that they should not hinder, but cause and procure some suitable means of instruction for them in the knowledge of the Christian religion. And agreeable to the late *royal
Proclamation, for the Encouragement of Piety and Virtue, and for
the preventing and punishing of Vice, Profaneness and Immoral-
ity;*[164] that by no means, under any pretence whatsoever, either for
themselves or their masters, the slaves under their subjection
should not be suffered to work on the Sabbath days, unless it be
such works as necessity and mercy may require. But that those

days, as well as some other hours selected for the purpose, should
be appropriated for the time of their instruction; and that if any of
their owners should not provide such suitable instructors for
them, that those slaves should be taken away from them and given
to others who would maintain and instruct them for their labour.
And that it should be made known to the slaves, that those who
had been above seven years in the islands or elsewhere, if they had
obtained any competent degree of knowledge of the Christian religion, and the laws of civilization, and had behaved themselves
honestly and decently, that they should immediately become free;
and that their owners should give them reasonable wages and
maintenance for their labour, and not cause them to go away unless they could find some suitable employment elsewhere. And accordingly, from the date of their arrival to seven years, as they
arrive at some suitable progress in knowledge, and behaved themselves honestly, that they should be getting free in the course of
that time, and at the end of seven years to let every honest man
and woman become free; for in the course of that time, they
would have sufficiently paid their owners by their labour, both for
their first purpose, and for the expences attending their education.
By being thus instructed in the course of seven years, they would
become tractable and obedient, useful labourers, dutiful servants
and good subjects; and Christian men might have the honor and
happiness to see many of them vieing with themselves to praise
the God of their salvation. And it might be another necessary duty
for Christians, in the course of that time, to make enquiry concerning some of their friends and relations in Africa; and if they
found any intelligent persons amongst them, to give them as good
education as they could, and find out a way of recourse to their
friends; that as soon as they had made any progress in useful
learning and the knowledge of the Christian religion, they might
be sent back to Africa, to be made useful there as soon, and as
many of them as could be made fit for instructing others. The rest
would become useful residentors in the colonies; where there
might be employment enough given to all free people, with suitable wages according to their usefulness, in the improvement of
land; and the more encouragement that could be given to agricul-
ture, and every other branch of useful industry, would thereby en-

crease the number of the inhabitants; without which any country, however blessed by nature, must continue poor.

And, thirdly, I would propose, that a fleet of some ships of war should be immediately sent to the coast of Africa, and particularly where the slave trade is carried on, with faithful men to direct that none should be brought from the coast of Africa without their own consent and the approbation of their friends, and to intercept all merchant ships that were bringing them away, until such a scrutiny was made, whatever nation they belonged to. And, I would suppose, if Great-Britain was to do any thing of this kind, that it would meet with the general approbation and assistance of other Christian nations; but whether it did or not, it could be very lawfully done at all the British forts and settlements on the coast of Africa; and particular remonstrances could be given to all the rest, to warn them of the consequences of such an evil and enormous wicked traffic as is now carried on. The Dutch have some crocodile settlers at the Cape,[165] that should be called to a particular account for their murders and inhuman barbarities. But all the present governors of the British forts and factories should be dismissed, and faithful and good men appointed in their room; and those forts and factories, which at present are a den of thieves, might be turned into shepherd's tents, and have good shepherds sent to call the flocks to feed beside them. Then would doors of hospitality in abundance be opened in Africa to supply the weary travellers, and that immense abundance which they are enriched with, might be diffused afar; but the character of the inhabitants on the west coast of Africa, and the rich produce of their country, have been too long misrepresented by avaricious plunderers and merchants who deal in slaves; and if that country was not annually ravished and laid waste, there might be a very considerable and profitable trade carried on with the Africans.[166] And, should the noble Britons, who have often supported their own liberties with their lives and fortunes, extend their philanthropy to abolish the slavery and oppression of the Africans, they might have settlements and many kingdoms united in a friendly alliance with themselves, which might be made greatly to their own advantage, as well as they might have the happiness of being useful to promoting the prosperity and felicity of others, who have been cruelly in-

jured and wrongfully dealt with. Were the Africans to be dealt
with in a friendly manner, and kind instruction to be administered
unto them, as by degrees they became to love learning, there
would be nothing in their power, but what they would wish to
render their service in return for the means of improving their
understanding; and the present British factories, and other settlements, might be enlarged to a very great extent. And as Great-
Britain has been remarkable for ages past, for encouraging arts and
sciences, and may now be put in competition with any nation in
the known world, if they would take compassion on the inhabitants of the coast of Guinea, and to make use of such means as
would be needful to enlighten their minds in the knowledge of
Christianity, their virtue, in this respect, would have its own reward. And as the Africans became refined and established in light
and knowledge, they would imitate their noble British friends, to
improve their lands, and make use of that industry as the nature of
their country might require, and to supply those that would trade
with them, with such productions as the nature of their climate
would produce; and, in every respect, the fair Britons would have
the preference with them to a very great extent; and, in another
respect, they would become a kind of first ornament to Great-
Britain for her tender and compassionate care of such a set of distressed poor ignorant people. And were the noble Britons, and
their august Sovereign, to cause protection and encouragement to
be given to those Africans, they might expect in a short time, if
need required it, to receive from thence great supplies of men in a
lawful way, either for industry or defence; and of other things in
abundance, from so great a source, where every thing is luxurious
and plenty, if not laid waste by barbarity and gross ignorance. Due
encouragement being given to so great, so just, and such a noble
undertaking, would soon bring more revenue in a righteous way
to the British nation, than ten times its share in all the profits that
slavery can produce;[167] and such a laudable example would inspire
every generous and enterprizing mind to imitate so great and worthy a nation, for establishing religion, justice, and equity to the
Africans, and, in doing this, would be held in the highest esteem
by all men, and be admired by all the world.

These three preceding considerations may suffice at present to

shew, that some plan might be adopted in such a manner as effectually to relieve the grievances and oppression of the Africans, and
to bring great honour and blessings to that nation, and to all men
whosoever would endeavour to promote so great good to mankind; and it might render more conspicuous advantages to the noble Britons, as the first doers of it, and greater honour than the
finding of America was at first to those that made the discovery:
Though several difficulties may seem to arise at first, and the good
to be sought after may appear to be remote and unknown, as it
was to explore the unknown regions of the Western Ocean;
should it be sought after, like the intrepid Columbus, if they do
not find kingdoms of wealth by the way, they may be certain of
finding treasures of happiness and of peace in the end. But should
there be any yet alive deserving the infamy and character of all the
harsh things which I have ascribed to the insidious carriers on of
the slavery and commerce of the human species, they will certainly object to any thing of this kind being proposed, or ever
thought of, as doing so great a good to the base Black Negroes
whom they make their prey. To such I must say again, that it
would be but a just commutation for what cannot be fully restored, in order to make restoration, as far as could be, for the injuries already done to them. And some may say, that if they have
wages to pay to the labourers for manufacturing the West-India
productions, that they would not be able to sell them at such a
price as would suit the European market, unless all the different
nations agreed to raise the price of their commodities in proportion. Whatever bad neighbours men may have to deal with, let the
upright shew themselves to be honest men, and that difficulty,
which some may fear, would be but small, as there can be no reason for men to do wrong because others do so; but as to what is
consumed in Great-Britain, they could raise the price in proportion, and it would be better to sip the West-India sweetness by
paying a little more money for it (if it should be found needful)
than to drink the blood of iniquity at a cheaper rate. I know several ladies in England who refuse to drink sugar in their tea,[168] because of the cruel injuries done to the Black People employed in
the culture of it at the West-Indies. But should it cost the West-
Indians more money to have their manufactories carried on[169] by

the labour of freemen than with slaves, it would be attended with greater blessings and advantages to them in the end. What the wages should be for the labour of freemen, is a question not so easily determined; yet I should think, that it always should be something more than merely victuals and cloaths; and if a man works by the day, he should have the three hundredth part of what might be estimated as sufficient to keep him in necessary cloaths and provisions for a year, and, added to that, such wages of reward as their usefulness might require. Something of this kind should be observed in free countries, and then the price of provisions would be kept at such a rate as the industrious poor could live, without being oppressed and screwed down to work for nothing, but only barely to live. And were every civilized nation, where they boast of liberty, so ordered by its government, that some general and useful employment were provided for every industrious man and woman, in such a manner that none should stand still and be idle, and have to say that they could not get employment, so long as there are barren lands at home and abroad sufficient to employ thousands and millions of people more than there are. This, in a great measure, would prevent thieves and robbers, and the labour of many would soon enrich a nation. But those employed by the general community should only have their maintenance either given or estimated in money, and half the wages of others, which would make them seek out for something else whenever they could, and half a loaf would be better than no bread. The men that were employed in this manner, would form an useful militia, and the women would be kept from a state of misery and want, and from following a life of dissolute wickedness. Liberty and freedom, where people may starve for want, can do them but little good. We want many rules of civilization in Africa; but, in many respects, we may boast of some more essential liberties than any of the civilized nations in Europe enjoy; for the poorest amongst us are never in distress for want, unless some general and universal calamity happen to us. But if any nation or society of men were to observe the laws of God, and to keep his commandments, and walk in the way of righteousness, they would not need to fear the heat in sultry hot climates, nor the freezing inclemency of the cold, and the storms and hurricanes would not hurt them at all; they might soon see blessings and plenty in abundance showered down upon their mountains and vallies; and if his beneficence was sought after, who martials out the drops of the dew, and bids the winds to blow, and to carry the clouds on their wings to drop down their moisture and fatness on what spot soever he pleaseth, and who causeth the genial rays of the sun to warm and cherish the productions of the earth in every place according to that temperature which he sees meet; then might the temperate climes of Great-Britain be seen to vie with the rich land of Canaan of old, which is now, because of the wickedness of its inhabitants, in comparison of what it was, as only a barren desart.

Particular thanks is due to every one of that humane society of worthy and respectful gentlemen, whose liberality hath supported many of the Black poor about London.[170] *Those that honor their Maker have mercy on the poor; and many blessings are upon the head of the just; may the fear of the Lord prolong their days, and cause their memory to be blessed, and may their number be encreased to fill their expectation with gladness;* for they have not only commiserated the poor in general, *but even those which are accounted as beasts, and imputed as vile in the sight of others.*[171] The part that the British government has taken, to co-operate with them, has certainly a flattering and laudable appearance of doing some good; and the fitting out ships to supply a company of Black People with clothes and provisions, and to carry them to settle at Sierra Leona, in the West coast of Africa, as a free colony to Great-Britain, in a peaceable alliance with the inhabitants, has every appearance of honour, and the approbation of friends. According to the plan, humanity hath made its appearance in a more honorable way of colonization, than any Christian nation have ever done before, and may be productive of much good, if they continue to encourage and support them. But after all, there is some doubt whether their own flattering expectation in the manner as set forth to them, and the hope of their friends may not be defeated and rendered abortive; and there is some reason to fear, that they never will be settled as intended, in any permanent and peaceable way at Sierra Leona.[172]

This prospect of settling a free colony to Great-Britain in a peaceable alliance with the inhabitants of Africa at Sierra Leona, has neither altogether met with the credulous approbation of the Africans here, nor yet been sought after with any prudent and right plan by the promoters of it. Had a treaty of agreement been first made with the inhabitants of Africa, and the terms and nature of such a settlement fixed upon, and its situation and boundary pointed out; then might the Africans, and others here, have embarked with a good prospect of enjoying happiness and prosperity themselves, and have gone with a hope of being able to render their services, in return, of some advantage to their friends and benefactors of Great-Britain. But as this was not done, and as they were to be hurried away at all events, come of them after what would; and yet, after all, to be delayed in the ships before they were set out from the coast, until many of them have perished with cold, and other disorders, and several of the most intelligent among them are dead, and others that, in all probability, would have been most useful for them were hindered from going, by means of some disagreeable jealousy of those who were appointed as governors, the great prospect of doing good seems all to be blown away.[173] And so it appeared to some of those who are now gone, and at last, hap hazard, were obliged to go; who endeavoured in vain to get away by plunging into the water, that they might, if possible wade ashore, as dreading the prospect of their wretched fate, and as beholding their perilous situation, having every prospect of difficulty and surrounding danger.

What with the death of some of the original promoters and proposers of this charitable undertaking, and the death and deprivation of others that were to share the benefit of it, and by the adverse motives of those employed to be the conductors thereof, we think it will be more than what can be well expected, if we ever hear of any good in proportion to so great, well-designed, laudable and expensive charity. Many more of the Black People still in this country would have, with great gladness, embraced the opportunity, longing to reach their native land; but as the old saying is, A burnt child dreads the fire, some of these unfortunate sons and daughters of Africa have been severally unlawfully dragged away from their native abodes, under various pretences, by the insidious treachery of others, and have been brought into the hands of barbarous robbers and pirates, and, like sheep to the market, have been sold into captivity and slavery, and thereby have been deprived of their natural liberty and property, and every connection that they held dear and valuable, and subjected to the cruel service of the hard-hearted brutes called planters. But some of them, by various services either to the public or to individuals, as more particularly in the course of last war, have gotten their liberty again in this free country. They are thankful for the respite, but afraid of being ensnared again; for the European seafaring people in general, who trade to foreign parts, have such a prejudice against Black People, that they use them more like asses than men, so that a Black Man is scarcely ever safe among them. Much assiduity was made use of to perswade the Black People in general to embrace the opportunity of going with this company of transports; but the wiser sort declined from all thoughts of it, unless they could hear of some better plan taking place for their security and safety.[174] For as it seemed prudent and obvious to many of them taking heed to that sacred enquiry, *Doth a fountain send forth at the same place sweet water and bitter?*[175] They were afraid that their doom would be to drink of the bitter water. For can it be readily conceived that government would establish a free colony for them nearly on the spot, while it supports its forts and garrisons, to ensnare, merchandize, and to carry others into captivity and slavery.

Above fifty years ago, P. Gordon, in his Geography, though he was no advocate against slavery, complains of the barbarities committed against the Heathen nations, and the base usage of the negro slaves subjected to bondage as brutes, and deprived of religion as men. His remark on the religion of the American islands, says: "As for the negroe slaves, their lot has hitherto been, and still is, to serve such Christian masters, who sufficiently declare what zeal they have for their conversion, by unkindly using a serious divine some time ago, for only proposing to endeavour the same."[176] This was above half a century ago, and their unchristian barbarity is still continued. Even in the little time that I was in Grenada, I saw a slave receive twenty-four lashes of a whip for being seen at a church on a Sunday, instead of going to work in the fields; and those whom they put the greatest confidence in, are often served

in the same manner. The noble proposals offered for instructing
the heathen nations and people in his Geography, has been attended to with great supineness and indifference. The author
wishes, that "sincere endeavours might be made to extend the lim-
its of our Saviour's kingdom, with those of our own dominions;
and to spread the true religion as far as the British sails have done
for traffic." And he adds, "Let our planters duly consider, that to
extirpate natives, is rather a supplanting than planting a new
colony; and that it is far more honourable to overcome paganism
in one, than to destroy a thousand pagans. Each convert is a conquest."[177]

To put an end to the wickedness[178] of slavery and merchandizing of men, and to prevent murder, extirpation and dissolution, is
what every righteous nation ought to seek after; and to endeavour
to diffuse knowledge and instruction to all the heathen nations
wherever they can, is the grand duty of all Christian men. But
while the horrible traffic of slavery is admitted and practiced,
there can be but little hope of any good proposals meeting with
success anywhere; for the abandoned carriers of it on have spread
the poison of their iniquity wherever they come, at home and
abroad. Were the iniquitous laws in support of it, and the whole of
that oppression and injustice abolished, and the righteous laws of
Christianity, equity, justice and humanity established in the room
thereof, multitudes of nations would flock to the standard of
truth, and instead of revolting away, they would count it their
greatest happiness to be under the protection and jurisdiction of a
righteous government. And in that respect, *in the multitude of the
people is the King's honour; but in the want of people, is the destruction of the Prince.*[179]

We would wish to have the grandeur and fame of the British
empire to extend far and wide; and the glory and honor of God to
be promoted by it, and the interest of Christianity set forth among
all the nations wherever its influence and power can extend; but
not to be supported by the insidious pirates, depredators, murderers and slave-holders. And as it might diffuse knowledge and instruction to others, that it might receive a tribute of reward from
all its territories, forts and garrisons, without being oppressive to
any. But contrary to this the wickedness of many of the White

People who keep slaves, and contrary to all the laws and duties of Christianity which the Scriptures teach, they have in general endeavoured to keep the Black People in total ignorance as much as they can, which must be a great dishonor to any Christian government, and injurious to the safety and happiness of rulers.

But in order to diffuse any knowledge of Christianity to the unlearned Heathens, those who undertake to do any thing therein ought to be wise and honest men. Their own learning, though the more the better, is not so much required as that they should be men of the same mind and principles of the apostle Paul; men that would hate covetousness, and who would hazard their lives for the cause and gospel of our Lord and Saviour Jesus Christ. "I think it needless to express how commendable such a design would be in itself, and how desirable the promotion thereof should be to all who stile themselves Christians, of what party or profession soever they are."[180] Rational methods might be taken to have the Scriptures translated into many foreign languages; "and a competent number of young students of theology might be educated at home in these foreign languages, to afford a constant supply of able men, who might yearly go abroad, and be sufficiently qualified at their first arrival to undertake the great work for which they were sent."[181] But as a hindrance to this, the many Anti-christian errors which are gone abroad into the world, and all the popish superstition and nonsense, and the various assimilations unto it, with the false philosophy which abounds among Christians, seems to threaten with an universal deluge; but God hath promised to fill the world with a knowledge of himself, and he hath set up his bow, in the rational heavens, as well as in the clouds, as a token that he will stop the proud ways of error and delusion, that hitherto they may come, and no farther. The holy arch of truth is to be seen in the azure paths of the pious and wise, and conspicuously painted in crimson over the martyrs tombs. These, with the golden altars of truth, built up by the reformed churches,[182] and many pious, good and righteous men, are bulwarks that will ever stand against all the sorts of error. Teaching would be exceeding necessary to the pagan nations and ignorant people in every place and situation; but they do not need any unscriptural forms and ceremonies to be taught unto them; they can devise superstitions enough among themselves, and church government too, if ever they need any.

And hence we would agree in this one thing with that erroneous philosopher, who has lately wrote *An Apology for Negro Slavery*, "But if the slave is only to be made acquainted with the form, without the substance; if he is only to be decked out with the external trappings of religion; if he is only to be taught the uncheering principles of gloomy superstition; or, if he is only to be inspired with the intemperate frenzy of enthusiastic fanaticism, it were better that he remained in that dark state, where he could not see good from ill."[183] But these words *intemperate, frenzy, enthusiastic,* and *fanaticism* may be variously applied, and often wrongfully; but, perhaps never better, or more fitly, than to be ascribed as the genuine character of this author's brutish philosophy; and he may subscribe it, and the meaning of these words, with as much affinity to himself, as he bears a relation to a *Hume,*[184] or to his friend *Tobin.* The poor negroes in the West-Indies, have suffered enough by such religion as the philosophers of the North produce; Protestants, as they are called, are the most barbarous slave-holders, and there are none can equal the Scotch floggers and negroe-drivers, and the barbarous Dutch cruelties. Perhaps as the church of Rome begins to sink in its power, its followers may encrease in virtue and humanity; so that many, who are the professed adherents thereof, would even blush and abhor the very mention of the cruelty and bloody deeds that their ancestors have committed; and we find slavery itself more tolerable among them, than it is in the Protestant countries.

But I shall add another observation, which I am sorry to find among Christians, and I think it is a great deficiency among the clergy in general, when covetous and profligate men are admitted among them, who either do not know, or dare not speak the truth, but neglect their duty much, or do it with such supineness, that it becomes good for nothing. Sometimes an old woman selling matches, will preach a better, and a more orthodox sermon, than some of the clergy, who are only decked out (as Mr. Turnbul [sic] calls it) with the external trappings of religion. Much of the great wickedness of others lieth at their door, and these words of the Prophet are applicable to them: *And first, saith the Lord, I will rec-*

ompence their iniquity, and their sin double; because they have defiled my land, they have filled mine inheritance with the carcases
of their detestable and abominable things.[185] Such are the errors of
men. Church, signifies an assembly of people; but a building of
wood, brick or stone, where the people meet together, is generally
called so; and should the people be frightened away by the many
abominable dead carcases which they meet with, they should follow the multitudes to the fields, to the vallies, to the mountains, to
the islands, to the rivers, and to the ships, and compel them to
come in, that the house of the Lord may be filled. But when we
find some of the covetous connivers with slave-holders, in the
West-Indies, so ignorant as to dispute whether a Pagan can be
baptized without giving him a Christian name, we cannot expect
much from them, or think that they will follow after much good.
No name, whether Christian or Pagan, has any thing to do with
baptism; if the requisite qualities of knowledge and faith be found
in a man, he may be baptized let his name be what it will. And
Christianity does not require that we should be deprived of our
own personal name, or the name of our ancestors; but it may very
fitly add another name unto us, Christian, or one anointed. And it
may as well be answered so to that question in the English liturgy,
What is your name?—A Christian.[186]

> "*A Christian is the highest stile of man!*
> *And is there, who the blessed cross wipes off*
> *As a foul blot, from his dishonor'd brow?*
> *If angels tremble, 'tis at such a sight:*
> *The wretch they quit disponding of their charge,*
> *More struck with grief or wonder who can tell?*"[187]

And let me now hope that you will pardon me in all that I have
been thus telling you, O ye inhabitants of Great-Britain! to whom
I owe the greatest respect; to your king! to yourselves! and to
your government! And tho' many things which I have written
may seem harsh, it cannot be otherwise evaded when such horrible iniquity is transacted: and tho' to some what I have said may
appear as the rattling leaves of autumn, that may soon be blown
away and whirled in a vortex where few can hear and know: I

must yet say, although it is not for me to determine the manner, that the voice of our complaint implies a vengeance, because of the great iniquity that you have done, and because of the cruel injustice done unto us Africans; and it ought to sound in your ears as the rolling waves around your circum-ambient shores; and if it is not hearkened unto, it may yet arise with a louder voice, as the rolling thunder, and it may encrease in the force of its volubility, not only to shake the leaves of the most stout in heart, but to rend the mountains before them, and to cleave in pieces the rocks under them, and to go on with fury to smite the stoutest oaks in the forest; and even to make that which is strong, and wherein you think that your strength lieth, to become as stubble, and as the fibres of rotten wood, that will do you no good, and your trust in it will become a snare of infatuation to you!

FINIS.

THOUGHTS AND SENTIMENTS

ON THE

EVIL OF SLAVERY;

OR, THE

NATURE OF SERVITUDE

AS ADMITTED BY THE

LAW OF *GOD*,

COMPARED TO THE

MODERN SLAVERY

OF THE

AFRICANS

IN THE WEST-INDIES;

In an Answer to the
ADVOCATES for Slavery and Oppression.
Addressed to the SONS of AFRICA,

BY

A NATIVE.

London:

Printed for, and sold by, the AUTHOR, No. 12, *Queen-Street,*
Grosvenor-Square. Sold also by Mr. KIRBY, *Oxford-*
Street; Mr. BELL, *Strand;* Mr. SIMONDS, *Pater-*
Noster-Row; Mr. STEEL, *Tower-Hill;* and
Mr. TAYLOR, *Royal-Exchange.*

M,DCC,XCI.

Thoughts and Sentiments on the Evil of Slavery.[1]

Gentlemen Countrymen and brother Sufferers.

AS SEVERAL GENTLEMEN of distinguished abilities, as well as eminent for their great humanity, liberality and candour, have written various essays against the infamous traffic of the African Slave Trade, carried on with the West-India planters and merchants, to the great shame and disgrace of all Christian nations wherever it has been admitted in any of their territories, or situations amongst them; it cannot be amiss that I should thankfully acknowledge these truly worthy & humane gentlemen (viz. Mr. WM. WILBERFORCE,[2] and Mr. GRENVILLE [sic] SHARP) with the warmest sense of gratitude, for their beneficent and laudatory endeavours towards a total suppression of that infamous traffic of buying, selling, and cruelly inslaving Men!

Those who have endeavoured to restore to their fellow-creatures the common rights of nature, of which especially the poor unfortunate Black People have been so unjustly deprived, cannot fail in meeting with the approbation and applause of all good men, and the approbation of that which will forever redound to their lasting memory; they have the warrant of that which is divine: *Open thy mouth, judge righteously, plead the cause of the poor and needy; for the liberal deviseth liberal things, and by liberal things it shall stand.*

The kind exertions of many benevolent and humane gentlemen, against the iniquitous traffic of slavery and oppression, has been attended with great good to many, and must redound with great honor to themselves, to humanity and their country; their laudable endeavours have been productive of the most beneficent effects in preventing that savage barbarity from taking place in free countries at home. For so it was considered as criminal, by the laws of Englishmen, when the tyrannical paw and the monster of slavery took the man by the neck, in the centre of the British freedom, and thought henceforth to compel him to his involuntary subjection of slavery and oppression; it was wisely determined by some of the most eminent and learned counsellors in the land. The whole of that affair rested solely upon that humane and indefatigable friend of mankind, GRENVILLE SHARP esq. whose name we should always mention with the greatest reverence and honor. The noble decision, thereby, before the Right Hon. Lord Chief Justice MANSFIELD, and the parts taken by the learned Counsellor HARGRAVE,[3] are the surest proofs of the most amiable disposition of the laws of Englishmen.

That part that has been taken lately by the generous senator WILLIAM WILBERFORCE esq. to co-operate with the British parliament, in behalf of the oppressed Africans, and many other gentlemen, who have joined him in sentiments, in behalf of us injured sable, from Africa, shews the amiable intentions of that august and much revered Assembly; we, as part of the sufferers, cannot but rest with the strongest confidence, and hope that the end of so laudable exertions, are the total abolition of that horrible traffic, so long practised. In this, as well as in many other respects, there is one class of people whose virtues of probity and humanity are well known, and worthy of universal approbation and imitation, because, like other men of honor and humanity, they have jointly agreed to carry on no slavery and savage barbarity among them; and, since last war, some mitigation of slavery has been obtained in some respective districts in America, though not in proportion to their own vaunted claims of freedom; but it is to be hoped, that they will still go on to make a further and greater reformation.

We need not say at present that we are able to reward them, for this kind and laudable exertion, as many of us having been long absent from our native country, and cannot forsee the future events; however, this we would aver, should the abolition of that horrible traffic take place, as it ought, next sessions of Parliament; that there may be a plan adopted to meet the general approbation of our African friends, who would be ready in renewing any instruction that might be adopted for the future, that may tend to the happiness of mankind, with every advantage and honor to the British nation.

Should the noble and generous Britions [sic] seek us with that cheerfulness and spirit of the intrepid Columbus, if they do not find kingdoms of wealth by the way, they would be sure to find treasures of happiness in the end; and this should be expected wherever the British sails has reached, or can extend for commerce. And in this advanced æra, when the kings of Europe become more conspicuous for their manly virtues, than any before them have been, it is to be hoped that they will not any longer suffer themselves to be imposed upon, beguiled, and brought into guilt and shame, by any instigations of the cunning craftiness, and evil policy of the avaricious enslavers of men. And as their wisdom and understanding is great and exalted as high dignity, it is also to be hoped that they will exert themselves, in the cause of righteousness and justice, and be like the wisest and greatest monarchs of old, to hearken to the counsel of the wise men that know the times, and to the righteous laws of God, and to deliver the oppressed, and put an end to the iniquitous commerce and slavery of men. And as we hear tell of the kings of Europe having almost abolished the infernal invention of the bloody tribunal of the inquisition, and the Emperor and others making some very grand reformations, for the good and happiness of their subjects; it is to be hoped also that these exalted and liberal principles will lead them on to greater improvements in civlization and felicitation, and next to abolish that other diabolical invention of the African Slave Trade, and the West-India slavery.

But the supporters and favourers of slavery make use of many things as a pretence and an excuse in their own defence; such as, that they find that it was admitted under the Divine institution by Moses, as well as the long continued practice of different nations for ages; and that the Africans are peculiarly marked out by some signal prediction in nature and complection for that purpose.

This seems to be the greatest bulwark of defence which the advocates and favourers of slavery can advance, and what is generally talked of in their favour by those who do not understand it. I shall consider it in that view, whereby it will appear, that they deceive themselves and mislead others. Men are never more liable to be drawn into error, than when truth is made use of in a guileful manner to seduce them. Those who do not believe the scriptures to be a Divine revelation, cannot, consistently with themselves, make the law of Moses, or any mark or prediction they can find respecting any particular set of men, as found in the sacred writings, any reason that one class of men should enslave another. In that respect, all that they have to enquire into should be whether it be right, or wrong, that any part of the human species should enslave another; and when that is the case, the Africans, though not so learned, are just as wise as the Europeans; and when the matter is left to human wisdom, they are both liable to err. But what the light of nature, and the dictates of reason, when rightly considered, teach, is, that no man ought to enslave another; and some, who have been rightly guided thereby, have made noble defences for the universal natural rights and privileges of all men. But in this case, when the learned take neither revelation nor reason for their guide, they fall into as great, and worse errors, than the unlearned; for they only make use of that system of Divine wisdom, which should guide them into truth, when they can find or pick out any thing that will suit their purpose, or that they can pervert to such—the very means of leading themselves and others into error. And, in consequence thereof, the pretences that some men make use of for holding of slaves, must be evidently the grossest perversion of reason, as well as an inconsistent and diabolical use of the sacred writings. For it must be a strange perversion of reason, and a wrong use or disbelief of the sacred writings, when any thing found there is so perverted by them, and set up as a precedent and rule for men to commit wickedness. They had better have no reason, and no belief in the scriptures, and make no use of them at all, than only to believe, and make use of that which leads them into the most abominable evil and wickedness of dealing unjustly with their fellow men.

But this will appear evident to all men that believe the scriptures, that every reason necessary is given that they should be believed; and, in this case, that they afford us this information: "That all mankind did spring from one original, and that there are no different species among men. For God who made the world, hath made of one blood all the nations of men that dwell on all the face of the earth." Wherefore we may justly infer, as there are no inferior species, but all of one blood and of one nature, that there does not an inferiority subsist, or depend, on their colour, features or form, whereby some men make a pretence to enslave others;

and consequently, as they have all one creator, one original, made of one blood, and all brethren descended from one father, it never could be lawful and just for any nation, or people, to oppress and enslave another.

And again, as all the present inhabitants of the world sprang from the family of Noah, and were then all of one complexion, there is no doubt, but the difference which we now find, took its rise very rapidly after they became dispersed and settled on the different parts of the globe. There seems to be a tendency to this, in many instances, among children of the same parents, having different colour of hair and features from one another. And God alone who established the course of nature, can bring about and establish what variety he pleases; and it is not in the power of man to make one hair white or black. But among the variety which it hath pleased God to establish and caused to take place, we may meet with some analogy in nature, that as the bodies of men are tempered with a different degree to enable them to endure the respective climates of their habitations, so their colours vary, in some degree, in a regular gradation from the equator towards either of the poles. However, there are other incidental causes arising from time and place, which constitute the most distinguishing variety of colour, form, appearance and features, as peculiar to the inhabitants of one tract of country, and differing in something from those in another, even in the same latitudes, as well as from those in different climates. Long custom and the different way of living among the several inhabitants of the different parts of the earth, has a very great effect in distinguishing them by a difference of features and complexion. These effects are easy to be seen; as to the causes, it is sufficient for us to know, that all is the work of an Almighty hand. Therefore, as we find the distribution of the human species inhabiting the barren, as well as the most fruitful parts of the earth, and the cold as well as the most hot, differing from one another in complexion according to their situation; it may be reasonably, as well as religiously, inferred, that He who placed them in their various situations, hath extended equally his care and protection to all; and from thence, that it becometh unlawful to counteract his benignity, by reducing others of different complexions to undeserved bondage.

According, as we find that the difference of colour among men
is only incidental, and equally natural to all, and agreeable to the
place of their habitation; and that if nothing else be different or
contrary among them, but that of features and complexion, in that
respect, they are all equally alike entitled to the enjoyment of
every mercy and blessing of God. But there are some men of that
complexion, because they are not black, whose ignorance and insolence leads them to think, that those who are black, were
marked out in that manner by some signal interdiction or curse, as
originally descending from their progenitors. To those I must say,
that the only mark which we read of, as generally alluded to, and
by them applied wrongfully, is that mark or sign which God gave
to Cain, to assure him that he should not be destroyed. Cain understood by the nature of the crime he had committed, that the
law required death, or cutting off, as the punishment thereof. But
God in his providence doth not always punish the wicked in this
life according to their enormous crimes, (we are told, by a sacred
poet, that he saw the wicked flourishing like a green bay tree)
though he generally marks them out by some signal token of his
vengeance; and that is a sure token of it, when men become long
hardened in their wickedness. The denunciation that passed upon
Cain was, that he should be a fugitive and a vagabond on the earth,
bearing the curse and reproach of his iniquity; and the rest of men
were prohibited as much from meddling with him, or defiling
their hands by him, as it naturally is, not to pull down the dead
carcase of an atrocious criminal, hung up in chains by the laws of
his country. But allow the mark set upon Cain to have consisted in
a black skin, still no conclusion can be drawn at all, that any of the
black people are of that descent, as the whole posterity of Cain
were destroyed in the universal deluge.

Only Noah, a righteous and just man, who found grace in the
sight of God, and his three sons, Shem, Ham, and Japheth, and
their wives, eight persons, were preserved from the universal deluge, in the ark which Noah was directed to build. The three sons
of Noah had each children born after the flood, from whom all the
present world of men descended. But it came to pass, in the days
of Noah, that an interdiction, or curse, took place in the family of
Ham, and that the descendants of one of his sons should become

the servants of servants to their brethren, the descendants of Shem and Japheth. This affords a grand pretence for the supporters of the African slavery to build a false notion upon, as it is found by history that Africa, in general, was peopled by the descendants of Ham; but they forget, that the prediction has already been fulfilled as far as it can go.

There can be no doubt, that there was a shameful misconduct in Ham himself, by what is related of him; but the fault, according to the prediction and curse, descended only to the families of the descendants of his younger son, Canaan. The occasion was, that Noah, his father, had drank wine, and (perhaps unawares) became inebriated by it, and fell asleep in his tent. It seems that Ham was greatly deficient of that filial virtue as either becoming a father or a son, went into his father's tent, and, it may be supposed, in an undecent manner, he had suffered his own son, Canaan, so to meddle with, or uncover, his father, that he saw his nakedness; for which he did not check the audacious rudeness of Canaan, but went and told his brethren without in ridicule of his aged parent. This rude audacious behaviour of Canaan, and the obloquy of his father Ham, brought on him the curse of his grandfather, Noah, but he blessed Shem and Japheth for their decent and filial virtues, and denounced, in the spirit of prophecy, that Canaan should be their servant, and should serve them.

It may be observed, that it is a great misfortune for children, when their parents are not endowed with that wisdom and prudence which is necessary for the early initiation of their offspring in the paths of virtue and righteousness. Ham was guilty of the offence as well as his son; he did not pity the weakness of his father, who was overcome with wine in that day wherein, it is likely, he had some solemn work to do. But the prediction and curse rested wholly upon the offspring of Canaan, who settled in the land known by his name, in the west of Asia, as is evident from the sacred writings. The Canaanites became an exceeding wicked people, and were visited with many calamities, according to the prediction of Noah, for their abominable wickedness and idolatry.

Chederluomer, a descendant of Shem, reduced the Canaanitish kingdoms to a tributary subjection; and some time after, upon their revolt, invaded and pillaged their country. Not long after

Sodom, Gomorrah, Admah and Zeboim, four kingdoms of the Canaanites were overthrown for their great wickedness, and utterly destroyed by fire and brimstone from heaven. The Hebrews, chiefly under Moses, Joshua and Barak, as they were directed by God, cut off most of the other Canaanitish kingdoms, and reduced many of them to subjection and vassalage. Those who settled in the north-west of Canaan, and formed the once flourishing states of Tyre and Sidon, were by the Assyrians, the Chaldeans, and the Persians successively reduced to great misery and bondage; but chiefly by the Greeks, the Romans, and the Saracens, and lastly by the Turks, they were compleatly and totally ruined, and have no more since been a distinct people among the different nations. Many of the Canaanites who fled away in the Time of Joshua, became mingled with the different nations, and some historians think that some of them came to England, and settled about Cornwall, as far back as that time; so that, for any thing that can be known to the contrary, there may be some of the descendants of that wicked generation still subsisting among the slaveholders in the West-Indies. For if the curse of God ever rested upon them, or upon any other men, the only visible mark thereof was always upon those who committed the most outrageous acts of violence and oppression. But colour and complexion has nothing to do with that mark; every wicked man, and the enslavers of others, bear the stamp of their own iniquity, and that mark which was set upon Cain.

Now, the descendants of the other three sons of Ham, were not included under the curse of his father, and as they dispersed and settled on the different parts of the earth, they became also sundry distinct and very formidable nations. Cush, the oldest, settled in the south-west of Arabia, and his descendants were anciently known to the Hebrews by the name of Cushites, or Cushie; one of his sons, Nimrod, founded the kingdom of Babylon, in Asia; and the others made their descent southward, by the Red Sea, and came over to Abyssinia and Ethiopia, and, likely, dispersed themselves throughout all the southern and interior parts of Africa; and as they lived mostly under the torrid zone, or near the tropics, they became black, as being natural to the inhabitants of those sultry hot climates; and, in that case, their complexion bears the signification of the name of their original progenitor, Cush, as known by the Hebrews by that name, both on the east and on the west, beyond the Red Sea; but the Greeks called them Ethiopians, or black faced people. The Egyptians and Philistines were the descendants of Mizraim, and the country which they inhabited was called the land of Mizraim, and Africa, in general, was anciently called the whole land of Ham. Phut, another of his sons, also settled on the west of Egypt, and as the youngest were obliged to emigrate farthest, afterwards dispersed themselves chiefly up the south of the Mediterranean sea, towards Lybia and Mauritania, and might early mingle with some of the Cushites on the more southern, and, chiefly, on the western parts of Africa. But all these might be followed by some other families and tribes from Asia; and some think that Africa got its name from the King of Lybia marrying a daughter of Aphra, one of the descendants of Abraham, by Keturah.

But it may be reasonably supposed, that the most part of the black people in Africa, are the descendants of the Cushites, towards the east, the south, and interior parts, and chiefly of the Phutians towards the west; and the various revolutions and changes which have happened among them have rather been local than universal; so that whoever their original progenitors were, as descending from one generation to another, in a long continuance, it becomes natural for the inhabitants of that tract of country to be a dark black, in general, resembling the original progenitor Noah, for according to the researchers of the most learned, it is evidently that Noah was of an olive black in colour. The learned and thinking part of men, who can refer to history, must know, that nothing with respect to colour, nor any mark or curse from any original prediction, can in any-wise be more particularly ascribed to the Africans than to any other people of the human species, so as to afford any pretence why they should be more evil treated, persecuted and enslaved, than any other. Nothing but ignorance, & the dreams of a viciated imagination arising from the general countenance given to the evil practice of wicked men, to strengthen their hands in wickedness, could ever make any person to fancy otherwise, or ever to think that the stealing, kidnapping, enslaving, persecuting or killing a black man, is in any way

& manner less criminal, than the same evil treatment of any other man of another complexion.

But again, in answer to another part of the pretence which the favourers of slavery make use of in their defence, that slavery was an ancient custom, and that it became the prevalent and universal practice of many different barbarous nations for ages: This must be granted; but not because it was right, or any thing like right and equity. A lawful servitude was always necessary, and became contingent with the very nature of human society. But when the laws of civilization were broken through, and when the rights and properties of others were invaded, that brought the oppressed into a kind of compulsive servitude, though often not compelled to it by those whom they were obliged to serve. This arose from the different depredations and robberies which were committed upon one another; the helpless were obliged to seek protection from such as could support them, and to give unto them their service, in order to preserve themselves from want, and to deliver them from the injury either of men or beasts. For while civil society continued in a rude state, even among the establishers of kingdoms, when they became powerful and proud, as they wanted to enlarge their territories, they drove and expelled others from their peaceable habitations, who were not so powerful as themselves. This made those who were robbed of their substance, and drove from the place of their abode, make their escape to such as could and would help them; but when such a relief could not be found, they were obliged to submit to the yoke of their oppressors, who, in many cases, would not yield them any protection upon any terms. Wherefore, when their lives were in danger otherwise, and they could not find any help, they were obliged to sell themselves for bond servants to such as would buy them, when they could not get a service that was better. But as soon as buyers could be found, robbers began their traffic to ensnare others, and such as fell into their hands were carried captive by them, and were obliged to submit to their being sold by them into the hands of other robbers, for there are few buyers of men, who intend thereby to make them free, and such as they buy are generally subjected to hard labour and bondage. Therefore at all times, while a man is a slave, he is still in captivity, and under the jurisdiction of robbers; and every man who keeps a slave, is a robber, whenever he compels him to his service without giving him a just reward. The barely supplying his slave with some necessary things, to keep him in life, is no reward at all, that is only for his own sake and benefit; and the very nature of compulsion and taking away the liberty of others, as well as their property, is robbery; and that kind of service which subjects men to a state of slavery, must at all times, and in every circumstance, be a barbarous, inhuman and unjust dealing with our fellow men. A voluntary service and slavery are quite different things; but in ancient times, in whatever degree slavery was admitted, and whatever hardships they were, in general, subjected to, it was not nearly so bad as the modern barbarous and cruel West-India slavery.

Now, in respect to that kind of servitude which was admitted into the law of Moses, that was not contrary to the natural liberties of men, but a state of equity and justice, according as the nature and circumstances of the times required. There was no more harm in entering into a covenant with another man as a bond-servant, than there is for two men to enter into partnership the one with the other; and sometimes the nature of the case may be, and their business require it, that the one may find money and live at a distance and ease, and the other manage the business for him: So a bond-servant was generally the steward in a man's house, this is a particular custom in the country of Fantee, a faithful servant, or slave, as so called, generally becomes steward of his master's household, and frequently his heir. There was no harm in buying a man who was in a state of captivity and bondage by others, and keeping him in servitude till such time as his purchase was redeemed by his labour and service. And there could be no harm in paying a man's debts, and keeping him in servitude until such time as an equitable agreement of composition was paid by him. And so, in general, whether they had been bought or sold in order to pay their just debts when they became poor, or were bought from such as held them in an unlawful captivity, the state of bondage which they and their children fell under, among the Israelites, was into that of a vassalage state, which rather might be termed a deliverance from debt and captivity, than a state of slavery. In that vassalage state which they were reduced to, they had a tax of some service to pay, which might only be reckoned equivalent to a poor man in England paying rent for his cottage. In this fair land of liberty, there are many thousands of the inhabitants who have no right to so much land as an inch of ground to set their foot upon, so as to take up their residence upon it, without paying a lawful and reasonable vassalage of rent for it—and yet the whole community is free from slavery. And so, likewise, those who were reduced to a state of servitude, or vassalage, in the land of Israel, were not negociable like chattels and goods; nor could they be disposed of like cattle and beasts of burden, or ever transferred or disposed of without their own consent; and perhaps not one man in all the land of Israel would buy another man, unless that man was willing to serve him. And when any man had gotten such a servant, as he had entered into a covenant of agreement with, as a bond-servant, if the man liked his master and his service, he could not oblige him to go away; and it sometimes happened, that they refused to go out free when the year of jubilee came. But even that state of servitude which the Canaanites were reduced to, among those who survived the general overthrow of their country, was nothing worse, in many respects, than that of poor labouring people in any free country. Their being made hewers of wood and drawers of water, were laborious employments; but they were paid for it in such a manner as the nature of their service required, and were supplied with abundance of such necessaries of life as they and their families had need of; and they were at liberty, if they chose, to go away, there was no restriction laid on them. They were not hunted after, and a reward offered for their heads, as it is the case in the West-Indies for any that can find a strayed slave; and he who can bring such a head warm reeking with his blood, as a token that he had murdered him—inhuman and shocking to think!—he is paid for it; and, cruel and dreadful as it is, that law is still in force in some of the British colonies.

But the Canaanites, although they were predicted to be reduced to a state of servitude, and bondage to that poor and menial employment, fared better than the West-India slaves; for when they were brought into that state of servitude, they were often employed in an honourable service. The Nethenims, and others, were to assist in the sacred solemnities and worship of God at the Temple of Jerusalem. They had the same laws and immunities respecting the solemn days and sabbaths, as their masters the Israelites, and they were to keep and observe them. But they were not suffered, much less required, to labour in their own spots of useful ground on the days of sacred rest from worldly employment; and that, if they did not improve the culture of it, in these times and seasons, they might otherwise perish for hunger and want; as it is the case of the West-India slaves, by their inhuman, infidel, hard-hearted masters. And, therefore, this may be justly said, that whatever servitude that was, or by whatever name it may be called, that the service which was required by the people of Israel in old time, was of a far milder nature than that which became the prevalent practice of other different and barbarous nations; and, if compared with modern slavery, it might be called liberty, equity, and felicity, in respect to that abominable, mean, beastly, cruel, bloody slavery carried on by the inhuman, barbarous Europeans, against the poor unfortunate Black Africans.

But again, this may be averred, that the servitude which took place under the sanction of the divine law, in the time of Moses, and what was enjoined as the civil and religious polity of the people of Israel, was in nothing contrary to the natural rights and common liberties of men, though it had an appearance as such for great and wise ends. The Divine Law Giver, in his good providence, for great and wise purposes intended by it, has always admitted into the world riches and poverty, prosperity and adversity, high and low, rich and poor; and in such manner, as in all their variety and difference, mutation and change, there is nothing set forth in the written law, by Moses, contrary, unbecoming, or inconsistent with that goodness of himself, as the wise and righteous Governor of the Universe. Those things admitted into the law, that had a seeming appearance contrary to the natural liberties of men, were only so admitted for a local time, to point out, and to establish, and to give instruction thereby, in an analogous allusion to other things.

And therefore, so far as I have been able to consult the law written by Moses, concerning that kind of servitude admitted by it, I can find nothing imported thereby, in the least degree, to warrant the modern practice of slavery. But, on the contrary, and what was principally intended thereby, and in the most particular manner, as respecting Christians, that it contains the strongest prohibition against it. And every Christian man, that can read his Bible, may find that which is of the greatest importance for himself to know, implied even under the very institution of bond-servants; and that the state of bondage which the law denounces and describes, was thereby so intended to point out something necessary, as well as similar to all the other ritual and ceremonial services; and that the whole is set forth in such a manner, as containing the very essence and foundation of the Christian religion. And, moreover, that it must appear evident to any Christian believer, that it was necessary that all these things should take place, and as the most beautiful fabric of Divine goodness, that in all their variety, and in all their forms, they should stand recorded under the sanction of the Divine law.

And this must be observed, that it hath so pleased the Almighty Creator, to establish all the variety of things in nature, different complexions and other circumstances among men, and to record the various transactions of his own providence; with all the ceremonial economy written in the books of Moses, as more particularly respecting and enjoined to the Israelitish nation and people, for the use of sacred language, in order to convey wisdom to the fallen apostate human race. Wherefore, all the various things established, admitted and recorded, whether natural, moral, typical or ceremonial, with all the various things in nature referred to, were so ordered and admitted, as figures, types and emblems, and other symbolical representations, to bring forward, usher in, hold forth and illustrate that most amazing transaction, and the things concerning it, of all things the most wonderful that ever could take place amongst the universe of intelligent beings; as in that, and the things concerning it, of the salvation of apostate men, and the wonderful benignity of their Almighty Redeemer.

Whoever will give a serious and unprejudiced attention to the various things alluded to in the language of sacred writ, must see reason to believe that they imply a purpose and design far more glorious and important, than what seems generally to be understood by them; and to point to objects and events far more extensive and interesting, than what is generally ascribed to them. But

as the grand eligibility and importance of those things, implied
and pointed out in sacred writ, and the right understanding
thereof, belongs to the sublime science of metaphysics and theology to enforce, illustrate and explain, I shall only select a few instances, which I think have a relation to my subject in hand.

Among other things it may be considered, that the different
colours and complexions among men were intended for another
purpose and design, than that of being only eligible in the variety
of the scale of nature. And, accordingly, had it been otherwise, and
if there had never been any black people among the children of
men, nor any spotted leopards among the beasts of the earth, such
an instructive question, by the prophet could not have been proposed, as this, *Can the Ethiopian change his skin, or the leopard his
spots? Then, may ye also do good, that are accustomed to do evil.*
Jer[emiah] xiii. 23. The instruction intended by this is evident, that
it was a convincing and forcible argument to shew, that none
among the fallen and apostate race of men, can by any effort of
their own, change their nature from the blackness and guilt of the
sable dye of sin and pollution, or alter their way accustomed to do
evil, from the variegated spots of their iniquity; and that such a
change is as impossible to be totally and radically effected by
them, as it is for a black man to change the colour of his skin, or
the leopard to alter his spots. But these differences of a natural variety amongst the things themselves, is in every respect equally innocent, and what they cannot alter or change, was made to be so,
and in the most eligible and primary design, were so, intended for
the very purposes of instructive language to men. And by these
extreme differences of colour, it was intended to point out and
shew to the white man, that there is a sinful blackness in his own
nature, which he can no more change, than the external blackness
which he sees in another can be rendered otherwise; and it likewise holds out to the black man, that the sinful blackness of his
own nature is such, that he can no more alter, than the outward
appearance of his colour can be brought to that of another. And
this is imported by it, that there is an inherent evil in every man,
contrary to that which is good; and that all men are like Ethiopians (even God's elect) in a state of nature and unregeneracy, they
are black with original sin, and spotted with actual transgression,

which they cannot reverse. But to this truth, asserted of blackness, I must add another glorious one. All thanks and eternal praise be to God! His infinite wisdom and goodness has found out a way of renovation, and has opened a fountain through the blood of Jesus, for sin and for uncleanness, wherein all the stains and blackest dyes of sin and pollution can be washed away for ever, and the darkest sinner be made to shine as the brightest angel in heaven. And for that end and purpose, God alone has appointed all the channels of conveyance of the everlasting Gospel for these healing and purifying streams of the water of life to run in, and to bring life and salvation, with light and gladness to men; but he denounces woe to those who do not receive it themselves, but hinder and debar others who would, from coming to those salutary streams for life: Yet not alone confined to these, nor hindered in his purpose by any opposers, HE, who can open the eyes of the blind, and make the deaf to hear, can open streams in the desert, and make his benignity to flow, and his salvation to visit, even the meanest and most ignorant man, in the darkest shades of nature, as well as the most learned on the earth; and he usually carries on his own gracious work of quickening and redeeming grace, in a secret, sovereign manner. To this I must again observe, and what I chiefly intended by this similitude, that the external blackness of the Ethiopians, is as innocent and natural, as spots in the leopards; and that the difference of colour and complexion, which it hath pleased God to appoint among men, are no more unbecoming unto either of them, than the different shades of the rainbow are unseemly to the whole, or unbecoming to any part of that apparent arch. It does not alter the nature and quality of a man, whether he wears a black or a white coat, whether he puts it on or strips it off, he is still the same man. And so likewise, when a man comes to die, it makes no difference whether he was black or white, whether he was male or female, whether he was great or small, or whether he was old or young; none of these differences alter the essentiality of the man, any more than he had wore a black or a white coat and thrown it off for ever.

Another form of instruction for the same purpose, may be taken from the slavery and oppression which men have committed upon one another, as well as that kind of bondage and servitude which was admitted under the sanction of the Divine law. But there is nothing set forth in the law as a rule, or any thing recorded therein that can stand as a precedent, or make it lawful, for men to practice slavery; nor can any laws in favour of slavery be deduced from thence, for to enslave men, be otherwise, than as unwarrantable, as it would be unnecessary and wrong, to order and command the sacrifices of beasts to be still continued. Now the great thing imported by it, and what is chiefly to be deduced from it in this respect, is, that so far as the law concerning bondservants, and that establishment of servitude, as admitted in the Mosaical institution, was set forth, it was thereby intended to prefigure and point out, that spiritual subjection and bondage to sin, that all mankind, by their original transgression, were fallen into. All men in their fallen depraved state, being under a spirit of bondage, sunk into a nature of brutish carnality, and by the lusts thereof, they are carried captive and enslaved; and the consequence is, that they are sold under sin and in bondage to iniquity, and carried captive by the devil at his will. This being the case, the thing proves itself; for if there had been no evil and sin amongst men, there never would have been any kind of bondage, slavery and oppression found amongst them; and if there was none of these things to be found, the great cause of it could not, in the present situation of men, be pointed out to them in that eligible manner as it is. Wherefore it was necessary that something of that bondage and servitude should be admitted into the ritual law for a figurative use, which, in all other respects and circumstances, was, in itself, contrary to the whole tenure of the law, and naturally in itself unlawful for men to practice.

Nothing but heavenly wisdom, and heavenly grace, can teach men to understand. The most deplorable of all things is, that the dreadful situation of our universal depraved state, which all mankind lyeth under, is such, that those who are not redeemed in time, must for ever continue to be the subjects of eternal bondage and misery. Blessed be God! he hath appointed and set up a deliverance, and the Saviour of Men is an Almighty Redeemer. When God, the Almighty Redeemer and Saviour of his people, brought his Israel out of Egypt and temporal bondage, it was intended and designed thereby, to set up an emblematical representation of their

deliverance from the power and captivity of sin, and from the dominion of that evil and malignant spirit, who had with exquisite
subtilty and guile at first seduced the original progenitors of
mankind. And when they were brought to the promised land, and
had gotten deliverance, and subdued their enemies under them,
they were to reign over them; and their laws respecting bond-
servants, and other things of that nature, were to denote, that they
were to keep under and in subjection the whole body of their evil
affections and lusts. This is so declared by the Apostle, that the
law is spiritual, and intended for spiritual uses. The general state of
slavery which took place in the world, among other enormous
crimes of wicked men might have served for an emblem and similitude of our spiritual bondage and slavery to sin; but, unless it had
been admitted into the spiritual and divine law, it could not have
stood and become an emblem that there was any spiritual restoration and deliverance afforded to us. By that which is evil in captivity and slavery among men, we are thereby so represented to be
under a like subjection to sin; but by what is instituted in the law
by Moses, in that respect we are thereby represented as Israel to
have dominion over sin, and to rule over and keep in subjection all
our spiritual enemies. And, therefore, any thing which had a seeming appearance in favour of slavery, so far as it was admitted into
the law, was to shew that it was not natural and innocent, like that
of different colours among men, but as necessary to be made an
emblem of what was intended by it, and, consequently, as it stands
enjoined among other typical representations, was to shew that
every thing of any evil appearance of it was to be removed, and to
end with the other typical and ceremonial injunctions, when the
time of that dispensation was over. This must appear evident to all
Christian believers; and since therefore all these things are fulfilled
in the establishment of Christianity, there is now nothing remaining in the law for a rule of practice to men, but the ever abiding
obligations, and ever binding injunctions of moral rectitude, justice, equity and righteousness. All the other things in the Divine
law, are for spiritual uses and similitudes, for giving instruction
to the wise, and understanding to the upright in heart, that the
man of God may be perfect, thoroughly furnished unto all good
works.

Among other things also, the wars of the Israelites, and the extirpation of the Canaanites, and other circumstances as recorded
in sacred history, were intended to give instruction to men, but
have often been perverted to the most flagrant abuse, and even inverted to the most notorious purposes, for men to embolden
themselves to commit wickedness. Every possession that men enjoy upon earth are the gifts of God, and he who gives them, may
either take them away again from men, or he may take men away
themselves from the earth, as it pleaseth him. But who dare, even
with Lucifer, the malignant devourer of the world, think to imitate
the most High? The extirpation of the Canaanites out of their
land, was so ordered, not only to punish them for their idolatry
and abominable wickedness, but also to shew forth the honour of
his power, and the sovereignty of him who is the only potent one
that reigneth over the nations; that all men at that time might learn
to fear and know him who is Jehovah; and ever since that it might
continue a standing memorial of him, and a standard of honor
unto him who doth according to his will among the armies of
heaven, and whatever pleaseth him with the inhabitants of the
earth. And, in general, these transactions stand recorded for an
emblematical use and similitude, in the spiritual warfare of every
true Israelite throughout all the ages of time. Every real believer
and valiant champion in the knowledge and faith of their Omnipotent Saviour and Almighty Deliverer, as the very nature of
Christianity requires and enjoins, knoweth the use of these things,
*and they know how to endure hardness as good soldiers of Jesus
Christ.* They have many battles to fight with their unbelief, the
perverseness of their nature, evil tempers and besetting sins, these
Canaanites which still dwell in their land. They are so surrounded
with adversaries, that they have need always to be upon their
guard, and to have all their armour on. They are *commanded to
cast off the works of darkness, and to put on the whole armour of
righteousness and light; and that they may be strong in the Lord,
and in the power of his might.* For it is required *that they should
be able to stand against the wiles of the devil, the powers of the
rulers of the darkness of this world, against spiritual wickedness in
high places.* And as their foes are *mighty and tall like the Anakims,
and fenced up to heaven,* they must be mighty warriors, *men of*

*renown, valiant for the truth, strong in the faith, fighting the
Lord's battles, and overcoming all their enemies, through the dear
might of the Great Captain of their salvation.* In this warfare,
should they meet with some mighty *Agag,* some strong corruption, or besetting sin, they are commanded *to cut it down,* and
with the sword of Samuel *to hew it to pieces before the Lord.* This,
in its literal sense, may seem harsh, as if Samuel had been cruel;
and so will our sins, and other sinners insinuate and tell us not to
mind such things as the perfect law of God requires. But if we
consider that the Lord God who breathed into man the breath of
life, can suspend and take it away when he pleaseth, and that there
is not a moment we have to exist, wherein that life may not be suspended before the next: it was therefore of an indifferent matter
for that man Agag, when the Lord, who hath the breath and life of
every man in his hand, had appointed him at that time to die, for
his great wickedness and the murders committed by him, whether
he was slain by Samuel or any other means. But what Samuel, the
servant of the Lord, did in that instance, was in obedience to his
voice, and in itself a righteous deed, and a just judgment upon
Agag. And the matter imported by it, was also intended to shew
that all our Amalekite sins, and even the chief and darling of them,
the avaricious and covetous Agags, should be cut off for ever. But
if we spare them, and leave them to remain alive in stubborn disobedience to the law and commandments of God, we should in
that case; be like Saul, cut off ourselves from the kingdom of his
grace. According to this view, it may suffice to shew (and what infinite wisdom intended, no doubt) that a wise and righteous use
may be made of those very things, which otherwise are generally
perverted to wrong purposes.

And now, as to these few instances which I have collected from
that sacred hypothesis, whereby it is shewn, that other things are
implied and to be understood by the various incidents as recorded
in sacred writ, with a variety of other things in nature, bearing an
analogous allusion to things of the greatest importance for every
Christian man to know and understand; and that the whole of the
ritual law, though these things themselves are not to be again repeated, is of that nature and use as never to be forgot. And therefore to suppose, or for any Christians to say, that they have

nothing to do with those things now in the right use thereof, and what was intended and imported thereby respecting themselves, would be equally as absurd as to hear them speaking in the language of devils; and they might as well say as they did, when speaking out of the demoniac, that they have nothing to do with Christ.

Having thus endeavoured to shew, and what, I think, must appear evident and obvious, that none of all these grand pretensions, as generally made use of by the favourers of slavery, to encourage and embolden them, in that iniquitous traffic, can have any foundation or shadow of truth to support them; and that there is nothing in nature, reason, and scripture can be found, in any manner or way, to warrant the enslaving of black people more than others.

But I am aware that some of these arguments will weigh nothing against such men as do not believe the scriptures themselves, nor care to understand; but let them be aware not to make use of these things against us which they do not believe, or whatever pretence they may have for committing violence against us. Any property taken away from others, whether by stealth, fraud, or violence, must be wrong; but to take away men themselves, and keep them in slavery, must be worse. *Skin for skin, all that a man hath would he give for his life;* and would rather lose his property to any amount whatever, than to have his liberty taken away, and be kept as a slave. It must be an inconceivable fallacy to think otherwise: none but the inconsiderate, most obdurate and stubborn, could ever think that it was right to enslave others. *But the way of the wicked is brutish: his own iniquity shall take the wicked himself, and he shall be holden with the cords of his sins: he shall die without instruction, and in the greatness of his folly he shall go astray.*

Among the various species of men that commit rapine, and violence, and murders, and theft, upon their fellow-creatures, like the ravenous beasts of the night, prowling for their prey, there are also those that set out their heads in the open day, opposing all the obligations of civilization among men, and breaking through all the laws of justice and equity to them, and making even the very things which are analogous to the obligations, which ought to warn and prohibit them, a pretence for their iniquity and injustice.

Such are the insidious merchants and pirates that gladen their oars with the carnage and captivity of men, and the vile negociators and enslavers of the human species. The prohibitions against them are so strong, that, in order to break through and to commit the most notorious and flagrant crimes with impunity, they are obliged to oil their poisonous pretences with various perversions of sundry transactions of things even in sacred writ, that the acrimonious points of their arsenic may be swallowed down the better, and the evil effects of their crimes appear the less. In this respect, instead of *the sacred history of the Israelitish nation being made profitable to them, for doctrine, for reproof, for correction, and for instruction in righteousness,* as it was intended, *and given to men* for that purpose; but, instead thereof, the wars of the Israelites, the extirpation and subjection of the Canaanites, and other transactions of that kind, are generally made use of by wicked men as precedents and pretences to encourage and embolden themselves to commit cruelty and slavery on their fellow-creatures: and the merciless depredators, negociators, and enslavers of men, revert to the very ritual law of Moses as a precedent for their barbarity, cruelty, and injustice; which law, though devoid of any iniquity, as bearing a parallel allusion to other things signified thereby, can afford no precedent for their evil way, in any shape or view: what was intended by it is fulfilled, and in no respect, or any thing like it, can be repeated again, without transgressing and breaking through every other injunction, precept, and command of the just and tremendous law of God.

The consequence of their apostacy from God, and disobedience to his law, became a snare to those men in times of old, who departed from it; and because of their disobedience and wickedness, the several nations, which went astray after their own abominations, were visited with many dreadful calamities and judgments. But to set up the ways of the wicked for an example, and to make the laws respecting their suppression, and the judgments that were inflicted upon them for their iniquity, and even the written word of God, and the transactions of his providence, to be reversed and become precedents and pretences for men to commit depredations and extirpations, and for enslaving and negociating or merchandizing the human species, must be horrible wickedness indeed, and sinning with a high hand. And it cannot be thought otherwise, but that the abandoned aggressors, among the learned nations will, in due time, as the just reward of their aggravated iniquity, be visited with some more dreadful and tremendous judgments of the righteous vengeance of God, than what even befel to the Canaanites of old.

And it may be considered further, that to draw any inferences in favour of extirpation, slavery, and negociation of men, from the written word of God, or from any thing else in the history and customs of different nations, as a precedent to embolden wicked men in their wickedness; cannot be more wicked, ridiculous, and absurd to shew any favour to these insidious negociators and enslavers, than it would be to stand and laugh, and look on with a brutal and savage impunity, at beholding the following supposition transacted. Suppose two or three half-witted foolish fellows happened to come past a crowd of people, gazing at one which they had hung up by the neck on a tree, as a victim suffering for breaking the laws of his country; and suppose these foolish fellows went on a little way in a bye path, and found some innocent person, not suspecting any harm till taken hold of by them, and could not deliver himself from them, and just because they had seen among the crowd of people which they came past, that there had been a man hung by the neck, they took it into their foolish wicked heads to hang up the poor innocent man on the next tree, and just did as they had seen others do, to please their own fancy and base foolishness, to see how he would swing. Now if any of the other people happened to come up to them, and saw what they had done, would they hesitate a moment to determine between themselves and these rascals which had done wickedness? Surely not; they would immediately take hold of such stupid wicked wretches, if it was in their power, and for their brutishness-sake, have them chained in a Bedlam, or hung on a gibbet. But what would these wretches say for themselves? That they saw others do so, and they thought there had been no harm in it, and they only did as they had seen the crowd of people do before. A poor rascally excuse indeed! But not a better excuse than this, can the brutish enslavers and negociators of men find in all the annals of history. The ensnarers, negociators, and oppressors

of men, have only to become more abandoned in wickedness than
these supposed wretches could be; and to pass on in the most
abominable bye paths of wickedness, and make every thing that
they can see an example for their brutal barbarity; and whether it
be a man hanged for his crimes, or an innocent man for the
wretched wickedness of others; right or wrong it makes no difference to them, if they can only satisfy their own wretched and brutal avarice. Whether it be the Israelites subjecting the Canaanites
for their crimes, or the Canaanites subjecting the Israelites, to
gratify their own wickedness, it makes no difference to them.
When they see some base wretches like themselves ensnaring, enslaving, oppressing, whipping, starving with hunger, and cruelly
torturing and murdering some of the poor helpless part of mankind, they would think no harm in it, they would do the same.
Perhaps the Greeks and Romans, and other crowds of barbarous
nations have done so before; they can make that a precedent, and
think no harm in it, they would still do the same, and worse than
any barbarous nations ever did before; and if they look backwards
and forwards they can find no better precedent, ancient or modern,
than that which is wicked, mean, brutish, and base. To practise
such abominable parallels of wickedness of ensnaring, negociating,
and enslaving men, is the scandal and shame of mankind; and what
must we think of their crimes? Let the groans and cries of the murdered, and the cruel slavery of the Africans tell!

They that can stand and look on and behold no evil in the infamous traffic of slavery must be sunk to a wonderful degree of insensibility; but surely those that can delight in that evil way for
their gain, and be pleased with the wickedness of the wicked, and
see no harm in subjecting their fellow-creatures to slavery, and
keeping them in a state of bondage and subjection as a brute, must
be wretchedly brutish indeed. But so bewitched are the general
part of mankind with some sottish or selfish principle, that they
care nothing about what is right or wrong, any farther than their
own interest leads them to; and when avarice leads them on they
can plead a thousand excuses for doing wrong, or letting others do
wickedly, so as they have any advantage by it, to their own gratifi-
cation and use. That sottish and selfish principle, without concern
and discernment among men is such, that if they can only prosper

themselves, they care nothing about the miserable situation of others: and hence it is, that even those who are elevated to high rank of power and affluence, and as becoming their eminent stations, have opportunity of extending their views afar, yet they can shut their eyes at this enormous evil of the slavery and commerce of the human species, and, contrary to all the boasted accomplishments, and fine virtues of the civilized and enlightened nations, they can sit still and let the torrent of robbery, slavery, and oppression roll on.

There is a way which seemeth good unto a man, but the end thereof are the ways of death. Should the enslavers of men think to justify themselves in their evil way, or that it can in any possible way be right for them to subject others to slavery; it is but charitable to evince and declare unto them, that they are those who have gone into that evil way of brutish stupidity as well as wickedness, that they can behold nothing of moral rectitude and equity among men but in the gloomy darkness of their own hemisphere, like the owls and night-hawks, who can see nothing but mist and darkness in the meridian blaze of day. When men forsake the paths of virtue, righteousness, justice, and mercy, and become vitiated in any evil way, all their pretended virtues, sensibility, and prudence among men, however high they may shine in their own, and of others estimation, will only appear to be but specious villainy at last. That virtue which will ever do men any good in the end, is as far from that which some men call such, as the gaudy appearance of a glow-worm in the dark is to the intrinsic value and lustre of a diamond: for if a man hath not love in his heart to his fellow-creatures, with a generous philanthropy diffused throughout his whole soul, all his other virtues are not worth a straw.

The whole law of God is founded upon love, and the two grand branches of it are these: *Thou shalt love the Lord thy God with all thy heart and with all thy soul; and thou shalt love thy neighbour as thyself.* And so it was when man was first created and made: they were created male and female, and pronounced to be in the image of God, and, as his representative, to have dominion over the lower creation: and their Maker, who is love, and the intellectual Father of Spirits, blessed them, and commanded them to arise in a bond of union of nature and of blood, each being a brother

and a sister together, and each the lover and the loved of one another. But when they were envied and invaded by the grand enslaver of men, all their jarring inconsistency arose, and those who
adhered to their pernicious usurper soon became envious, hateful,
and hating one another. And those who go on to injure, ensnare,
oppress, and enslave their fellow-creatures, manifest their hatred
to men, and maintain their own infamous dignity and vassalage, as
the servants of sin and the devil: but the man who has any honour
as a man scorns their ignominious dignity: the noble philan-
thropist looks up to his God and Father as his only sovereign; and
he looks around on his fellow men as his brethren and friends; and
in every situation and case, however mean and contemptible they
may seem, he endeavours to do them good: and should he meet
with one in the desert, whom he never saw before, he would hail
him my brother! my sister! my friend! how fares it with thee?
And if he can do any of them any good it would gladden every
nerve of his soul.

But as there is but *one law and one manner* prescribed universally for all mankind, *for you, and for the stranger that sojourneth
with you,* and wheresoever they may be scattered throughout the
face of the whole earth, the difference of superiority and inferiority which are found subsisting amongst them is no way incompatible with the universal law of love, honor, righteousness, and
equity; so that a free, voluntary, and sociable servitude, which is
the very basis of human society, either civil or religious, whereby
we serve one another that we may be served, or do good that good
may be done unto us, is in all things requisite and agreeable to all
law and justice. But the taking away the natural liberties of men,
and compelling them to any involuntary slavery or compulsory
service, is an injury and robbery contrary to all law, civilization,
reason, justice, equity, and humanity: therefore when men break
through the laws of God, and the rules of civilization among men,
and go forth to steal, to rob, to plunder, to oppress and to enslave,
and to destroy their fellow-creatures, the laws of God and man require that they should be suppressed, and deprived of their liberty,
or perhaps their lives.

But justice and equity does not always reside among men, even
where some considerable degree of civilization is maintained; if it

had, that most infamous reservoir of public and abandoned merchandizers and enslavers of men would not have been suffered so
long, nor the poor unfortunate Africans, that never would have
crossed the Atlantic to rob them, would not have become their
prey. But it is just as great and as heinous a transgression of the
law of God to steal, kidnap, buy, sell, and enslave any one of the
Africans, as it would be to ensnare any other man in the same
manner, let him be who he will. And suppose that some of the
African pirates had been as dextrous as the Europeans, and that
they had made excursions on the coast of Great-Britain or elsewhere, and though even assisted by some of their own insidious
neighbours, for there may be some men even among them vile
enough to do such a thing if they could get money by it; and that
they should carry off their sons and their daughters, wives and
friends, to a perpetual and barbarous slavery, you would certainly
think that those African pirates were justly deserving of any punishment that could be put upon them. But the European pirates
and merchandizers of the human species, let them belong to what
nation they will, are equally as bad; and they have no better right
to steal, kidnap, buy, and carry away and sell the Africans, than
the Africans would have to carry away any of the Europeans in
the same barbarous and unlawful manner.

But again, let us follow the European piracy to the West-Indies,
or any where among Christians, and this law of the *Lord Christ*
must stare every infidel slave-holder in the face, *And as ye would
that men should do to you, do ye also to them likewise.* But there is
no slave-holder would like to have himself enslaved, and to be
treated as a dog, and sold like a beast; and therefore the slave-
holders, and merchandizers of men, transgress this plain law, and
they commit a greater violation against it, and act more contrary
unto it, than it would be for a parcel of slaves to assume authority
over their masters, and compel them to slavery under them; for, if
that was not doing as they would wish to be done to, it would be
doing, at least, as others do to them, in a way equally as much and
more wrong. But our Divine Lord and *Master Christ* also teacheth
men to *forgive one another their trespasses,* and that we are not to
do evil because others do so, and to revenge injuries done unto us.
Wherefore it is better, and more our duty, to suffer ourselves to be

lashed and cruelly treated, than to take up the task of their barbarity. The just law of God requires an equal retaliation and restoration for every injury that men may do to others, to shew the greatness of the crime; but the law of forbearance, righteousness and forgiveness, forbids the retaliation to be sought after, when it would be doing as great an injury to them, without any reparation or benefit to ourselves. For what man can restore an eye that he may have deprived another of, and if even a double punishment was to pass upon him, and that he was to lose both his eyes for the crime, that would make no reparation to the other man whom he had deprived of one eye. And so, likewise, when a man is carried captive and enslaved, and maimed and cruelly treated, that would make no adequate reparation and restitution for the injuries he had received, if he was even to get the person who had ensnared him to be taken captive and treated in the same manner. What he is to seek after is a deliverance and protection for himself, and not a revenge upon others. Wherefore the honest and upright, like the just Bethlehem Joseph, cannot think of doing evil, nor require an equal retaliation for such injuries done to them, so as to revenge themselves upon others, for that which would do them no manner of good. Such vengeance belongeth unto the Lord, and he will render vengeance and recompence to his enemies and the violaters of his law.

But thus saith the law of God: *If a man be found stealing any of his neighbours, or he that stealeth a man (let him be who he will) and selleth him or that maketh merchandize of him, or if he be found in his hand, then that thief shall die.* However, in all modern slavery among Christians, who ought to know this law, they have not had any regard to it. Surely if any law among them admits of death as a punishment for robbing or defrauding others of their money or goods, it ought to be double death, if it was possible, when a man is robbed of himself, and sold into captivity and cruel bondage.

The crying sin of tolerating slavery has long need[ed] redress, and many pious men who are raising up as bulwarks of defence against the efforts of error, has made some laudable exertions towards a total suppression of that horrible traffic; but, whilst the hearts of mankind are allured by the goddess of avarice and infidelity, combined together. We need not suppose that there can be much good done, in proportion to the laudable exertions now made. But, let men remember, that the judgment of God slumbereth not.

The higher any man is exalted in power and dignity, the more eminent is his danger, though he may not live to see the evil that may eventually contribute to his country, because of his disobedience to the law and commandments of God. All men in authority, kings in general, who are exalted to the most conspicuous offices of superiority, while they take upon themselves to be the administrators of righteousness and justice to others, they become equally responsible for admitting or suffering others under their authority to do wrong. Wherefore the highest offices of authority among men, are not so desirable as some may be apt to conceive; it was so considered by the virtuous queen Anne, when she was called to the royal dignity, as she declared to the council of the nation, that it was a heavy weight and burden brought upon her. For kings are the ministers of God, to do justice, and not to bear the sword in vain, but to revenge wrath upon them that do evil. But if they do not in such a case as this, the cruel oppressions of thousands, and the blood of the murdered Africans who are slain by the sword of cruel avarice, must rest upon their own guilty heads; and therefore they ought to let no companies of insidious merchants, or any guileful insinuations of wicked men, prevail upon them to establish laws of iniquity, and to carry on a trade of oppression and injustice; but they ought to consider such as the worst of foes and rebels, and greater enemies than any that can rise up against their temporal dignity. From all such enemies, good Lord, deliver the kings! for it is far better to lose a temporal kingdom, than only to endanger the happiness and enjoyment of an eternal one. Should this small Abstract obtain the approbation of my Readers, I shall publish the remainder of the Work, in a short time.

QUOBNA OTTOBOUH [sic] CUGOANO,
A Native of the Gold Coast,
AFRICA.

F I N I S.

THE Author *begs Leave to inform his Friends and the Public in general, particularly those humane and charitable Gentlemen, who Supported his original Thoughts and Sentiments on the* Evil of Slavery, *that he has only printed this Abstract, merely to convey Instructions to his* oppressed Countrymen, *and as much as possible to excite their Attention to the religious Observance of the* Laws *of* GOD.

He further proposes to open a School, *for all such of his Complexion as are desirous of being acquainted with the Knowledge of the* Christian Religion *and the* Laws *of* Civilization.[4] *His sole Motive for these Undertakings, are, that he finds several of his Countrymen, here in England, who have not only been in an unlawful Manner brought away from their peaceable Habitations, but also deprived of every Blessing of the Christian Knowledge, by their various Masters and Mistresses, either through the motives of Avarice, or the want of the Knowledge of their own Religion, which must be a great Dishonor to Christianity.*

Nothing engages my desire so much as the Descendants of my Countrymen, so as to have them educated in the Duties and Knowledge of that Religion which all good Christian People enjoy; these Blessings cannot be well conveyed without Learning, *and as most of my Countrymen are Poor and cannot afford it, and others are so much engaged in Servitude, that they have little Time to attend to it; my Design, therefore, is to open a Place for the Instruction of such as can attend; but to accomplish it, I must wholly depend on the humane and charitable* Contributions *of those* Ladies *and* Gentlemen *who are inclinable to Support this Undertaking. I am not excluding some other young Persons, who need to be taught* Reading, *&c. but my Design is chiefly intended for my Countrymen.*

SUBSCRIBERS NAMES.

A

Mr. Adams, Mount-street, Berkley square.

Mrs. Allen, Oxford-street.

Mr. Allam, Carmile-buildings Portman-square.

Mr. Allwood, Great Russel-street, Bloomsbury.

Mr. Alexander, St. Anne's-court, Soho.

B

The Right Hon. Lord and Lady Barnard, St. James's-square.

Mr. Becket, Old Bond-street.

Mr. Barrat, Paddington-green.

Mr. Baptize, Ogle-street, Mary-le-bone.

Mr. Burkeny Young, Crown-court, St. Anne.

Mr. Brablytroy, John-street, Oxford-market.

Mr. Bowie, Edgware-road.

Mr. Baily, Adam-street, Portman-square.

Mr. Bovie, Titchfield-street, Mary-le-bone.

Mr. Brown, Edgware-road.

Mr. Brewer, ditto.

Mr. Bennet, ditto.

Mr. and Mrs. Bradbury, ditto.

Mr. Boston, Cheapside.

Mr. Browne, Oxford-street.

Mr. Bridgewater, Barclay-buildings, Holborn.

Mr. Beckford, Oxford-street.

C

Mr. Campbell, Oxford-street.

Mr. Cosway, Stratford-place.

Mr. Cuzons, Paddington-green.

Mr. Carry, Oxford-street.

Mr. Camburn, Edgware-road.

Mr. Charpontiare, Cumberland-street.

Mr. Crook, Carmile-buildings.

Mr. Crossland, James-street, Oxford-street.

Mr. Crigg, Holborn.

Mr. Collings, Cheapside.

D

Mr. Dumanuduc, Bloomsbury-square.

Mr. Davison, Great Warner-street, Hatton-garden.

Mr. Douglass, Leicester-fields.

Mr. Daves, Jermyn-street, St. James's.

Mr. Davise, Cheapside.

Mr. Durnford, Cumberland-street.

Mr. Dent, Royal-exchange.

Mr. Daves, Queen-street,
　Southwark.
Mr. Dodsly, Cumberland-street.

E
Mr. Ellis, Upper Rathbone-place.
Mr. Elliott, [sic]
Mr. Enoch, Oxford-street.
Mr. Ebdon, Crispin-street,
　Mary-le-bone.
Mr. Emery, Wardour-street,
　Soho.

F
The Right Hon. Viscount Field-
　ing, Chesterfield-street,
　May-fair.
Mr. Fox, Edgware-road.
Mr. Followes, Warwick-street,
　Golden-square.
Mr. Frall, Oxford-street.
Mr. Ferral, Portman-street,
　Portman-square.
Mr. Fleece, St. George's row,
　Oxford-street.
Mr. Flanders, Oxford-street.
Mr. Frances, Mary-le-bone-lane.
Mrs. Fletcher, Castle-street,
　Oxford-street.
Mr. George Fancy, Long-acre.

G
Mr. Goodram.
Mr. Gray, Oxford-street.
Mr. Gray, ditto.
Dr. Gartshore, St. Martins-lane.
Mr. Gill, Lower Brook-street.
Mr. Green, Wood-street,
　Cheapside.
Mr. Glover, Carmile-buildings.
Mr. Graves, Oxford-street.

Mr. Gibbs, Upper Broynstone-
　street.
Mr. Gibson, Adam-street,
　Portman-square.
Mr. Glade, Oxford-street.

H
Earl Harrington, Stable-yard, St.
　James's.
Mr. Hoyle, Portman-street,
　Portman-square.
Mr. Harris, Union-court,
　Mary-le-bone.
Mr. Higgings, Little Portland-
　street.
Mr. Haynes, Edgware-road.
Mr. Hazzard, Broynstone-street.
Mr. Hunt, Edgware-road.
Mr. Harding, Berwick-street,
　Soho.
Mr. Harris, Jermyn-street.
Mr. Harris, Charles-street.
Mr. Hayward, Adam-street,
　Portman-square.
Mr. Harris, Rebbecca-court, Well-
　street.
Mr. Hern, Oxford-street.
Mr. Howell, Oxford-street.
Mrs. Hart, Woodstock-street,
　Mary-le-bone.
Dr. Houston, Brewer-street,
　Golden-square.

J
Mr. Jerard, Oxford-street.
Mr. Jerningham, Green-street,
　Grosvenor-square.
Mr. Jones, Duke-street,
　Grosvenor-square.
Mr. Jefferys, Piccadilly.
Mr. Jacobs, Edgware-road.

K

Mr. King, King-street, St. James's.
Mr. Knill, Oxendon-street, Hay-market.
Mrs. Kenlock, Oxford-street.

L

Mr. Land, Mary-le-bone-inn.
Mr. Longland, Queen-square, Westminster.
Mr. Leslie, Charlotte-street, Bloomsbury.
Mr. Landreff, Cheapside.
Mr. Lambart, St. Martin's-Lane.
Mr. Linsay, Queen-street, Grosvenor-square.

M

Mr. Morgin, Hackney.
Mr. Morgin, King-street, Covent-garden.
Mr. Martini, Warwick-street, Golden-square.
Mr. Morgin, Cheapside.
Mr. Mandivill, Carnaby-street, Carnaby-market.
Mr. Myers.
Mr. Martin.
Mr. Morris, Great Russell-street.
Mr. Mobbs, Berwick-street, Soho.
Mr. Mosly, New-court, Fleet-market.
Mr. Maish, Oxford-street.
Mr. Mare, ditto.
Mr. Martlock, ditto.
Mr. Moor, ditto.
Mr. Maddleton, St. Martin's-lane.
Mr. Miller, St. Anne's-court, Soho.

N

Mr. Nolekins [*sic*], Mortimore-street, Cavendish-square.
Mr. Northcot, Argyle-street, Oxford-street.
Mr. Norman, Duke-street, Grosvenor-square.

P

Mr. Paine, Old Bond-street.
Mr. Philpot, Oxford-street.
Mr. Partriacks, Cheapside.
Mr. Pinkes, Broynstone-street, Portman-square.
Mr. Pierce, Queen-street, Grosvenor-square.
Mr. Potter, Cheapside.
Mr. Pitt, Ogle-street, Mary-le-bone.
Mrs. Proudlove, Woodstock-street.
Mr. Phillips, Edgware-road.
Mr. Parkinson, Devonshire-street, Queen-square.
Mr. Petters, Carmile-build-ings.
Mr. Papera, Mary-le-bone-street, Golden-sqr.

R

Sir Joshua Reynolds, Leicester-fields.
Mr. Robinson, Cheapside.
Mr. Ross, Great Portland-street, Oxford-street.
Mr. Roberts, Fleet-lane.
Mr. Robinson, Charles-street.
Mr. Roe, St. Martin's-lane.
Mr. Robertson, Mary-le-bone-lane.

S

Messrs. Stedman and Co. Princes-
street.
Mr. Salter, Southampton-street.
Mr. Sastrass, Edgware-road.
Mr. Samel, Little Wild-street.
Mr. Sartini, New Compton-street.
Mr. Stephenson, Brown-street,
Grosvenor-sqr.
Mr. Sparkes, Castle-mews,
Oxford-street.
Mr. Shan, Adam-street, Portman-
square.
Mr. Sutherland, Vigo-lane, Bond-
street.
Mrs. Smith, Oxford-street.
Mr. Sanby, St. Georges-row,
Oxford-street.
Mrs. Smith, Oxford-market.
Mr. Simpson, Great St. Andrew-
street.
Mr. Shee, Jermyn-street.

T

Mr. Towne, St. Georges-market.
Mr. Thompson.

Mr. Thomas, Paddington.
Mr. Taite, Oxford-street.
Mr. Thornton, Lower Grosvenor-
street.
Mr. Tarry.
Mr. Thomas, Stratford-place,
Oxford-street.
Mr. Tassier, Leicester-fields.

W

Mr. Winter, Portman-square.
Mr. Walker, Oxford-street.
Mr. Warborn, ditto.
Mr. Woodfall, Salsbury-square.
Mr. Williams, Great Waner-street,
Hatton-garden.
Mr. Wood, Broynston-street,
Portman-square.
Mr. and Miss Wesley, Chester-
field-street, May-fair.
Mr. William Hall, No. 25,
Princes-street, 40 copies.

EXPLANATORY NOTES
TO THE 1787 PUBLICATION

1. The following *"N[ota] B[ene]"* is pasted into some issues of the 1787 edition: see "A Note on the Text."

2. Alexander Campbell, Esq . . . the end of the year 1772: probably the same Alexander Campbell, Esq., who testified before Parliament on 13–18 February 1790 against the abolition of the slave trade. A native of Scotland, Campbell lived in North America from 1753 to 1759, with the exceptions of a four-month period spent in the West Indies and a year in England. After purchasing two sugar estates on Grenada with more than three hundred slaves for more than £40,000 in 1763, Campbell divided his time about equally between Britain and the Caribbean until June 1788, when he retired to Britain after having served in the legislature of Grenada. Since 1763 he had purchased an estimated twelve hundred new slaves, and from 1766 to 1790 he owned between five hundred and one thousand slaves on his various West Indian plantations. At the time of his testimony, he owned more than nine hundred slaves, more than 180 of whom were children. Of Grenada's more than eighty thousand acres, Campbell owned three estates totalling 1,230 acres and employing 559 slaves. He also owned smaller estates on other West Indian islands.

Campbell and Cugoano arrived in England at the end of 1772; the hurricane season generally precluded travel from the West Indies to England between July and November. On the significance of the timing of Cugoano's arrival in England, see note 55.

3. Cugoano refers to the long-standing, though mistaken, belief that conversion to Christianity merited emancipation from slavery, a belief so strong that it led to colonial statutes denying its validity. A prohibition against Christians enslaving fellow Christians would have paralleled the prohibition in Leviticus 25:39ff. of Hebrews enslaving fellow Hebrews, as well as the Muslim prohibition against enslaving coreligionists. The Muslim policy was familiar to many pagan Africans who, perhaps including Cugoano, had been enslaved by their Muslim neighbors. Historically, societies that practiced slavery generally did not enslave members of their own people. Emphasizing ethnic difference as a ground for slavery be-

came increasingly important to the pro-slavery argument because conversion to Christianity meant that religion no longer served as a defining difference between enslaver and enslaved in the Atlantic trade.

By 1706 the British colonies of the Carolinas, New Jersey, and New York all had declared conversion and baptism irrelevant to a slave's status. But faith in the effects of conversion abided, especially in England itself, where no positive law (formulated and passed by Parliament) specifically addressed the issue of slavery. In 1768 Sir John Fielding (1721–1780), the leading magistrate in Middlesex county where Cugoano was baptized, complained about the continuing belief in the equation of Christianity and freedom and its disruptive social effects in cases like Cugoano's:

> There are already a great Number of black Men and Women who have made themselves so troublesome and dangerous to the Families who brought them over [to England from the American colonies] as to get themselves discharged; they enter into Societies, and make it their Business to corrupt and dissatisfy the Mind of every fresh black Servant that comes to *England*; first, by getting them christened or married, which they inform them makes them free (tho' it has been adjudged by our most able Lawyers, that neither of these Circumstances alter the Master's Property in a Slave). *Extracts from Such of the Laws, as Particularly Relate to the Peace and Good Order of this Metropolis. . . .* (London)

4. Dr. Skinner: the clergyman Thomas Skinner, who voted in the 1774 Westminster election and who lived in Marylebone Street, a few blocks from St. James's Church, where he was Clerk in Orders.

5. I was baptized . . . in the year 1773: the parish register entry for 20 August 1773 reads: "John Stuart—a Black, aged 16 Years."

6. The Black People sent to Sierra Leona: see notes 170–174.

7. But still I fear . . . slavery is carried on by them: see note 172.

8. O earth! . . . negro slaves: Compare John Wesley (1703–1791), *Thoughts upon Slavery* (London, 1774), 23: "O Earth, O Sea, cover not thou their blood!" Italic type is sometimes used in Cugoano's works for emphasis alone, and sometimes—as here—to indicate a quoted passage as well.

Henri Grégoire (1750–1831) offers differing as well as additional biographical data on Cugoano in *An Enquiry Concerning the Intellectual and Moral Faculties and Literature of Negroes: Followed with an Account of the Life and Works of Fifteen Negroes and Mulattoes Distinguished in Science, Literature and the Arts* (Brooklyn, New York, 1810), translated by David Bailie Warden from the original French edition (1808): "[Cugoano] was a slave at Grenada, and was indebted for his liberty to the generosity of Lord Hoth, who carried him to England. He was there in 1788, in the service of [Richard] Cosway [1742–1821], the first painter of the Prince of Wales [the future George IV (1762–1830)]. [Scipione] Piatoli [*sic*] [1749–1809], author of a treatise in Italian, on the *situation* and *dangers* of burial grounds. . . . [,] who, during a long residence at London, was particularly acquainted with Cugoano, then about forty years of age, and whose wife was an Englishwoman, praises highly this African; and speaks in strong terms of his piety, his mild character and modesty, his integrity and talents" (189).

Unfortunately, Grégoire is often unreliable. I have not been able to discover anything about a Lord Hoth. Piàttoli, an Italian abbot, was a longtime supporter of Poland's struggle for independence, a drafter of the Polish Constitution of 1791, and a friend of Richard Cosway's wife, Maria (1760–1838), also a painter. Since Piàttoli was in an Austrian prison from 1794 to 1800 and resumed his political activities in St. Petersburg, Russia, by 1803, if he did meet Cugoano he must have been in London between 1800 and 1803.

9. Proverbs 31:9 and Isaiah 32:8. I have not attempted to trace every possible allusion in Cugoano's quasi-Biblical diction.

10. Job 30:25.

11. There is one class of people . . . agreed to carry on no slavery and savage barbarity among them: Cugoano undoubtedly refers to the Society of Friends, or Quakers, which put increasing pressure on its members to renounce slavery, eventually threatening slave dealers and owners with expulsion. In 1783, the London Quaker Meeting for Sufferings created an Abolition Committee to oppose the slave trade and to petition Parliament to abolish it, and Quakers formed the majority of the Society to Effect the Abolition of the Slave Trade at its founding in 1787. (During the eighteenth century, an abolitionist was someone who opposed the slave trade; far fewer in number were those who, like Cugoano, were emancipationists opposed to the institution of slavery as well.) The Society used the Quaker printer James Phillips (1745–1799) and the national and international Quaker distribution system to circulate anti-slave-trade publications. Phillips produced one of the printings of Cugoano's *Thoughts and Sentiments* but appears to have distributed the book without the official support of either the Quaker Abolition Committee or the Society to Effect the Abolition of the Slave Trade.

12. Some mitigation . . . and greater reformation: Cugoano refers to such recent laws as those in Vermont (1777) and Pennsylvania (1780) banning slavery or legislating the gradual emancipation of slaves. These laws

were part of what has been called the first emancipation—the anti-slavery movement in the northern states that developed during and after the American Revolution. The first emancipation did not affect the southern states, where the vast majority of North American slaves lived. Unfortunately, Articles I and IV of the Constitution of the new United States, which went into effect on 4 March 1789, recognized the legality of slavery. The proposed Constitution was published in the *Public Advertiser* on 31 October 1787.

13. Inquisition: the institution within the Roman Catholic Church established in the Middle Ages to identify and prosecute heretics. The Inquisition was still operating in Spain and Portugal in the eighteenth century. Spain introduced both the Inquisition and African slavery into its colonial American empire at the beginning of the sixteenth century.

14. The bloody edicts of Popish massacres: prior to the Protestant Reformation of the sixteenth century, papal edicts against heretics frequently led to large-scale persecution and even extermination of the accused.

15. Matthew 19:19; 7:12.

16. Chain: the Great Chain of Being, the idea that all created things are arranged in an order of descending complexity, from the fully human to inert matter. Some of the defenders of slavery contended that Africans were placed between the human and the monkey on the Chain.

17. That an African . . . to be a slave: as he often does, Cugoano places within quotation marks imagined statements. Conversely, he often fails to identify by punctuation statements directly quoted from other sources.

18. Factory: a European trading post on the coast of Africa.

19. I was born . . . Assinee: all of the places Cugoano mentions in this sentence were located on the Gold Coast of the Gulf of Guinea, in present-day Ghana. Cape Coast, mentioned in the next paragraph, was the British administrative center on the Gold Coast.

20. Eat: a common alternative spelling of *ate*.

21. Jehovah Sabaoth: the Lord of Hosts.

22. Good: corrected from "great" in "ERRATA."

23. Stouter ones: stronger ones.

24. A gentleman coming to England: Alexander Campbell.

25. *The Prince of the Kings of the earth:* Revelation 1:5.

26. I may say with Joseph . . . intended for my good: see Genesis 45:4–8. Cugoano probably mentions Joseph here because, as William Bollan (d. 1776) says in *Britannia Libera, or a Defence of the Free State of Man in England, against the Claim of any Man there as a Slave. Inscribed and Submitted to the Jurisconsulti, and the Free People of England* (London, 1772), a text Cugoano later quotes (see note 114), "[t]he first man certainly known by name, or otherwise, to have been sold for a *slave*, was *Joseph*" (2).

27. [Cugoano's note.] The justly celebrated Dr. [Edward] Young [1683–1765], in recommending this divine book of heavenly wisdom to the giddy and thoughtless world, in his Night Thoughts, has the following elegant lines:

> *Perhaps thou'dst laugh but at thine own expence,*
> *This counsel strange should I presume to give;*
> *Retire and read thy Bible to be gay;*
> *There truths abound of sov'reign aid to peace.*
> *Ah, do not prize it less because inspired.*
> *Read and revere the sacred page; a page,*
> *Where triumphs immortality; a page,*
> *Which not the whole creation could produce;*
> *Which not the conflagration shall destroy;*
> *In nature's ruin not one letter's lost,*
> *'Tis printed in the mind of gods for ever,*
> *Angels and men assent to what I sing!*

[Quoted from Young's *The Complaint; or Night-Thoughts on Life, Death, & Immortality* (London, 1742–1746). Cugoano misquotes and transposes lines from various parts of the poem: the first five lines, slightly misquoted, are from Book 8:769–773; the next four are from 7:1360–1363; the last three are 7:1365, 7:1364, and 7:1368.]

28. The Cursory Remarker: James Tobin (d. 1817), a West Indian planter from the island of Nevis. His *Cursory Remarks upon the Reverend Mr. Ramsay's Essay.* . . . (London, 1785) is an attack on James Ramsay (1733–1789), *An Essay on the Treatment and Conversion of African Slaves in the British Sugar Colonies* (London, 1784). Thomas Clarkson (1760–1846), in *An Essay on the Slavery and Commerce of the Human Species, Particularly the African* (London, 1786), calls Tobin "the Cursory Remarker." Olaudah Equiano, or Gustavus Vassa (1745?–1797), also responded to Tobin in his autobiography, as well as his review of Tobin's *Cursory Remarks* in the *Public Advertiser* (28 January 1788): see the Penguin edition of Equiano's *The Interesting Narrative and Other Writings* (New York, 1995), ed. Vincent Carretta, 328–330.

29. Demetrius: see Acts 19:23–41.

30. Diana: the Roman goddess of chastity and hunting, to whom the temple at Ephesus was dedicated.

31. [Cugoano's note.] The worthy and judicious author of "An Essay on the Treatment and Conversion of the African Slaves in the British Sugar Colonies."

[Cugoano quotes Tobin, *Cursory Remarks*, 5.]

32. An event . . . horse: *Cursory Remarks*, 22. Images of the natural order inverted by the pursuit of folly—the world turned upside down—were common in popular visual prints and chapbooks during the eighteenth century.

33. A conflation of lines from John Dryden (1631–1700), *The Hind and the Panther* (London, 1687), 1:33–34 ("Truth has such a face and such a mien / As to be loved needs but to be seen"), and Alexander Pope (1688–1744), *Essay on Man* (London, 1733–1734), 2:217–218 ("Vice is a monster of so frightful mien / As to be hated needs but to be seen").

34. To dedicate . . . parish: *Cursory Remarks*, 88.

35. A man . . . his own senses: *Cursory Remarks*, 149. Cugoano applies Tobin's description of Ramsay to Tobin himself. The parenthetical phrase is Cugoano's own editorial comment.

36. Some pretend . . . their own native country: rather than quoting a particular source, Cugoano is apparently paraphrasing an accusation frequently made by defenders of the slave trade and often found in the writings of those who questioned the equality of Africans. For example, in "Of National Characters," in *Three Essays: Moral and Political* (Edinburgh and London, 1748), David Hume (1711–1776) says, "You may obtain any thing of the NEGROES by offering them strong drink; and may easily prevail with them to sell, not only their children, but their wives and mistresses, for a cask of brandy." Cugoano cites Hume later in *Thoughts and Sentiments*—see note 184. The assertion that slavery brought Africans to a better material existence in the Americas is commonly found in contemporaneous arguments in favor of the trade.

37. Ukawsaw Groniosaw: James Albert Ukawsaw Gronniosaw (ca. 1710–ca. 1772), author of *A Narrative of the Most Remarkable Particulars in the Life of James Albert Ukawsaw Gronniosaw, an African Prince, as Related by Himself* (Bath, 1772), reproduced in Vincent Carretta, ed., *Unchained Voices: An Anthology of Black Authors in the English-speaking World of the Eighteenth Century* (Lexington, University Press of Kentucky, 1996), 32–58.

38. A. Morrant in America: John Marrant (1755–1791), author of *A Narrative of the Lord's Wonderful Dealings with John Marrant, a Black* (London, 1785), reproduced in Carretta, ed., *Unchained Voices*, 110–133.

39. [Cugoano's note.] It may be true, that some of the slaves transported from Africa, may have committed crimes in their own country, that require some slavery as a punishment; but, according to the laws of equity and justice, they ought to become free, as soon as their labour has paid for their purchase in the West-Indies or elsewhere.

40. Gewgaws: trinkets.

41. Æthiopian: African.

42. That all mankind ... face of the earth: again, apparently an imagined quotation. Like most abolitionists, Cugoano embraces the theologically orthodox belief in the monogenetic development of the human race from a single source: Adam and Eve. Some proponents of slavery argued that humans developed polygenetically, maintaining that Africans and Europeans descended from separate pairs of original parents.

43. That mark or sign which God gave to Cain: see Genesis 4:1–16. God punishes Cain for having murdered his brother, Abel:

> 12. When thou tillest the ground, it shall not henceforth yield unto thee her strength; a fugitive and a vagabond shalt thou be in the earth.
>
> 13. And Cain said unto the LORD, My punishment *is* greater than I can bear.
>
> 14. Behold, thou hast driven me out this day from the face of the earth; and from thy face shall I be hid; and I shall be a fugitive and a vagabond in the earth; and it shall come to pass, *that* every one that findeth me shall slay me.
>
> 15. And the LORD said unto him, Therefore whosoever slayeth Cain, vengeance shall be taken on him sevenfold. And the LORD set a mark upon Cain, lest any finding him should kill him.

44. A sacred poet ... green bay tree: Cugoano refers to Psalm 37:35: "I have seen the wicked in great power, and spreading himself like a green bay tree." The "sacred poet" is David, traditionally identified as the author of the Psalms.

45. Only Noah ... directed to build: the story of Noah, his children, and the ark is found in Genesis 5:30–9:29.

46. And denounced ... should serve them: Noah's curse on Canaan is found in Genesis 9:20–27. The apparent substitution of the name Canaan for Ham in Genesis 9:25–27 explains Cugoano's seeming confusion of Canaan, the son, with his father, Ham, as the one who discovered the nakedness of the inebriated Noah, Canaan's grandfather:

> 22. And Ham, the father of Canaan, saw the nakedness of his father, and told his two brethren without.
>
> 23. And Shem and Japheth took a garment, and laid *it* upon both their shoulders, and went backward, and covered the nakedness of their father; and their faces *were* backward, and they saw not their father's nakedness.

24. And Noah awoke from his wine, and knew what his younger son had done unto him.

25. And he said, Cursed *be* Canaan; a servant of servants shall he be unto his brethren.

Seeking a religious justification for the practice despite the absence of any biblical foundation, defenders of the enslavement of Africans since the middle of the fifteenth century increasingly embraced the notion that God cursed the descendants of Cain and/or of Ham/Canaan with blackness. This "curse of Ham" was the twelfth-century invention of Benjamin of Tudeal, who published his idea in *The Itinerary of Benjamin of Tudella*. Apologists for slavery argued that sub-Saharan Africans, as the descendants of Ham, cursed with a dark complexion and the condition of servitude, were destined to slavery. Hence, by the late eighteenth century in pro-slavery discourse, blackness and slavery were often synonymous.

47. Chedorlaomer: corrected from "Chederluomer" in "ERRATA." See Genesis 14:1ff.

48. Many of the Canaanites . . . as far back as that time: commentators on the Bible generally accepted the identification of the Phoenicians as the Canaanites expelled by the Jews from Canaan. The idea that Phoenicians probably settled in Cornwall was first implied by the Greek Strabo (ca. 60 B.C.E.–ca. 21 C.E.), who, in his *Geographica*, apparently describes the Phoenician discovery of the Scilly Islands off Cornwall's coast. The argument that Phoenicians were the first settlers of Britain is elaborated, discussed and rejected, or simply accepted by a number of later historians: Thomas Twyne (1501?–1581), in *De Rebus Albionicis* (London, 1590); Aylett Sammes (1636?–1679?), in *Britannia Antiqua Illustrata: or, the Antiquities of Ancient Britain, Derived from the Phoenicians* (London, 1676); Samuel Bochart (1591–1667), in *Geographia Sacra* (Paris, 1646); Edmund Gibson (1669–1748), in his 1695 edition of William Camden's (1551–1623) *Britannia* (London, 1586); Charles Leigh (1662–1701), in *The Natural History of Lancashire, Chesire and the Peak in Derbyshire, with an Account of the British, Phoenician, Armenian, Greek and Roman Antiquities in those Parts* (London, 1700); and William Stukeley (1687–1765), in *Stonehenge, a Temple Restor'd to the British Druids* (London, 1740) and *Abury, a Temple of the British Druids* (London, 1743).

49. Now, the descendants . . . very formidable nations: Noah's descendants are identified in Genesis 10:1ff. This genealogy of Noah and his sons is frequently called the Table of Nations. According to a traditional inter-

pretation, Japheth fathered the Indo-Europeans; Shem the Semites; and Ham the Africans and non-Hebrew inhabitants of Asia Minor.

50. To: corrected from "by" in the "ERRATA."

51. Ethiopians . . . people: according to mistaken popular etymology, *Ethiopia* meant "burnt-facedom."

52. Aphra . . . Keturah: Keturah was a wife of Abraham. Aphra, not included among Keturah's children in Genesis 25:1–4 and 1 Chronicles 1:32–33, is a creation of later commentators on the Bible who saw Africans as descendants of Ham. For example, in *An Exposition of the Old Testament, in Which Are Recorded the Original of Mankind, of the Several Nations of the World, and of the Jewish Nation in Particular* (London, 1788), John Gill (1697–1771) remarks, "all *Africa* and a considerable part of *Asia* were possessed by the four sons of Ham and their descendants" (73).

53. Bond-servant: a person obligated by contract to work without wages, usually for a specified period of time. Limited bond service, or slavery, of fellow Hebrews for debt is mentioned in Exodus 21:1–6; Leviticus 25:39ff.; and Deuteronomy 15:12ff. But these Hebrew slaves were to be treated as servants, not to be resold, and at the end of the time limit, the slave could choose either liberty or perpetual servitude.

54. Deliverance . . . slavery: Cugoano offers an overly positive view of ancient slavery in the Near East. The Hebrew word *ebed* covers a wide range of statuses, including the fellow Hebrew bond servant (see note 53), the favored servant Moses in Numbers 12:7, the suffering servant in Isaiah 42:1, and the chattel slave in Leviticus 25:44–46 lacking the human rights accorded fellow Hebrews:

44. Both thy bondmen, and thy bondmaids, which thou shalt have, *shall be* of the heathen that are round about you; of them shall ye buy bondmen and bondmaids.

45. Moreover of the children of the strangers that do sojourn among you, of them shall ye buy, and of their families that *are* with you, which they begat in your land: and they shall be your possession.

46. And ye shall take them as an inheritance for your children after you, to inherit *them for* a possession; they shall be your bondmen for ever; but over your brethren the children of Israel, ye shall not rule one over another with rigour.

The Mishnah, the Jewish interpretation of Scripture developed after the destruction of the Temple in 70 C.E., uses the terms *Hebrews* and *Canaanites* to refer, respectively, to "the children of Israel" and "strangers."

The only apparent objection in the Old Testament to the institution of slavery on the grounds of common humanity is Job 31:13–15:

> 13. If I did despise the cause of my manservant or of my maidservant, when they contended with me;
> 14. What then shall I do when God riseth up? and when he visiteth, what shall I answer him?
> 15. Did not he that made me in the womb make him? and did not one fashion us in the womb?

Nor is slavery explicitly condemned in the New Testament. Indeed, apologists for slavery found support for their position in Ephesians 6:5–8:

> 5. Servants [slaves], be obedient to them that are *your* masters according to the flesh, with fear and trembling, in singleness of your heart, as unto Christ;
> 6. Not with eye-service, as men-pleasers; but as the servants [slaves] of Christ, doing the will of God from the heart;
> 7. With good will doing service, as to the Lord, and not to men:
> 8. Knowing that whatsoever good thing any man doeth, the same shall he receive of the Lord, whether *he be* bond or free.

55. And yet the whole community is free from slavery: Cugoano was apparently one of many people who believed that the Mansfield decision in the Somerset case on 22 June 1772 rendered slavery illegal in England by liberating a slave the moment he or she set foot on English soil. Lord Mansfield (1705–1793), Lord Chief Justice of the King's Bench, ruled that James Somerset, a slave brought to England from Massachusetts by his master, Charles Stewart, a customs official, could not legally be forced by his owner back to the colonies. Mansfield's judgment was quickly disseminated throughout Britain and the colonies through newspapers and magazines. Granville Sharp (1735–1813) had convinced several lawyers to argue Somerset's case free of charge, and the inexperienced Francis Hargrave (1741?–1821) had also volunteered his legal services on Somerset's behalf. Cugoano praises Mansfield, Grenville [*sic*] Sharp, and Hargrave in his 1791 *Thoughts and Sentiments.* In his 1787 letter to George, Prince of Wales (1762–1830) and the patron of Cugoano's employer, Richard Cosway (see Appendix), Cugoano calls Hargrave "a great Counsellor" and quotes from his *An Argument in the Case of James Somersett, a Negro, Lately Determined by the Court of King's Bench: Wherein It Is At-*

tempted to Demonstrate the Present Unlawfulness of Domestic Slavery in England. To Which Is Prefixed a State of the Case (London, 1772).

The timing of Cugoano's arrival in England at "the end of the year 1772" means that he may have taken advantage of the Mansfield decision to emancipate himself from his West Indian master, Alexander Campbell. And when Cugoano was baptized in 1773 in an attempt to assure his freedom (see note 3), he may have been hedging his bet on the applicability of the Mansfield ruling to his own situation.

56. *The year of jubilee came*: every fiftieth year was legally a year of rest for the Israelites, when slaves were freed, land left untilled, and alienated property returned to the former owners. The law was probably not put into practice. See Leviticus 25:8–17, 29–31. Rather than the year of jubilee, Cugoano probably means the Mosaic law of Exodus 21:2, 5–6:

> 2. If thou buy an Hebrew servant, six years he shall serve; and in the seventh he shall go out free for nothing.
>
> 5. And if the servant shall plainly say, I love my master, my wife, and my children; I will not go out free:
>
> 6. Then his master shall bring him unto the judges; he shall also bring him to the door, or unto the door post; and his master shall bore his ear through with an awl; and he shall serve him for ever.

57. *Their being made hewers of wood and drawers of water*: during the conquest of Canaan by the Jews, Joshua tells the Gibeonites that they will serve the Jews: "Now therefore ye *are* cursed, and there shall none of you be freed from being bondmen, and hewers of wood and drawers of water for the house of my God" (Joshua 9:23).

58. Cugoano may be thinking of a passage in John Wesley, *Thoughts upon Slavery* (Philadelphia, 1774): "The author of the history of *Jamaica*, wrote about the year 1740 . . . [says,] 'Those that go out in parties to reduce the negroes, shall receive from the treasurer for every rebellious negro that shall be killed, bringing in his head to any justice, forty pounds; for every negro taken and brought in alive, and not maimed, ten pounds, to be paid by the owner . . .' " (27, 29, note). The quotation is from Charles Leslie, *A New History of Jamaica, from the Earliest Accounts, to the Taking of Porto Bello by Vice-Admiral Vernon* (London, 1740), 238. The equivalent passage in the London edition (1774) of Wesley's *Thoughts* published by Robert Hawes reads, "The Law of *Jamaica* ordains, 'Every slave that shall run away, and continue absent from his master twelve months, shall be *deemed rebellious*:' And by another law, fifty pounds are allowed, to those who kill or bring in alive a *rebellious* slave" (27).

59. The Nethenims ... Temple of Jerusalem: the Nethinims (usually translated "temple slaves" or "temple servants") were probably originally prisoners of war who eventually gained either freedom or Israelite status. They are mentioned in 1 Chronicles 9:2, Ezra 2:43–54, 7:7, 8:17–20; and Nehemiah 7:46ff.

60. God's elect: the doctrine that God has chosen, or elected, some relatively few people—the "elect"—who are predestined to be saved while the great majority are doomed to eternal damnation was most often associated with the teachings of John Calvin (1509–1564). See Romans 8:27–9:21.

61. Declared by the Apostle, that the law is spiritual: "For we know that the law is spiritual: but I am carnal, sold under sin" (Romans 7:14). The "Apostle" is Paul.

62. 2 Timothy 2:3.

63. A conflation of Romans 13:12 and 2 Corinthians 6:7.

64. A conflation of Romans 13:12, 2 Corinthians 6:7, and Ephesians 6:11–13.

65. *Anakims*: see Joshua 11:21–22 and 2 Samuel 21:16–22.

66. A conflation of texts, including Jeremiah 9:3 and Hebrews 2:10.

67. *Agag*: for Agag, King of the Amalekites, see 1 Samuel 15:8ff.

68. Adapted from 1 Samuel 15:33.

69. Saul: Cugoano's reference could be to either the Old Testament Saul (see 1 Samuel 28:6, 15) or the New Testament Saul (Paul before his conversion; see Acts 9).

70. Job 2:4.

71. Proverbs 5:22.

72. Adapted from 2 Timothy 3:16.

73. Bedlam: madhouse.

74. Proverbs 14:12.

75. Matthew 22:37, 39.

76. Numbers 15:16.

77. Matthew 7:12.

78. Matthew 6:14.

79. The just Bethlehem Joseph: presumably the husband of Mary, mother of Jesus, called "a just *man*" (Matthew 1:19).

80. Such vengeance ... violaters of his law: compare "To me *belongeth* vengeance, and recompence; their foot shall slide in *due* time: for the day of their calamity *is* at hand, and the things that shall come upon them make haste" (Deuteronomy 32:35).

81. Adapted from Deuteronomy 24:7.

82. Who is the righteous fulfiller of the law: Christ.

83. When the accusers of a woman . . . sin no more: see John 7:53–8:11.

84. Deuteronomy 19:19.

85. Genesis 9:5–6.

86. Compare Deuteronomy 4:2.

87. David: for David's role in the death of Uriah, see 2 Samuel 11.

88. Solomon: see 1 Kings 2:27–34.

89. Cromwell: Oliver Cromwell (1599–1658): leader of the victorious Puritan forces in the English Civil War that led to the execution of Charles I, the Martyr King. Cromwell became the dictatorial Protector of the new government.

90. Charles the Second [1630–1685, ruled 1660–1685]: Cugoano no doubt refers to Charles's having granted a royal charter in 1662 to the Royal Adventurers to Africa, creating a monopoly to conduct the slave trade between Africa and the American colonies. The Royal African Company was formed in 1672 as the successor to the Royal Adventurers.

91. Queen Mary [1516–1558]: called Bloody Mary because of the persecution of Protestants under her Roman Catholic reign.

92. Late rebellion . . . in Britain: the Jacobite rebellion in Scotland in 1745–1746, during the reign of George II (1683–1760), grandfather of George III (1738–1820).

93. [Cugoano's note.] A great part of this law is strictly observed in Africa, and we make use of sacrifices, and keep a sabbath every seventh day, more strictly than Christians generally do.

[Cugoano's quotation is adapted from Exodus 22.]

94. [Cugoano's note.] This confessional minstrel may be often repeated, but, I fear, seldom regarded: "We have offended against thy holy laws; we have left undone those things which we ought to have done; and we have done those things which we ought not to have done."

[Cugoano quotes from the General Confession of the Anglican *Book of Common Prayer*, whose language is adapted from Christ's words in Matthew 23:23 and Luke 11:42.]

95. Specie: coin of the realm.

96. Onesimus: Onesimus, a slave who ran away from his master, Philemon of Colossae, was converted to Christianity by the apostle Paul in Rome. Paul sent him back to Philemon with a letter calling Onesimus "a faithful and beloved brother, who is *one* of you" and enjoining Philemon to receive him "Not now as a servant, but above a servant, a brother beloved, specially to me, but how much more unto thee, both in the flesh, and in the Lord." See Colossians 4:9 and the Epistle of Paul to Philemon.

Onesimus was a central figure in arguments during the eighteenth century
over whether Christianity condemns or condones slavery.

97. For he who leadeth into captivity . . . should die with the sword:
compare "He that leadeth into captivity shall go into captivity: he that
killeth with the sword must be killed with the sword. Here is the patience
and the faith of the saints" (Revelation 13:10), and "Then said Jesus unto
him, Put up again thy sword into his place: for all they that take the
sword shall perish with the sword" (Matthew 26:52).

98. *Woe is me . . . be far removed:* compare Micah 7:1–11.

99. At Hispaniola . . . horrible and lamentable: Cugoano relies, without acknowledgement, on William Robertson (1721–1793), *The History
of America* (London, 1777), for his account of the New World. Robertson, in turn, relies on acknowledged sixteenth-century Spanish historians.
Anacoana, cazique, or ruler, of the western part of Hispaniola (the island
that comprises present-day Haiti and the Dominican Republic) entertained Nicolas de Ovando (1460–1511) and his men, who, under the guise
of a military parade, seized her and her attendants. Taken in chains to
Saint Domingo, she was tried and publicly hanged. Ovando became Governor of Hispaniola in 1501 and the principal political rival of Christopher Columbus (1451–1506). Robertson adds, "Ovando governed the
Spaniards with wisdom and justice, not inferior to the rigour with which
he treated the Indians" (1:180–182). Ovando introduced the extensive im-
portation of African slaves to the Americas.

Robertson's views on slavery, expressed in *The History of America* and
The History of the Reign of the Emperor Charles V (London, 1769), are
similar to Cugoano's.

100. Cortes: Hernán Cortés (1485–1547), Spanish conqueror of the
Aztec empire in what is present-day Mexico.

101. Montezuma II (1466–1520), monarch of the Aztecs.

102. Pizarra: Francisco Pizarro (ca. 1475–1541), Spanish conqueror of
the Inca empire in what is present-day Peru.

103. A great monarch: through military conquest and marriage to Isabella (1451–1504), King Ferdinand (1452–1516) consolidated his rule
over Spain as King of Castile, Aragon and Sicily, and Naples. Ferdinand
and Isabella sponsored Columbus's explorations.

104. Atahualpa (ca. 1502–1533).

105. The arch fanatic . . . chaplain to the expedition: Vincente de
Valverde (1490?–1543).

**106. The fabulous notion of St. Peter's viceregency . . . continued in
the succession of the Popes:** as a Protestant, Cugoano rejects the Roman
Catholic doctrine that the popes (fathers), beginning with Christ's apostle

Peter, inherit Christ's authority and thus are Christ's vicars, or vicere-
gents.

107. The then Pope, Alexander . . . the sole Monarch of all the New
World: In 1493, Alexander VI (1431–1503, pope, 1492–1503) divided the
New World between Spain and Portugal by drawing a line on the globe,
unintentionally granting most of the landmass to Spain. Pope Alexander's
division was confirmed in 1494 by the Treaty of Tordesillas.

108. He desired to know. . . . to the ground: quoted directly from
Robertson, 2:175. An account of Atahualpa's throwing the book down in
anger appears in the anonymous *La Conquista del Peru* (Seville, 1534),
the first published history of the conquest of Peru. But the idea that he
does so because it doesn't speak to him is found only in later histories.
The anecdote made its way into popular accounts of the fall of the Incan
Empire in English as early as 1581, in the translation by Thomas Nicholas
(b. ca. 1532, fl. 1560–1596) of Augustín de Zárate (1514–ca. 1560), *Histo-
ria del Descubrimiento y Conquista del Peru* (Antwerp, 1555). Ironically,
Pizarro himself was illiterate.

As Paul Edwards first pointed out, the trope of the book that does not
speak to the illiterate appears as well in the writings of Gronniosaw (see
note 37), Marrant (see note 38), and Equiano (see note 28). For these and
additional uses of the trope by Afro-British writers, see Carretta, ed., *The
Interesting Narrative*, 254–256, note 143. Henry Louis Gates, Jr., dis-
cusses the trope at length in *The Signifying Monkey: A Theory of African-
American Literary Criticism* (New York: Oxford University Press, 1988).

109. Their hell-invented enginery of thunder, fire and smoke: attribu-
tion to the devil of the invention of gunpowder and firearms was a literary commonplace, found, for example, in Edmund Spenser (1552–1599),
The Faerie Queene (1590), bk 1, canto 7, stanza 13, lines 1–4; John Milton
(1608–1674), *Paradise Lost* (1667), 6:484–489.

110. It is said . . . this beneficent character: Robertson 2:166, with minor changes.

111. At that time . . . Newton: I have not found Cugoano's citation in
*Observations upon the Prophecies of Daniel, and the Apocalypse of St.
John* (London, 1733) by Sir Isaac Newton (1642–1727). But, in *Dissertations on the Prophecies, Which Have Remarkably Been Fulfilled, and at
this Time Are Fulfilling in the World* (London, 1754–1758), Thomas Newton (1704–1782) expresses a sentiment similar to the one Cugoano cites:
"and who were the persons to whom this commission [to spread the
Word of God] was given? those who were best qualified and able to carry
it into execution? the rich, the wise, the mighty of this world? No, they
were chiefly a few poor fishermen, of low parentage and education, of no

learning or eloquence, of no policy or address, of no repute or authority, despised as Jews by the rest of mankind and as the meanest and worst of Jews by the Jews themselves" (1:237).

112. With whom the kings of the earth . . . and souls of men: compare Revelation 18:2–3:

> 2. . . . Babylon the great is fallen, is fallen, and is become the habitation of devils, and the hold of every foul spirit, and a cage of every unclean and hateful bird.

> 3. For all nations have drunk of the wine of the wrath of her fornication, and the kings of the earth have committed fornication with her, and the merchants of the earth are waxed rich through the abundance of her delicacies.

113. One of its umbrageous horns . . . has extended itself over all the Mahometan nations in the East . . . the other horn of apostacy . . . has extended itself over all the Christian nations in the West: Cugoano interprets imagery in Revelation allegorically to identify the theologies of Islam and Roman Catholicism as perversions, respectively, of the Old and New Testaments. To call the Islamic nations "Mahometan" wrongfully implies that they worship the human prophet rather than the God Allah.

Cugoano's application of the prophecies of Revelation is consistent with earlier Protestant interpretations. For example, compare Thomas Newton's comments on Mohammed in *Dissertations*: "At the sounding of the fifth trumpet *a star fallen from heaven*, meaning the imposter Mohammed, *opened the bottom-less pit, and there arose a smoke out of the pit, and the sun and the air were darkened* by it; that is, a false religion was set up, which filled the world with darkness and error; and swarms of Saracen or Arabian *locusts* overspread the earth. A false prophet is very fitly typified by a blazing *star* or meteor" (3:84–85). Or Isaac Newton's comment in *Observations* on the Pope: "By the conversion of the ten kingdoms to the *Roman* religion, the Pope only enlarged his spiritual dominion, but did not rise up as a horn of the beast. It was his temporal dominion which made him one of the horns" (113).

114. The learned and ingenious author . . . the encrease of future glory: William Bollan, *Britannia Libera*, 40. Although Cugoano quotes approvingly from *Britannia Libera*, one wonders how he reacted to Bollan's concluding sentence: "We have no law of the land to warrant the use of *slaves* upon it; and as the institution of *slavery* would break up the entirety of the free state of the kingdom, and so nearly affect it various

ways, the authority of parliament, I conceive, would be absolutely necessary to make it, together with the laws proper to regulate this new order of men; whereas parliaments, it is hoped, will ever be sollicitous to preserve the kingdom entirely free, and moreover to prevent *Britannias* [*sic*] pure and noble blood from being polluted by the multiplicity of those conjunctions which produce such a motley disagreeable race, instead of establishing *slavery*, to the great and lasting prejudice of her honour and welfare" (47).

115. A world of debt at home . . . continued heavy annual load of taxes: taxes had been increased to pay for the high national debt incurred in fighting the American Revolution.

116. All stock-jobbing, lotteries, and useless business: Cugoano is an economic conservative who distrusts the financial innovations of the past century, especially the development of the stock market, in which wealth was created by speculation in paper credit rather than investment in land or the production of material goods, and the creation of the national lottery, used by the government between 1694 and 1826 to raise funds.

117. Compare Isaiah 3:15.

118. Deuteronomy 15:6.

119. Colonians: those in Britain deriving income from the slavery-based economies of the British colonies in America, as well as the colonists themselves.

120. That base traffic . . . begun by the Portuguese on the coast of Africa: in 1482, the Portuguese established Fort São Jorge da Mina, on the coast of present-day Ghana, to buy gold and slaves.

121. The Spaniards followed their infamous example: the first African slaves were brought to the Caribbean in 1502.

122. From Salle . . . Cape of Good Hope: the whole west coast of Africa, from north to south.

123. Laid open . . . Anno 1697: because the Royal African Company was unable to protect its granted monopoly of the slave trade along the length of the western coast of Africa, the trade was officially opened to those who were already illegally engaged in it.

124. Viz.: videlicet, namely.

125. North part of Guinea . . . &c.: during the eighteenth century *Guinea* included all the African lands along the Gulf of Guinea, roughly from present-day Guinea in the north to at least Nigeria in the south and extending many miles inland all along the coast.

126. Here daughters are clinging . . . breasts with tears: compare Wesley, *Thoughts on Slavery*: "Here you may see mothers hanging over their daughters, bedewing their naked breasts with tears, and daughters cling-

ing to their parents, till the whipper soon obliges them to part" (23).

127. The emancipation of a few . . . cannot make that horrible traffic one bit the less criminal: besides himself, Cugoano is probably thinking of other prominent Afro-British writers such as Ignatius Sancho (1729?–1780), whose *Letters* had been published in 1782.

128. The worthy and judicious author of the Historical account of Guinea: Anthony Benezet (1713–1784), *Some Historical Account of Guinea, Its Situation, Produce, and the General Disposition of Its Inhabitants. With an Inquiry into the Rise and Progress of the Slave Trade, Its Nature, and Lamentable Effects* (London, 1771, with frequent reprintings).

129. The African slave-trade . . . the English have taken the lead . . . in carrying it on: Cugoano is correct. During the 1780s, the Atlantic slave trade was at its peak, with an annual average of about eighty thousand Africans being brought to the British, Danish, Dutch, French, Portuguese, and Spanish colonies, as well as to the United States. Britain, whose own population reached about ten million in 1800, had by the 1780s become the single largest dealer in slaves, transporting an estimated 38,000 Africans in 1787 alone.

Between 1500 and 1900 approximately twelve million enslaved Africans crossed the Atlantic to the Americas, more than six million of them during the eighteenth century. Many of these transported Africans soon died aboard ship during the Middle Passage or during the period called the Seasoning—the first few months of exposure to labor and unfamiliar diseases in the Americas. Moreover, other millions of enslaved Africans died on their way to the coast of Africa. In addition, before, during, and after the Atlantic slave trade, the Islamic trade brought probably at least six million enslaved Africans to the Middle East, Asia, and the Mediterranean. So many Africans were enslaved by European and Islamic traders that historians calculate that the population of Africa, estimated to have been about 25,000,000 in 1850, would have been nearly 50,000,000 without the slave trade.

130. Seasoning: the period in which slaves newly arrived in the Americas were gradually acclimated and acculturated to their new land and status.

131. Gracious God . . . enormities deserve: Clarkson, *An Essa*, 252.

132. For while . . . individuals: Cugoano's transitional paraphrase of Clarkson.

133. Or as patronized . . . Almighty God: from "Sermon Preached before the University of Cambridge by the Reverend Peter Peckard [1718?–1797]," quoted in Clarkson, *Essay*, 254.

134. On this occasion . . . regard it: Cugoano's transitional paraphrase of Clarkson.

135. The violent and supernatural agitations . . . millions of their fellow-creatures: Clarkson, *Essay*, 254–255. Cugoano's note reads:

> See the excellent Mr. Clarkson's Essay on the Slavery and Commerce of the Human Species; and, I must add, the amiable and indefatigable friend of mankind, Granville Sharp, Esq. [1735–1813]; from whose writings I have borrowed some of the following observations. I am also indebted to several others, whose intrinsic virtues will equally shine in the same amiable manner, while ever there is any virtue and humanity amongst men; and when those of the enslavers of men will sink into abhorrence for ever.

136. In Babylon a little before Cyrus encamped against it: see Isaiah 45–47.

137. And it is not known . . . the poor Africans: Granville Sharp, *The Law of Retribution; or, a Serious Warning to Great Britain and her Colonies, Founded on Unquestionable Examples of God's Temporal Vengeance against Tyrants, Slave-holders, and Oppressors* (London, 1776), 262.

138. For national wickedness . . . partakers in their guilt: Sharp, *Law of Retribution*, 17.

139. And every man . . . does not avert it: Sharp, *Law of Retribution*, 261–262.

140. Must rest . . . slavery: the concluding words of Sharp's *Law of Retribution*.

141. For it is evident . . . great in temporal dignity: source not found.

Natural religion, and the revealed voice of God: "natural religion" refers to the belief that all humans, through the use of the five senses and reason, could recognize the existence of a benevolent creator by contemplating the supposed order of nature, which includes human nature, as if nature were a book to be read. But only "the revealed voice of God" in the Bible introduces humans to the whole truth of the Christian God, partially "read" in the book of nature.

142. Queen Anne: Anne (1665–1714), Queen of Great Britain, 1702–1714.

143. David that murdered Uriah: see 2 Samuel 11.

144. A conflation and paraphrase of various biblical passages, including Revelation 13:10.

145. Some men . . . protest against their measures then carried on: Cugoano no doubt is thinking of Bartolomé de Las Casas (1474–1556), who became a priest years after he had accompanied Columbus in 1502 on his third voyage to Hispaniola. He became known as the "Apostle of the Indians" because of his arguments against their enslavement in his written debates in 1550–1551 with Juan Ginés de Sepulveda, as well as in his *Brevísima relación de la destrucción de las Indias* (Seville, 1552), which was quickly translated into English (1583) and the other major European languages and remained available in English through the eighteenth century. In his debate with Sepulveda, Las Casas advocated substituting African for Indian slaves, a position he later recanted. Translated into English during the seventeenth and eighteenth centuries with such titles as *The Tears of the Indians* (London, 1656) and *Popery Truly Display'd in its Bloody Colours, or, A Faithful Narrative of the Horrid and Unexampled Massacres, Butcheries, and all Manner of Cruelties, that Hell and Malice Could Invent, Committed by the Popish Spanish Party on the Inhabitants of West-India* (London, 1689), Las Casas's work was used as evidence by English and Dutch Protestant propagandists to create the "black legend" of Spanish cruelty in the Americas.

Cugoano may also intend the Holy Roman Emperor Charles V (1500–1558), who tried without success to end slavery in Spanish America.

146. Proverbs 10:29.

147. Proverbs 11:5.

148. Proverbs 14:34.

149. The Emperor and others . . . good of their subjects: the Emperor is Joseph II (1741–1790) of Austria. *The Annual Register for 1782* (London, 1783) reports, on "26th [June]. Slavery is entirely abolished in Austrian Poland, and joy is seen in every peasant's countenance, for that he can now keep the fruit of his labour, unoppressed by a tyrannical lord" (211). The "slavery" found in Eastern Europe was serfdom, a system of forced labor in which the serfs were bound by birth to the land and thereby to the owner of the land. It was not the chattel slavery found in the Americas, under which the slave was the personal property of the master. In practice, however, the most severe forms of serfdom were very like American plantation slavery. The "others" Cugoano refers to include Frederick II, the Great (1712–1786), of Prussia, and Catherine II, the Great (1729–1796), of Russia. Frederick abolished serfdom in East and newly annexed West Prussia in 1773 and published his *Essay on the Forms of Government and Duties of Sovereigns* in 1777, calling on rulers to keep the best interests of their peasants in mind. Catherine's visionary reform program of 1767, the *Great Instruction*, though never enacted, was published in an English translation in 1768.

150. Amos 8:8.

151. A very melancholy instance ... about the year 1780: Cugoano refers to the *Zong* case of 1783, which was brought to Granville Sharp's attention by Equiano. On 19 March 1783, Sharp recorded in his journal that "Gustavus Vassa, a negro, called on me, with an account of 130 negroes being thrown alive into the sea" (Prince Hoare [1755–1834], *Memoirs of Granville Sharp* [London, 1820], 236). Equiano probably brought Sharp the report in the *Morning Chronicle, and London Advertiser* (18 March 1783) of the recent court hearing of the case. The slave ship *Zong*, owned by the Liverpool banker William Gregson and his associates and commanded by Luke Collingwood, sailed from the coast of present-day Gabon on 6 September 1781 with a crew of seventeen and a cargo of approximately 470 enslaved Africans. When seven of his crew and more than sixty of the Africans had died by 29 November, with many others in failing health, Collingwood explained to his officers that if the Africans died of natural causes the owners of the *Zong* (and Collingwood) would have to absorb the cost, but if they had to be thrown overboard to save the ship and its crew, the insurance underwriters would be obligated to cover the loss. Over the objection of his first mate, James Kelsal, who testified against him, Collingwood ordered that 133 of the sickest Africans be divided into groups and thrown alive into the ocean on the pretext that the ship lacked sufficient drinking water. The ship's records showed, however, that it had two hundred unrationed gallons of water on 29 November and 420 gallons when it arrived in Jamaica on 22 December. And Kelsal testified that Africans continued to be thrown overboard even after a heavy rain.

When the insurers challenged the claim made by the *Zong*'s owners, the court decided in favor of the owners, awarding them £30 for each murder victim. When the insurers still refused to pay the £3,960, the owners were granted a new trial before the Court of King's Bench, but its outcome is not recorded and whether the owners received payment is unknown.

Although Collingwood died during the proceedings, Granville Sharp sought to prosecute the remaining murderers in the Admiralty Court, but no action was ever taken against them.

152. Tied two and two together: the "ERRATA" reads "*for* tied together, *read* hand-cuffed."

153. The British Dan in the East-Indies, to her Beershebah in the West: because Dan and Beersheba were, respectively, the most northern and southern cities of the Holy Land, the phrase "from Dan to Beersheba" meant from one end of a political realm to another.

154. Adapted from Psalms 50:18.

155. Genesis 4:23.

156. Queen: Esther, who outwitted Haman, the son of Hammedatha, thus saving her Jewish brethren.

157. Shores: corrected from "shore" in "ERRATA."

158. The imagery in this paragraph is drawn primarily from the Book of Revelation.

159. Cugoano seems to be associating himself with the apostles John and Jude, who address their fellow early Christian converts as "beloved."

160. Amos 5:24.

161. Mordecai's: see Esther 4.

162. Aera: corrected from "era" in "ERRATA."

163. Proverbs 30:20.

164. *By the King, a Proclamation, for the Encouragement of Piety and Virtue, and for Preventing and Punishing of Vice* . . . (London, 1 June 1787).

165. The Cape: the Cape of Good Hope, South Africa.

166. And if that country was not annually ravished . . . trade carried on with the Africans: Daniel Defoe (1660–1731) and Malachy Postlethwayt (1707–1767) were among the many eighteenth-century economic theorists who anticipated Cugoano's commercial argument against the slave trade, though elsewhere in their writings they supported the slave trade. In his *Interesting Narrative*, Equiano makes a very similar argument to Cugoano's for the economic development of Africa freed from the slave trade. In a 1778 letter to a young friend who has gone to India to make his fortune, Ignatius Sancho also expresses his faith in the civilizing effects of commerce: "Commerce was meant by the goodness of the Deity to diffuse the various goods of the earth into every part—to unite mankind in the blessed chains of brotherly love—society—and mutual dependence:—the enlightened Christian should diffuse the riches of the Gospel of peace—with the commodities of his respective land—Commerce attended with strict honesty—and with Religion for its companion—would be a blessing to every shore it touched at."

167. [Cugoano's note.] A gentleman of my acquaintance told me that, if ever he hears tell of any thing of this kind taking place, he has a plan in contemplation, which would, in some equitable manner, produce from one million to fifteen millions sterling to the British government annually, as it might be required; of which a due proportion of that revenue would by paid by the Africans; and that it would prevent all smuggling and illicit traffic; in a great measure, prevent running into debt, long imprisonment, and all unlawful bankruptcies; effectually prevent all dishonesty and swindling, and almost put an end to all robbery, fraud and theft.

168. Several ladies in England who refuse to drink sugar in their tea: Cugoano's "ladies" anticipate the organized public boycott of sugar in 1791 to pressure Parliament to abolish the slave trade.

169. On: added in "ERRATA."

170. Particular thanks . . . Black poor about London: Cugoano refers to the Committee for the Relief of the Black Poor, organized by humanitarian businessmen in early 1786 to offer aid to indigent East Indian sailors, called lascars, who had been employed by the East India Company but abandoned in London. Since *Black* referred to complexion rather than ethnicity or origin, the recipients of the committee's charity soon included people of African descent as well. The committee raised more than £1,000 to provide relief, health care, clothing, food, and jobs to needy Blacks.

In February 1786 the committee was approached by Henry Smeathman (d. 1786), author of the *Plan of a Settlement to Be Made near Sierra Leone, on the Grain Coast of Africa. Intended more particularly for the Service and Happy Establishment of Blacks and People of Colour, to Be Shipped as Freemen under the Direction of the Committee for Relieving the Black Poor, and under the Protection of the British Government* (London, 1786). Smeathman had spent time in Africa conducting research for a treatise on termites and while there had married into the families of the local African rulers, King Tom and Cleveland. Smeathman's concern for the presence and plight of Blacks under British rule was prompted by Britain's defeat in the American Revolution: "And whereas many black persons, and people of Colour, Refugees from America, disbanded from his Majesty's Service by sea or land, or otherwise distinguished objects of British humanity, are at this time in the greatest distress, they are invited to avail themselves of the advantages of the plan proposed" (16–17). His charitable impulse was complemented by the desire to abolish the slave trade and to demonstrate that Africa could generate wealth without being forced to export its human resources.

The committee approved a version of Smeathman's plan in May 1786 and quickly received a promise from the Treasury of up to £14 per person to support transporting the settlers of the projected self-governing village of Granville Town (named in honor of Granville Sharp), in the Province of Freedom to be established on land bought for that purpose from local African authorities. Sharp published his political constitution for the projected community in *A Short Sketch of Temporary Regulations (until Better Shall Be Proposed), for the Intended Settlement on the Grain Coast of Africa, near Sierra Leone* (London, 1786).

A letter from the government to the Committee for the Black Poor reveals a sense of urgency:

> I am commanded by the Lords Commissioners of His Majesty's Treasury to acquaint you that they have taken Measures for the Civil Officers apprehending such Blacks as they may meet with committing any Act of Vagrancy who have received the Bounty of the public on Condition of their going to Serra [sic] Leona, with an Intention to have them sent from Time to Time on Board the Ships prepared to convey them to the place of their Destination and the better to enable My Lords to carry their Intentions into Execution, I am directed to desire you will send them a List of the Names of such as have received the said Bounty, and who are not now on board the Ships, and to request that You will favour them with any Observations that may occur to You or any other Plan that You are of Opinion may more effectually carry the Intentions of this Board respecting the sending the Blacks to Serra Leona into Execution with as little delay as possible. [PRO 27/38, dated 4 December 1786]

The *Morning Herald* (2 January 1787) reported that the authorities acted promptly:

> The Mayor has given orders to the City Marshals, the Marshalmen, and Constables, to take up all the blacks they find begging about the streets, and to bring them before him, or some other Magistrate, that they may be sent home, or to the new colony that is going to be established in Africa; near twenty are already taken up, and lodged in the two Compters [the Poultry and Wood Street jails in the City of London].

On 4 January 1787, the *Public Advertiser* applauded the Lord Mayor's action and called for similar edicts in other jurisdictions:

> The conduct of the Lord-Mayor in ordering the blacks who are found begging about the streets to be taken up, is highly commendable, and it is to be hoped will be imitated by the Magistrates of Westminster, Middlesex, Surrey, and the other counties. It is, however, humbly submitted to their judgment, whether instead of mere confinement in a gaol, it would not be preferable to put them to hard labour in Bridewell. The blacks, especially those of the East-Indies, are naturally indolent; nothing but the utmost necessity will make them work; and the very thought of being subjected to that would soon reconcile them to the plan proposed by Government.

171. Adapted from Job 18:3.

172. But after all . . . Sierra Leona: Cugoano's concerns about the settlement project were shared by others and perceived by the government as a threat to its success. On 1 January 1787, the *Public Advertiser* observed.

They must be enemies to public tranquility, to the police, and also to the Blacks, who studiously endeavour to fill the minds of these poor people with apprehensions of slavery, in the intended settlement on the banks of the Sierra Leona. No Ministry would think of breaking public faith with any body of men, however poor and abject they may be: Faith is kept by a nation, not because the persons to whom it is pledged are considerable and powerful, but because it is dishonourable to a nation to break its faith; and the precedent might be attended with consequences highly injurious to the State. The national honour would rouse its guardians, the House of Commons, to do it justice, and to punish those, who, by a breach of public faith, should tarnish its lustre. The Blacks, therefore, can have no real cause to apprehend that Government only wants to trepan [trick] them to Africa, in order to make them slaves. Ministers have no such view; cannot, dare not have such a view: they have too much virtue themselves to think of it, and they know there is too much virtue in the British nation to suffer them to accomplish what they are too just, too generous, and too polite to think of. The Blacks may therefore embark with confidence: their liberty, so far from being invaded, will be protected by Government; and if they are not deprived of their reason, they will quickly perceive how much more eligible it will be for them to go to a country where they will have lands assigned to them for their support, and all implements of husbandry supplied to them by the bounty of the nation, than to remain in indigence and want, strolling, wretched spectacles of distress, through our streets; constantly exposed to the temptation of committing felonies, for which they may be either hanged or transported to Africa, and left defenceless on the coast, where they will perish with hunger, be killed by their savage countrymen, or taken by them and sold as slaves: so that they may at length meet real slavery, in consequence of their ill-grounded apprehension of an imaginary one.

In the event, Cugoano's fears for the success of the settlement of Blacks in an area of Africa where the slave trade was still actively conducted were well founded. The British government's role ended with the payment of transportation costs. The Province of Freedom was conceived as a self-governing, free settlement, not as a British colony. The settlers left Britain on 9 April 1787, after having waited in port for five months,

and arrived at Sierra Leone on 10 May. Of the nearly four hundred settlers, including dozens of Whites, who survived the voyage, fifty-two had
died by 24 July 1787, with another 150 on the sick list. The survivors were
dispersed in December 1789, when a local African chieftain, King Jimmy,
destroyed the town in misdirected retaliation for the abduction of some
of his people by a United States slave trader.

173. Some disagreeable jealousy . . . all to be blown away: Cugoano no
doubt refers here to his friend and occasional collaborator Olaudah
Equiano, or Gustavus Vassa. Vassa was the only person of African descent to be involved with the organization and administration of the pró-
ject to settle Sierra Leone. He was appointed by the Navy Board in 1786
as "Commissary on the part of Government" to oversee the procurement
and dispersal of supplies and to act as the official representative of the
British government in its dealings with the local African authorities. In
part because of an awkward administrative structure that caused some of
his duties to overlap and even conflict with those of Joseph Irwin
(d. 1787), who had succeeded Smeathman as the "Agent" or "Superinten-
dent" of the expedition appointed by the Committee for the Relief of the
Black Poor, tension soon developed between Vassa and Irwin. Both administrators made mistakes in judgment and bookkeeping, and Vassa
leaked information to the *Morning Herald* that undercut confidence in
the project. Vassa was dismissed from his position on 24 March 1787 and
made the conflict public in a letter to Cugoano ("John Stewart") published in the *Public Advertiser* (4 April 1787) complaining of his treatment
and defending his conduct (see Appendix). On 6 April 1787, the *Public
Advertiser* reported

> We find his Majesty's servants have taken away the Commissary's com-
> mission from [Gustavus] Vasa [*sic*]. He came up from Plymouth to
> complain, and is now gone back again to take his effects on shore. The
> memorials [written petitions and/or statements of facts] of all the Black
> people, which they have sent up from Plymouth, represent that they
> are much wronged, injured, and oppressed natives of Africa, and under
> various pretences and different manners, have been dragged away from
> London, and carried captives to Plymouth, where they have nothing
> but slavery before their eyes, should they proceed to Africa or the
> West-Indies under the command of the persons who have the charge of
> them—That many of them served under Lord Dunmore [on 7 Novem-
> ber 1775, John Murray (1732–1809), fourth earl of Dunmore, royal
> governor of Virginia, issued a proclamation promising freedom to all
> rebel-owned slaves who joined the British forces. Five hundred of
> those who accepted his offer were organized into the "Ethiopian Regi-

ment." Tens of thousands of former slaves joined the British forces during the American Revolution], and other officers in America, in the
British army—Also on board the British Fleet in the West-Indies—
That the contract, on Mr. Smeathman's plan to settle them in Africa, has
not been fulfilled in their favour, but a Mr. Irwin has contrived to mo-
nopolize the benefit to himself—That they fear a right plan has not
been formed to settle them in Africa with any prospect of happiness to
themselves, or any hope of future advantage to Great-Britain.—They
cannot conceive, say they, that Government would establish a free
colony for them, whilst it supports its forts and factories to wrong and
ensnare, and to carry others of their colour and country into slavery
and bondage—They are afraid that their doom would be to drink of the
bitter water, and observe that it would be their prudence and safety to
take warning from the cautions in Scripture:—"Doth a fountain send
forth at the same place sweet water and bitter?"—That they say the design of some in sending them away, is only to get rid of them at all
events, come of them afterwards what will.—In that perilous situation
they see themselves surrounded with difficulties and danger; and what
gives them the most dreadful presage of their fate is that the white men
set over them have shewn them no humanity or good-will, but have
conspired to use them unjustly before they quitted the English coast—
And that they had better swim to shore, if they can, to preserve their
lives and liberties in Britain, than to hazard themselves at Sea with such
enemies to their welfare, and the peril of settling at Sierra Leona under
their government.

Vassa continued his self-defense in his *Interesting Narrative* (London,
1789). For Vassa's role in the Sierra Leone project and the press war it en-
gendered, see Carretta, ed., Olaudah Equiano's *The Interesting Narrative
and Other Writings*.

174. But the wiser sort declined . . . for their security and safety: in its
2–5 January 1787 issue, the *Morning Herald* had also reported the reluc-
tance of some Blacks to embrace the resettlement plan: "Six of the leaders
of these poor deceived people, Captains of hundreds and Captains of
fifties [the divisions of the intended settlers], came up last week from the
Belisarius and Atlantic [ships carrying the settlers to Sierra Leone], at
Gravesend, and waited upon Lord George Gordon, to pray the continuance of his protection, and to stop their sailing, till the meeting of parliament, that the public might know their unhappy situation. Their poverty
is made the pretence for their transportation, and the inferior orders of
them decoyed on board the ships, are already subjected to a treatment and
controul, little short of the discipline of Guinea-men [ships engaged in the
African slave trade]."

Gordon (1751–1793) gained notoriety in 1780 for his role in the anti–Roman Catholic Gordon Riots, but because of his opposition to the transportation of convicts to Australia he was seen as the champion of social underdogs. The Blacks were understandably frightened by rumors that their actual destination was Botany Bay.

175. James 3:11.

176. *P. Gordon . . . to endeavour the same:* Patrick Gordon (fl. 1700), *Geography Anatomized: or, a Compleat Geographical Grammar. . . . To Which Is Added, the Present State of the European Plantations in the East and West Indies, with a . . . Proposal for the Propagation of the Blessed Gospel in all Pagan Countries* (London, 1693; 20th ed., with revised title, 1754). Cugoano's quotations from Gordon are passages that first appear in the second edition, 1699. Given the facts that Cugoano refers to "above fifty years ago," and that the passages are not in the 1754 edition, he probably quotes from the fourteenth edition, 1735, 400–401.

177. *Let our planters . . . conquest:* Gordon, *Geography*, 416.

178. *Wickedness:* corrected from "nakedness" in "ERRATA."

179. Proverbs 14:28.

180. *I think . . . they are:* Gordon, *Geography*, 415.

181. *And a competent number . . . they were sent:* Gordon, *Geography*, 414.

182. *The reformed churches:* Protestants.

183. *That erroneous philosopher . . . not see good from ill:* Gordon Turnbull, *An Apology for Negro Slavery* (London, 1786), 42–43. Turnbull identifies himself in the second edition, 1786. Equiano's review in the *Public Advertiser* (5 February 1788) of Turnbull's *Apology* is reprinted in the Penguin edition of *Equiano's Interesting Narrative and Other Writings*. Turnbull also wrote *Letters to a Young Planter; or Observations on the Management of a Sugar-Plantation. To Which Is Added, The Planter's Kalendar. Written on the Island of Grenada, by an Old Planter* (London, 1785).

184. *Hume:* Cugoano probably refers to the notorious comment on race David Hume makes in a footnote added to "Of National Characters" (see note 36) in *Essays and Treatises on Several Subjects* (Edinburgh and London, 1753–1754): "In JAMAICA indeed they talk of one negroe as a man of parts and learning; but 'tis likely he is admired for very slender accomplishments, like a parrot who speaks a few words plainly." Hume refers to Francis Williams (ca. 1700–ca. 1770), whose poem, "An Ode" (1758) was published by Edward Long (1735–1813) in *The History of Jamaica* (London, 1774). Williams's poem and Long's hostile commentary on its author, which includes Hume's passage, are reproduced in Carretta, ed., *Unchained Voices*. Williams is also very probably the person referred to in the 19 June 1744 entry in the unpublished "Itinerarium" of Dr. Alexander Hamilton (1712–1756): "There, talking of a certain free negroe in Jamaica who was a man of estate, good sense, and education, the 'fore-mentioned gentleman [from the West Indies] who had entertained us in the morning about burying of souls, gravely asked if that negroe's parents were not whites, for he was sure that nothing good could come of the whole generation of blacks."

Cugoano seems to have been unaware of Hume's anti-slavery remarks in "Of the Populousness of Antient Nations," first published in *Political Discourses* (Edinburgh, 1752), where he attributes "the severe . . . barbarous manners of ancient times" to "the practice of domestic slavery; by which every man of rank was rendered a petty tyrant, and educated amidst the flattery, submission, and low debasement of his slaves."

185. Jeremiah 16:18, a fitting final Biblical quotation for a work that is itself a jeremiad.

186. That question . . . Christian: the question and answer begin the Anglican catechism for confirmation. Cugoano's suggested revision may have been inspired by Paul's Epistle to the Galatians 3:26–29:

26. For ye are all the children of God by faith in Christ Jesus.
27. For as many of you as have been baptized into Christ have put on Christ.
28. There is neither Jew nor Greek, there is neither bond nor free, there is neither male nor female: for ye are all one in Christ Jesus.
29. And if ye *be* Christ's, then are ye Abraham's seed, and heirs according to the promise.

187. Young, *Night Thoughts* 4:788–793.

EXPLANATORY NOTES
TO THE 1791 PUBLICATION

1. Since, with the exception of the first few paragraphs of his 1791 publication, Cugoano reuses portions of his earlier *Thoughts and Sentiments* in the later one, to avoid redundancy I annotate only those sections and references in the later text not found in the earlier.

2. William Wilberforce (1759–1833) led the crusade in the House of Commons to end the African slave trade in 1807, and after his retirement in 1825 he continued his support for the movement to end slavery.

3. For so it was considered as criminal . . . the parts taken by the learned Counsellor HARGRAVE: Francis Hargrave (1741?–1821). See *Thoughts and Sentiments* (1787), note 55. Cugoano was familiar with Hargrave's account of the proceedings of *Somerset v. Stewart: An Argument in the Case of James Sommersett a Negro, Lately Determined by the Court of King's Bench: Wherein it Is Attempted to Demonstrate the Present Unlawfulness of Domestic Slavery in England. To Which Is Prefixed a State of the Case. By Mr. Hargrave, One of the Counsel for the Negro* (London, 1772; 3rd ed. 1788).

4. *He further proposes to open a School* . . . Laws of Civilization: I have found no record of Cugoano's having opened a school.

APPENDIX

CORRESPONDENCE OF
QUOBNA OTTOBAH CUGOANO

1.   [To the Prince of Wales, the future George IV (1762–1830)]

MAY IT PLEASE YOUR HIGHNESS,
   To accept of these little tracts and pardon the freedom of recommending them to your Perusal.
   And may [He by] whom Kings Reign and Princes decree
Justice Influence your Highness to consider the Case of the
poor Africans who are most barbarously captured and unlawfully carried away from their own Country and cruelly
enslaved by many under the British Government and other
Nations of Europe and in many respects are treated in a
more unjust and inhuman manner than ever known among
any of the Barbarous Nations of the World.
   Should your Highness endeavour to release the oppressed
and put a stop to that iniquitous traffic of buying and selling
Men you would not equal the Virtuous Queen of Portugal[1]
in this respect but it would add Lustre and Greatness to
your aspiring Years[.] all generous minds would admire
you[;] the wise and virtuous would praise you[.] The
prayer of the oppressed would ascend to pour down those
Blessings upon you[,] and your Name would resound with
applause from Shore to Shore[,] and in all the records of
Fame be held in the highest Esteem throughout the Annals
of time.
   And should your Highness regard this Petition it would
be the ardent wish of Millions to behold in you [that] true

Greatness denotes Title great Permit me to be with the greatest Submission

> *Your Royal Highness['s] much oblig'd*
> *and most Obedient Humble Servant*
> [signed] John Stuart, 1786

*   *   *

2.   [To] Edmund Burke[2] Esqr. Gerard Street
Pall mall at Mr. Cosway's [undated, probably 1787]

HONOURED SIR,
Permit me to lay my thoughts and Sentiments before you,
the production of a Young man a Native of Africa, in a Domestic Employment, wherein it may appear rather harsh
against the Carriers on of such abandoned wickness, as the
affrican Slave trade, and West India Slavery. I hope the Arguments therein, will meet your approbation, and all good
Christians, if I should be so happy as to have your approbation of my small undertaking, a trifle towards the printing
will be acceptable. I have put my affrican Name to the Title
of the Book, But at present I must beg leave to Subscribe
myself.

> Honoured Sir,
> Your most Obedient
> and most humble Servant
> [signed] John Stuart

*   *   *

3.   [To the Prince of Wales]

May it, please your highness
To accept this little tract as being the thoughts and sentiments of an African against all manner of Slavery and
oppression as a great Counsellor[3] has asserted. "Slavery in
whatever light we view it may be deemed a most pernicious
institution immediately so to the unhappy Person who suffers under it finally to the Master who triumphs in it and ru-

inous to the State who allows it."[4] But because it is the custom of base minds to take the advantage of the weak and to
Build their Fortunes on the artless and helpless and whereas
we have no institution of Ambassadors to demand restitution for the injuries which the Europeans have pursued
against us we can no where lay our Case more fitly than at
the feet of your Highness and if it meets with your approbation we have no doubt of your proving our Advocate. This
meritorious act would rejoice the Hearts of all the true Sons
of Liberty throughout your Royal Fathers Dominions and it
may be hoped in Days yet remote but in Gods good time
that your Highness might thereby sway a greater and hap-
pier Empire than any British Monarch did before. This is a
Concern of great importance and to be a means under God
to endeavour to Exalt right virtue liberty and felicity to Millions would make your illustrious name resound from Shore
to Shore. And none can wish it more than He whose African
Name is in the title of the book.

But I must at present beg leave to subscribe myself your
Royal Highness['s] much obliged and most obedient Servant
[signed] John Stuart
1787

* * *

4. [Gustavus Vassa (Olaudah Equiano) to John Stewart
(Quobna Ottobah Cugoano)]

FOR THE PUBLIC ADVERTISER, 4 APRIL 1787.
We are sorry to find that his Majesty's Commissary for the
African Settlement[5] has sent the following letter to Mr. John
Stewart, Pall Mall:

At Plymouth, March 24, 1787.
SIR,
These with my respects to you. I am sorry you and some
more are not here with us. I am sure [Joseph] Irwin,[6] and

[Patrick] Fraser the Parson,[7] are great villains, and Dr. [Daniel] Currie [Curry]. I am exceeding much aggrieved at the conduct of those who call themselves gentlemen. They now mean to serve (or use) the blacks the same as they do in the West Indies. For the good of the settlement I have borne every affront that could be given, believe me, without giving the least occasion, or ever yet resenting any.

By Sir Charles Middleton's[8] letter to me, I now find Irwin and Fraser have wrote to the Committee and the Treasury, that I use the white people with arrogance, and the blacks with civility, and stir them up to mutiny: which is not true, for I am the greatest peace-maker that goes out. The reason for this lie is, that in the presence of these two I acquainted Captain Thompson[9] of the Nautilus sloop, our convoy, that I would go to London and tell of their roguery; and further insisted on Captain Thompson to come on board of the ships, and see the wrongs done to me and the people; so Captain Thompson came and saw it, and ordered the things to be given according to contract—which is not yet done in many things—and many of the black people have died for want of their due. I am grieved in every respect. Irwin never meant well to the people, but self-interest has ever been his end: twice this week [the Black Poor] have taken him, bodily, to the Captain, to complain of him, and I have done it four times.

I do not know how this undertaking will end; I wish I had never been involved in it; but at times I think the Lord will make me very useful at last.

                                              I am, dear Friend,
                                          With respect, your's,
                                                    "G. VASA."
                              The Commissary for the Black Poor.

                              *   *   *

5. The Address of Thanks of the Sons of Africa to the
Honourable Granville Sharp, Esq.[10]

December 15, 1787.

HONOURABLE AND WORTHY SIR,

Give us leave to say, that every virtuous man is a truly honourable man; and he that doth good hath honour to himself: and
many blessings are upon the head of the just, and their memory
shall be blessed, and their works praise them in the gate.

And we must say, that we, who are a part, or descendants,
of the much-wronged people of Africa, are peculiarly and
greatly indebted to you, for the many good and friendly services that you have done towards us, and which are now
even out of our power to enumerate.

Nevertheless, we are truly sensible of your great kindness
and humanity; and we cannot do otherwise but endeavour,
with the utmost sincerity and thankfulness, to acknowledge
our great obligations to you, and, with the most feeling sense
of our hearts, on all occasions to express and manifest our
gratitude and love for your long, valuable, and indefatigable
labours and benevolence towards using every means to rescue our suffering brethren in slavery.

Your writings, Sir, are not of trivial matters, but of great
and essential things of moral and religious importance, worthy the regard of all men; and abound with many great and
precious things, of sacred writ, particularly respecting the
laws of God, and the duties of men.

Therefore, we wish, for ourselves and others, that these
valuable treatises may be collected and preserved, for the
benefit and good of all men, and for an enduring memorial
of the great learning, piety, and vigilance of our good friend
the worthy Author. And we wish that the laws of God, and
his ways of righteousness set forth therein, may be as a path
for the virtuous and prudent to walk in, and as a clear shin-
ing light to the wise in all ages; and that these and other writ-

ings of that nature, may be preserved and established as a
monument or beacon to guide or to warn men, lest they
should depart from the paths of justice and humanity; and
that they may more and more become means of curbing the
vicious violators of God's holy law, and to restrain the avaricious invaders of the rights and liberties of men, whilever the
human race inhabits this earth below.

And, ever honourable and worthy Sir, may the blessing and
peace of Almighty God be with you, and long preserve your
valuable life, and make you abundantly useful in every good
word and work! And when God's appointed time shall come,
may your exit be blessed, and may you arise and for ever shine
in the glorious world above, when that Sovereign Voice, speaking with joy, as the sound of many waters, shall be heard, saying, "Well done, thou good and faithful servant: enter thou
into the joy of thy Lord!" It will then be the sweetest of all de-
lights for ever, and more melodious than all music! And such
honour and felicity will the blessed God and Saviour of his
people bestow upon all the saints and faithful servants who are
redeemed from among men, and saved from sin, slavery, misery, pain, and death, and from eternal dishonour and wrath de-
pending upon the heads of all the wicked and rebellious.

And now, honourable Sir, with the greatest submission,
we must beg you to accept this memorial of our thanks for
your good and faithful services towards us, and for your
humane commiseration of our brethren and countrymen unlawfully held in slavery.

And we have hereunto subscribed a few of our names, as
a mark of our gratitude and love. And we are, with the greatest esteem and veneration, honourable and worthy, Sir, your
most obliged and most devoted humble servants.

OTTOBAH CUGOANO.	JASPER GOREE.
JOHN STUART.	GUSTAVUS VASA.
GEORGE ROBERT MANDEVILLE.	JAMES BAILEY.
WILLIAM STEVENS.	THOMAS OXFORD.
JOSEPH ALMAZE.	JOHN ADAMS.
BOUGHWA GEGANSMEL.	GEORGE WALLACE.

* * *

6.   [To George III (1738–1820)]

May it please your Majesty to pardon an African particularly
concerned for the injurious treatment of his Countrymen To
present you with the inclosed Book. The cause of justice and
humanity are the only motives which induced me to collect
those thoughts and sentiments on the evil of Slavery with a
view to the natural liberties of Men which your Majesty as a
Sovereign will be pleased to support. I therefore presume to
lay them at your Majestys feet imploring mercy and pardon[.] If any Passage should appear inaccurate or so repre-
hensible a Subject your known Beneficence will construe the
influence which your Potent Power will have by preserving
Thousands of fellow sufferers from inevitable Destruction.

Permit me to be with the greatest Respect
Your Majesty's most Obedient Subject to Command
[signed] John Stuart 1788

* * *

7.   To Granville Sharp, Esq. [undated]

SIR,

Being assembled (few and insignificant as we are) for the
purpose of offering grateful thanks to our benefactors, it was
impossible to forget HIM who has been the great source and
support of our hopes. We need not use many words. We are
those who were considered as slaves, even in England itself,
till your aid and exertions set us free. We are those whose
minds and bodies are bartered from hand to hand on the
coast of Africa, and in the West Indies, as the ordinary commodities of trade. But it is said that we are the factors of our
own slavery, and sell one another at our own market for a
price. No doubt but in our uncivilized state we commit
much evil; but surely the trader cannot believe that the
strong on the coast of Africa are entitled to deprive the weak
of every right of humanity, and to devote to the most cruel
slavery them and their posterity for ever; or that it belongs
to him, more enlightened than we, to execute so horrid a

doom. But our cause is in better hands than our own; and
humbleness and sobriety, we are sensible, will best become
our condition: and this, also, we know to be the return desired by you, looking for your own peculiar reward in the
consciousness of doing good.

But yet, Sir, you may allow us to believe that the name of
GRANVILLE SHARP, our constant and generous friend,
will be drawn forth by our more enlightened posterity, and
distinguishingly marked in future times for gratitude and
praise.
[signed]

THOMAS COOPER	JOHN SCOT
GEO. ROBT. MANDEVILLE	JORGE DENT
JOHN STUART	THOS. OXFORD
DANIEL CHRISTOPHER	JAMES BAILEY
BERNARD ELLIOTT	JAMES FRAZER
JAMES FORSTER	THOMAS CARLISLE

* * *

8.   [To Sir William Dolben (1727–1814),[11] undated,
probably May–June 1788].

HONOURED SIR,
permit an african perticulary Concerned for the Injuraous
Treatments of his Countrymen to returned you His humble
and gratefull thanks for your Noble, bold, and Loudable Exertions in the Cause of Justice, Liberty—and filicety, And a
noble regulations you have proposed In our behalves. May
the almighty god Whose Merciful Eyes is ever opened on all
True acts of virtue, generousity, and Humanity Enable you
to meet with your Desired Success Infavour of the oppressed. No Doubt but it will [be] The means of saving
thousands from the Cruel Sword of the Cursed avarice, and
if ever Infedility Cease tobe no doubt your noble Name
Shall be revered from Shore to Shores, And also permit me
to recomend to your perusal these small tracts as a Collec-

tion of an african against all manner of Slavery, and oppression.—

And Honoured Sir,
with a Humble Submission
your Most obedient Humble
Servant
[signed] Ottobah Cugoano. John Stuart
at Richd Cosway Esqr. pall mall

* * *

9. For *The Morning Chronicle and London Advertiser*,
15 July 1788.

TO THE HONOURABLE SIR WILLIAM DOLBEN, BART.
SIR,

We beg your permission to lay in this manner our humble thankfulness before you, for a benevolent law obtained at your motion, by which the miseries of our unhappy brethren, on the coast of Africa, may be alleviated, and by which the lives of many, though destined for the present to a cruel slavery, may be preserved, as we hope, for future and for greater mercies.

Our simple testimony is not much, yet you will not be displeased to learn, that a few persons of colour, existing here, providentially released from the common calamity, and feeling for their kind, are daily pouring forth their prayers for you, Sir, and other noble and generous persons who will not (as we understand) longer suffer the rights of humanity to be confounded with ordinary commodities, and passed from hand to hand, as an article of trade.

We are not ignorant, however, Sir, that the best return we can make is, to behave with sobriety, fidelity, and diligence in our different stations, whether remaining here under the protection of the laws, or colonizing our native soil, as most of us wish to do, under the dominion of this country; or as free labourers and artizans in the West India islands, which, under equal laws, might become to men of colour places of voluntary and very general resort.

But in whatever station, Sir, having lived here, as we hope, without reproach, so we trust that we and our whole race shall endeavour to merit, by dutiful behaviour, those mercies, which, humane and benevolent minds seem to be preparing for us.

THOMAS COOPER.
GUSTAVUS VASSA.
OTTOBAH CUGOANA STEWARD.
GEORGE ROBERT MANDEVIL.
JOHN CHRISTOPHER.
THOMAS JONES.

FOR OURSELVES AND BRETHREN

Sir W. DOLBEN is highly gratified with the kind acceptance his endeavours to promote the liberal designs of the Legislature have met from the worthy natives of Africa; whose warm sense of benefits, and honourable resolution of showing their gratitude by their future conduct in steadiness and sobriety, fidelity, and diligence, will undoubtedly recommend them to the British Government, and he trusts, to other Christian powers, as most worthy of their further care and attention; yet as he is but one among many who are equally zealous for the accomplishment of this good work, he must earnestly desire to decline any particular address upon the occasion.

Duke-Street, Westminster, 1788.

* * *

10.   For *The Morning Chronicle and London Advertiser,*
15 July 1788.

TO THE RIGHT HONOURABLE WILLIAM PITT.[12]
SIR,

We will not presume to trouble you with many words. We are persons of colour, happily released from the common

calamity, and desirous of leaving at your door, in behalf of
our Brethren, on the Coast of Africa, this simple, but grateful acknowledgment of your goodness and benevolence towards our unhappy race.

THOMAS COOPER.
GUSTAVUS VASSA.
OTTOBAH CUGOANA STEWARD.
GEORGE ROBERT MANDEVIL.
JOHN CHRISTOPHER.
THOMAS JONES.
For ourselves and Brethren.

* * *

11. For *The Morning Chronicle and London Advertiser*,
15 July 1788.

TO THE RIGHT HONOURABLE CHARLES JAMES FOX.[13]
SIR,
We are men of colour, happily, ourselves, emancipated from
a general calamity by the laws of this place, but yet feeling
very sensibly for our kind, and hearing, Sir, that, in their
favour, you have cooperated with the minister [Pitt], and
have nobly considered the rights of humanity as a common
cause, we have thereupon assumed the liberty (we hope,
without offence) of leaving this simple, but honest token of
our joy and thankfulness at your door.

THOMAS COOPER.
GUSTAVUS VASSA.
OTTOBAH CUGOANA STEWARD.
GEORGE ROBERT MANDEVIL.
JOHN CHRISTOPHER.
THOMAS JONES.
For ourselves and Brethren.

* * *

12.   For *The Diary; or Woodfall's Register*, 25 April 1789.

TO MR. *WILLIAM DICKSON*,[14] FORMERLY PRIVATE
SECRETARY TO THE HON. EDWARD HAY, GOVERNOR OF THE
ISLAND OF BARBADOES.

SIR,

We who have perused your well authenticated Book, entitled
LETTERS ON SLAVERY, think it a duty incumbent on us
to confess, that in our opinion such a work cannot be too
much esteemed; you have given but too just a picture of the
Slave Trade, and the horrid cruelties practised on the poor
sable people in the West Indies, to the disgrace of Christianity. Their injury calls aloud for redress, and the day we hope
is not far distant, which may record one of the most glorious
acts that ever passed the British Senate—we mean an Act for
the total Abolition of the Slave Trade.

It is the duty of every man who is a friend to religion and
humanity (and such you have shewn yourself to be) to shew
his detestation of such inhuman traffick. Thank to God, the
nation at last is awakened to a sense of our sufferings, except
the Oran Otang philosophers, who we think will find it a
hard task to dissect your letters. Those who can feel for the
distresses of their own countrymen, will also commiserate
the case of the poor Africans.

Permit us, Sir, on behalf of ourselves and the rest of our
brethren, to offer you our sincere thanks for the testimony
of regard you have shewn for the poor and much oppressed
sable people.

With our best wishes that your praise-worthy publication
may meet with the wished-for success, and may the all-
bountiful Creator bless you with health and happiness, and
bestow on you every blessing of time and eternity.

We are,
Sir,
Your most obedient humble servants,
OLAUDAH EQUIANO, *or* GUSTAVUS VASA.
OTTOBAH CUGOANO, *or* JOHN S[T]UAR[T].

YAHNE AELANE, *or* JOSEPH SANDERS.
BROUGHWAR JOGENSMEL, *or* JASPER GOREE.
COJOH AMMERE, *or* GEORGE WILLIAMS.
THOMAS COOPER.
WILLIAM GREEK.
GEORGE MANDEVILLE.
BERNARD ELLIOT GRIFFITHS.

* * *

13.   [To] Granville Sharp Esqr., Leadenhall
[undated, probably 1791][15]

HONOURED SIR,
Pardon the liberty taken in troubling you with this few lines
but as there is Several Ships now going to new Brunswick I
could wish to have your answer that I might be able to gived
the black settlers there some kind of answer to their request,
the generality of them are mediately the natives of africa
who Join [perhaps *Is in*] the british forces Last war, they are
consisting of Different Macanicks such as Carpenters,
Smiths, Masons and farmers, this are the people that we have
imediate use for in the Provence of freedom. Most of them
are people of property and able to pay their own Passages,
and the familly, as well as the Country been by far the
cheapest market for victualling vessels, I am of opinion that
connections with them will be immediate service—should
think it proper to make lest interest for me I shall go over
with Cap. Younghusband who will sale for that province in a
few days my motive is this, I shall endeavour to know who
is able to pay their ways, and they that might be thought
useful to the free african settlers. This may be Complicated
in three months and then youll be able to Judge wether or
no, would be worth your while to send out a ship for that
purpose; the spruce is a native of these Country, which will
be Immediately valuable in african Climate, a tree which
Produce sugar equall with that which many thousands are
murdered for, is, here only by cutting down its branches and

setting a tubb under it, which is only Boild with every little trouble, equally with that of our West india brown sugar. but what encouragement has the poor unfortunate sables those Under sanction of freedom are worse off, than slaves. Eight months severe winter, to incounter and when bringh their little stock market oblidge sell for little or nothing at a white mans Price. these inhuman Distinctions of colours, has in every point, and in every view, spead its Predominant Power over all the northern Climes, that it puts me in the mind of the leaned Bollingbrook, who was some time at lost to know Distinction betwixt a man and a stone.

I have, within this last three months b[een] after upwards of fifty places but, Complexion is a Predominant Prejudice for a man to starve for want in a christian Country be will be a folly. I shall Call for your Answer to morrow.

I am Sincerly your Dutifull Ser
[signed] John Stuart [sic passim]

NOTES

1. Virtuous Queen of Portugal: Maria I (1734–1816), the first queen regnant of Portugal, who freed political prisoners when she ascended the throne in 1777.

2. Edmund Burke (1729–1797) expressed his disapproval of West Indian slavery in *An Account of the European Settlements in America* (London, 1757) and in 1765 opposed seating Americans in the House of Commons in 1765 because to do so would condone slavery. In the House of Commons, Burke supported the abolition of the slave trade.

3. A great Counsellor: Francis Hargrave.

4. Slavery in whatever light . . . and ruinous to the State who allows it: with the addition of "ruinous" and some changes in punctuation, Cugoano quotes from Hargrave's *An Argument in the Case of James Somersett A Negro, Lately Determined by the Court of King's Bench: Wherein It Is Attempted to Demonstrate the Present Unlawfulness of Domestic Slavery in England. To Which Is Prefixed a State of the Case. By Mr. Hargrave, One of the Counsel for the Negro* (London, 1772), 16–17.

5. His Majesty's Commissary for the African Settlement: Equiano was the only person of African descent to be involved in the organization of the project to settle Sierra Leone. His full title of "Commissary on the

part of the Government" expresses the importance of his position: in addition to overseeing supplies, he was to act as the official representative of the British government in dealings with the local African authorities in Sierra Leone.

6. [Joseph] Irwin: in 1786 Irwin was appointed leader of the expedition to settle Sierra Leone. He died on 12 July 1787.

7. [Patrick] Fraser: a minister accompanying the expedition who had published an attack on Equiano's conduct in the newspapers the *London Chronicle* and the *Morning Chronicle, and London Advertiser*.

8. Sir Charles Middleton (1726–1813), baronet, later Lord Barham, and from 1778 to 1790 comptroller of the navy. An active opponent of the slave trade, Middleton had appointed Equiano commissary, and he was an original subscriber to *The Interesting Narrative*.

9. Thomas Boulden Thompson (1766?–1828) was put in command of the naval vessel assigned to escort the expeditionary fleet. His command of the *Nautilus* was officially confirmed on 27 March 1786, two months after he had been given the commission. He did not receive the rank of post-captain until 22 November 1790.

10. Quoted from Prince Hoare (1755–1834), *Memoirs of Granville Sharp* (London, 1820), 374–375.

11. Dolben (1727–1814) led the legislative fight for passage of the Slave Limitation (or Middle Passage) Bill regulating the overcrowding of slave ships. The Bill passed the House of Commons on 13 May 1788 and the House of Lords on 24 June. Cugoano's letter to Dolben is in the Northamptonshire Record Office, Ref: (D)F 39.

12. William Pitt (1759–1806), prime minister of Great Britain, 1783–1801 and 1804–1806, supported in 1792 Wilberforce's proposed abolition of the slave trade.

13. Charles James Fox (1749–1806), a leader of Pitt's political opposition in the House of Commons, also opposed the slave trade.

14. William Dickson (fl. 1789–1815), *Letters on Slavery. . . . To Which Are Added, Addresses to the Whites, and to the Free Negroes of Barbadoes; and Accounts of Some Negroes Eminent for their Virtues and Abilities* (London, 1789). Dickson was a subscriber to Equiano's *Narrative*.

15. In 1790, before he learned that Granville Town had been destroyed, Sharp published anonymously *Free English Territory in Africa*, proposing the creation of the St. George's Bay Company for trade with Sierra Leone. His concept evolved into the design of a new settlement established by the Sierra Leone Company, incorporated by Parliament on 1 July 1791 to build Freetown on the physical and economic remains of

the Province of Freedom. Freetown was established in February 1792 by survivors of Granville Town and about twelve hundred Afro-Britons recruited for the Sierra Leone Company in Nova Scotia by its Agent, John Clarkson (1765–1828), a lieutenant in the royal navy and brother of the great abolitionist. The possibility of using Nova Scotian settlers arose when Thomas Peters (ca. 1738–1792), a former slave who had sought refuge in Nova Scotia after the American Revolution, came to London seeking redress for the complaints of the Afro-Britons in North America.

Clarkson's conduct so impressed the settlers and the company that the directors appointed him Governor of Sierra Leone. But tensions soon developed between the company and the settlers, leading to a confrontation between Clarkson and Peters on 8 April 1792, strikes by some settlers protesting their governance and the attempt by the company to collect quitrents on the settlers' lands, and an abortive rebellion in 1800. Parliament granted the company a charter in 1800, and in 1808 control of the settlement was transferred from the company to the British government, making Sierra Leone a crown colony.

Despite Cugoano's expression of interest in the resettlement plan, we do not know if his offer to join the expedition was accepted.